# NUTRITION SMART!

# NUTRITION SMART!

## *Ready-to-Use Lessons and Worksheets for the Primary Grades*

**Robin S. Bagby, M.Ed., R.D.**
**Shirley A. Woika, M.S.**
*of the Penn State Nutrition Center*

The Center for Applied Research in Education
West Nyack, New York

© 1991 by

THE CENTER FOR APPLIED
RESEARCH IN EDUCATION

West Nyack, New York

All rights reserved.

Permission is given for individual classroom teachers to reproduce the pages and illustrations for classroom use. Reproduction of these materials for an entire school system is strictly forbidden.

10 9 8 7 6 5 4 3 2 1

*Library of Congress Cataloging-in-Publication Data*

Bagby, Robin S.
    Nutrition smart! : ready-to-use lessons and worksheets for the primary grades / Robin S. Bagby, Shirley Woika.
      p.  cm.
    Includes bibliographical references.
    ISBN 0-87628-615-5
    1. Nutrition—Study and teaching (Primary)  I. Woika, Shirley.
II. Title.
QP143.B34  1991
372.3′7′043—dc20                                       91-3691
                                                                    CIP

ISBN 0-87628-615-5

THE CENTER FOR APPLIED
RESEARCH IN EDUCATION
BUSINESS & PROFESSIONAL DIVISION
A Simon & Schuster Company
West Nyack, New York 10995

Printed in the United States of America

To Julia and Jack Bagby
and
Benjamin and Nicholas Woika

# About the Authors

ROBIN S. BAGBY, M.ED., R.D., has taught in a number of elementary grades in Kansas, Ohio, and Pennsylvania. After joining the nutrition faculty at the Pennsylvania State University in 1985, she taught Introductory Nutrition, and in 1986 became In-House Coordinator for the Penn State Nutrition Center. She authored the print materials to accompany the multimedia program *Nutrition in Action* and was involved in the creation of two worksite programs for adults, *Food Works* and *Heart Healthy*. She also revised the seventh edition of Helen Guthrie's *Introductory Nutrition* and wrote the first and second editions of the related *Instructor's Manual*. She authored the Introductory Nutrition Student Manual for the Penn State Independent Learning Course. Robin received her Bachelor's degree in education from the University of Kansas in 1973, and her M.Ed. in nutrition education from the University of Cincinnati in 1983. She is a Registered Dietician and a member of the American Dietetic Association, the Pennsylvania Dietetic Association, and the Society for Nutrition Education.

SHIRLEY A. WOIKA, M.S., is certified in special education and elementary–kindergarten education and has taught gifted, special education, and regular education students in both public and private schools. She moved on to teach courses at the Pennsylvania State University in instructional design, development and implementation, and in mathematics education. She also supervised student teachers in a variety of elementary schools. After earning her M.S. in school psychology from Penn State, she supervised school psychology graduate students at the university's CEDAR clinic, and served as a certified school psychologist for Penn State's Program for Learning Disabled College Students. She currently works as a school psychologist for the Tuscarora (PA) Intermediate Unit, servicing five schools. To date, she has completed all degree requirements except the doctoral dissertation for her Ph.D. in School Psychology. She has presented at a number of in-service programs and state conferences, and she is a member of Phi Delta Kappa, a professional educational fraternity.

Shirley and her husband have gained much hands-on experience with children as the parents of two boys; they are also foster parents.

# About This Resource

The ready-to-use lessons and activity sheets in NUTRITION SMART! will help you teach students in grades K–3 how to make healthy food choices at a time in their lives when they are developing patterns and preferences that will affect their growth, development, and well-being for many years to come. NUTRITION SMART! provides over 75 completely reproducible black-line master activities that use simple, high-interest puzzles, word games, cut-and-paste activities, and more to introduce and reinforce basic nutrition knowledge and skills. The 25 lessons comprise a complete primary curriculum in nutrition, covering:

- How food provides energy for growth
- Why the body needs certain nutrients
- What digestion is and how it works
- What the basic food groups are and what they provide
- How to follow good dietary guidelines
- Why fats, sweets, and sodium should be eaten in moderation
- Why it is important to eat a variety of foods
- How to make good food choices throughout the day
- How it can be fun to try new foods
- How to choose snacks and convenience foods wisely
- What advertising is and how it can be misleading
- How different cultures eat different foods

You can follow the lessons sequentially, or pick and choose activities to supplement your existing curriculum. Each lesson provides full teacher background, and each activity is organized for easy use, listing the objective, materials needed, prerequisite skills, step-by-step directions for teaching the concepts, and suggested supplementary activities. A full answer key is provided in the back, as well as an appendix that lists recommended curriculum and activity books, children's books, audiovisual materials, posters, software, reference sources, and more.

NUTRITION SMART! doesn't use scare tactics or make children feel guilty about their food preferences; it recognizes the reality that snacks and convenience foods are part of the American diet, that families are eating fewer meals together, and that children tend to dislike new foods. Written by experienced classroom teachers and tested in real classrooms, it offers children nutrition knowledge and skills in a way that will allow them to *enjoy* making nutrition-smart food choices.

All information in this book accords with the most recent dietary guidelines developed by the USDA and the Red Cross, and reflects current research on nutrition and the role good eating patterns play in maintaining good health and preventing diseases later in life. For example, the activity "Clogged Pipes" uses a straw, some modeling clay, and a simple diagram to demonstrate the long-term dangers of excess fat in the diet, while "Fat Pats" helps children relate the abstract concept of grams of fat to the concrete reality of pats of butter. "Popcorn Percents" is just one activity that prompts students to recognize the common nutritional difference between processed and unprocessed versions of the same food.

Because children are already buying food and influencing purchases, activities like "Commercials" and "Slogan Power" teach them to be aware of typical advertising techniques and how some foods get a lot of advertising while others receive none. There is also an emphasis throughout these activities on making decisions about food packaging and waste disposal that are not only nutrition-smart, but environmentally sound.

Good nutrition now can make a world of difference to the children in your classroom today and the adults they become tomorrow. We hope that NUTRITION SMART! will help you show children how to make smart food choices for a lifetime of good health.

Robin Bagby
Shirley Woika

# Acknowledgments

The authors would like to acknowledge and thank the following people for their contributions and efforts given faithfully during the production of *Nutrition Smart!* First and foremost, our appreciation is extended to the Howard Heinz Endowment that generously funded this project, and to all members of the Penn State Nutritional Center who backed this project with encouragement and support. We thank Barbara Shannon for her leadership and guidance; Norma Woika for her patience, creative input, and competent computer skills; April Sherry for her graphic creativity; Janet Durrwachter and Mary Ann Pugh for their work to develop the proposal text and activities; Laura Walsh for her organization of materials and creative graphic skills on the design of the activities; and Karen Atkins for her input into the *Things to Know* section. In addition, Star Campbell, Sally Anger, Victoria Getty, Madeline Sigman, Helen Guthrie, and Renee Matich gave invaluable editorial comments. We also wish to extend our extreme thanks to the teachers and students of Mifflin County Schools and State College Area Schools who pilot tested these activities and provided useful feedback on ways to revise them. We wish to thank our husbands, Dale and John, for their encouragement, patience and understanding. And a special thank you to our children, Nicholas, Benjamin, Julia, and Jack for they have inspired us to make positive contributions to the field of education.

# Contents

## UNIT 1.   EATING TO GROW    1

### Lesson 1. Growing Up    2

Things to Know About Growing Up    2
Activity 1–1. Things That Grow    4
Activity 1–2. Growing Bigger    6
Activity 1–3. How Big Am I?    8

### Lesson 2. Nutrients to Grow On    12

Things to Know About Nutrients    12
Activity 2–1. Riddle    14
Activity 2–2. Food Energy    16
Activity 2–3. Nutrient Words    19

### Lesson 3. What's Inside Me?    21

Things to Know About What's Inside Me    21
Activity 3–1. Bone Smart    23
Activity 3–2. Muscle Smart    29
Activity 3–3. Body Smart    32

### Lesson 4. After I Swallow, What Happens?    34

Things to Know About Digestion    34
Activity 4–1. Fun Facts    36
Activity 4–2. Where Food Goes    38
Activity 4–3. Digestion Action    41

## UNIT 2.   EATING ALL KINDS OF FOOD    44

### Lesson 5. Introducing a Pattern for Daily Food Choices    45

Things to Know About *A Pattern for Daily Food Choices*    45
Activity 5–1. Beary-Good Eating    47
Activity 5–2. Eating Advice    49
Activity 5–3. Serving Numbers    51

### Lesson 6. The Meat Group    53

Things to Know About the Meat Group    53
Activity 6–1. Meat and Legume Scramble    56
Activity 6–2. Protein Smart    59
Activity 6–3. Green Eggs and Ham    61

### Lesson 7. Breads, Grains, and Cereal

    Things to Know About the Bread Group    64
    Activity 7–1. Grain Word Search    66
    Activity 7–2. What Is Enriched?    69
    Activity 7–3. Pockets for Eating    71

### Lesson 8. Fruits    *74*

    Things to Know About Fruit    74
    Activity 8–1. Try It! You'll Like It!    76
    Activity 8–2. Fruit Smart    79
    Activity 8–3. How Fruits Grow    81

### Lesson 9. Vegetables    *83*

    Things to Know About Vegetables    83
    Activity 9–1. Vegetable Taste Test    85
    Activity 9–2. Pizza Smart    88
    Activity 9–3. Vegetable Colors    90

### Lesson 10. Milk, Cheese, and Yogurt    *92*

    Things to Know About the Dairy Group    92
    Activity 10–1. Milk Product Maze    95
    Activity 10–2. Milk Sorting    97
    Activity 10–3. Milk Products    99

### Lesson 11. Fats and Sweets    *101*

    Things to Know About Fats and Sweets    101
    Activity 11–1. Food Group Smart    103
    Activity 11–2. Smart Choices    105
    Activity 11–3. Where's the Fat?    107

# UNIT 3.    EATING HEALTHY FOODS    109

### Lesson 12. Dietary Guidelines    *110*

    Things to Know About the Dietary Guidelines    110
    Activity 12–1. Nutrition-Smart Guidelines Game    112
    Activity 12–2. Guidelines Code    117
    Activity 12–3. Keeping Score    119

### Lesson 13. Eating a Variety of Foods    *121*

    Things to Know About Eating a Variety of Foods    121
    Activity 13–1. Cheeseburger Smart    123
    Activity 13–2. Food Diary    125
    Activity 13–3. Varietarian    128

### Lesson 14. Maintaining Healthy Weight    *130*

    Things to Know About Maintaining Healthy Weight    130
    Activity 14–1. Good Moves    133
    Activity 14–2. Using Energy    135
    Activity 14–3. Exercise Message    138

### Lesson 15. Eating Lowfat Foods    *140*

    Things to Know About Fat and Cholesterol    140
    Activity 15–1. Milk Carton Cutouts    142
    Activity 15–2. Clogged Pipes    145
    Activity 15–3. Fat Finder    149

### Lesson 16. Eating Plenty of Vegetables, Fruits, and Grains    *152*

    Things to Know About Eating Vegetables, Fruits, and Grain Products    152
    Activity 16–1. Starch and Fiber Chains    154
    Activity 16–2. Fiber Foods    157
    Activity 16–3. Fiber Count    159

### Lesson 17. Using Sugars in Moderation    *161*

    Things to Know About Sugars    161
    Activity 17–1. Tooth Smart    165
    Activity 17–2. Ingredient Smart    167
    Activity 17–3. Sugar Decoder    170

### Lesson 18. Using Salt and Sodium in Moderation    *174*

    Things to Know About Salt and Sodium    174
    Activity 18–1. Sodium Smart    176
    Activity 18–2. Sodium Inspector    179
    Activity 18–3. Sodium Vending    182

# UNIT 4.   EATING THROUGHOUT THE DAY    184

### Lesson 19. Breakfast    *184*

    Things to Know About Breakfast    185
    Activity 19–1. Mystery Message    187
    Activity 19–2. Time to Eat    189
    Activity 19–3. Breakfast on the Run    191

### Lesson 20. Lunch    *194*

    Things to Know About Lunch    194
    Activity 20–1. Bag Lunches    196
    Activity 20–2. Menu of Color    200
    Activity 20–3. Fill in the Menu    202

## Lesson 21. Supper  *204*

Things to Know About Supper   204
Activity 21–1. Families   206
Activity 21–2. Supper Steps   208
Activity 21–3. Microwaving   211

## Lesson 22. Snacks  *214*

Things to Know About Snacks   214
Activity 22–1. Choosing Snacks   216
Activity 22–2. Snack Track   218
Activity 22–3. Popcorn Percents   220

## Lesson 23. Convenience Foods and Vending Machines  *223*

Things to Know About Convenience Foods and Vending Machines   223
Activity 23–1A. Fat Pats   225
Activity 23–1B. Fat Pats (higher level)   228
Activity 23–2. Shopping   230
Activity 23–3. Snack Cents   232

## Lesson 24. Advertising  *235*

Things to Know About Advertising   235
Activity 24–1. Commercials   237
Activity 24–2. Slogan Power   239
Activity 24–3. Ads, Ads, Ads   243

## Lesson 25. Cultural Foods  *246*

Things to Know About Cultural Foods   246
Activity 25–1. Favorite Food Flags   247
Activity 25–2. Cultural Foods   249
Activity 25–3. Cultural Food Search   252

## *ANSWER KEY*  *255*

## *APPENDIX: Selected Nutrition Education Materials for Grades K–3*  *264*

# NUTRITION SMART!

# Unit 1. EATING TO GROW

Lesson 1 <u>Growing Up</u>
1-1. Things That Grow
1-2. Growing Bigger
1-3. How Big Am I?

Lesson 2 <u>Nutrients to Grow On</u>
2-1. Riddle
2-2. Food Energy
2-3. Nutrient Words

Lesson 3 <u>What's Inside Me?</u>
3-1. Bone Smart
3-2. Muscle Smart
3-3. Body Smart

Lesson 4 <u>After I Swallow, What Happens?</u>
4-1. Fun Facts
4-2. Where the Food Goes
4-3. Digestion Action

# Lesson 1. *Growing Up*

## Things to Know About Growing Up

*Key Points:*

- Children grow at different rates.

- Excesses or inadequacies in nutrients will be reflected in patterns of growth.

- Children should be encouraged to respect each other's individual growth patterns.

*At what rate do children grow?*

Children grow at different rates and come in a variety of shapes and sizes. Parents need to be reassured that children are very different in the way they grow and mature. There are differences in the rate of growth and development among individual children during any age period. Variations between slow and rapid growth do not necessarily indicate abnormal growth.

During the years between 5-9, the rate of growth slows and becomes erratic. Linear growth is approximately two inches per year until mid-puberty and weight gain about five pounds annually for boys and four pounds for girls. At some periods there are plateaus; at others small spurts of growth occur. The overall erratic rate affects appetite accordingly. At age six, boys are taller and heavier than girls. By age nine, the height of the average girl is the same as that of the nine-year-old male and her weight is slightly greater. Like growth in height, growth in weight settles into a steady annual increase until the onset of adolescence.

Parents may ask teachers if their child is too little, too short, or too tall. The National Center for Health Sciences has growth charts in which you and the parent can plot the child's growth to see if the child falls within the normal range.

*Why are growth charts an appropriate way to show parents that their child is growing normally?*

Children usually grow in height and weight in predictable ways that can be plotted on standard growth graphs. These graphs allow a parent to observe a child's growth over time to see if he or she is following one of the percentile lines on the charts. If there is a child that fails to follow the pattern he/she usually follows, especially if there is a significant change, the problem causing the varying growth pattern can be investigated. Growth charts should normally be used to compare the individual child's growth over time. There is no need to compare one child's growth with another child's because each will vary.

*Are there racial differences in the way children grow?*

Racial differences have been noted in rates of growth. Black Americans grow more rapidly during the first two years of life, and from that age through adolescence are taller than white American boys and girls of the same age. Asian children tend to be smaller than both black and white children.

*How do children's eating patterns affect their growth?*

Excesses or inadequacies in energy and nutrient intakes will be reflected in patterns of growth. The child who is not eating sufficient food will drop in his growth pattern if the food deprivation is severe enough. Some children grow very slowly at first and may seem skinny and lanky. In most cases, this pattern is normal and children will make up the growth difference in time.

Depending on the time of year, children's weight may fluctuate greatly. For example a child in the winter months may gain quite a few pounds due to lack of outdoor physical activity. Also, girls and boys often gain in percentage of body fat just before the growth spurt of puberty.

*How can the food a child eats in his early years have an impact of his lifelong health?*

The food a child eats during the early years can have a major impact on this lifelong health. The first priority is adequate calories and nutrients to allow growth and optimal development. The second priority is prevention of disease. Efforts to manage weight or control blood cholesterol must never be so vigorous that they keep children from growing properly.

The nutritional habits children learn at this age are likely to carry with them for the rest of their lives. If you present a positive attitude about nutrition-smart eating and how it benefits growth, the children in your classroom will also have a positive attitude about eating.

*How can teachers help students feel less anxious about their growth?*

Children want to grow up. They not only want to get bigger but they also want to get better at everything they do. But they don't all get bigger at the same rate. As a teacher, it is necessary to teach the children to respect each other's growth rates and individuality.

# Activity 1-1. Things That Grow

## DIRECTIONS TO THE TEACHER

**Objective** (Cognitive Domain: Comprehension Level)

Students will distinguish between things that grow and things that do not grow.

## Materials

Student Activity Sheet (1)
Pencil

## Prerequisite Skills

Can differentiate between living and nonliving.

## Procedure

1. Define growth. Things that grow get bigger. All living things grow (until they reach maturation). Nonliving things like rocks and pencils do not grow.

2. Discuss growth with students. Some sample questions are:
   - How can you tell that you have grown?
   - Is everyone in your family growing? Does everyone grow at the same rate?
   - Why do we grow?
   - Will everyone grow to the same size?
   - What other things grow?

3. Distribute the activity sheet and explain the directions.

## Supplementary Activities

1. Ask students to make a collage of living and nonliving things. Use pictures cut from magazines. Place cutouts of living things on one side and nonliving things on the other side.

2. Discuss Japanese bonsai plants. These are potted plants (such as a tree) that are dwarfed by special methods of culture. Show how things that normally grow are kept from growing just by changing conditions, such as the size of the environment, water, and nutrients.

3. Discuss and compare requirements for growth of different living things. Plants require sunlight, air, water, and nutrients. Animals require sunlight, air, water, and food.

Name _____ Date _____

## Activity 1-1. Things That Grow

**Directions:** Circle things that grow. Put an **X** through the things that don't grow.

How many of these things grow? _____

How many of these things don't grow? _____

Draw three more things that grow in the spaces below.

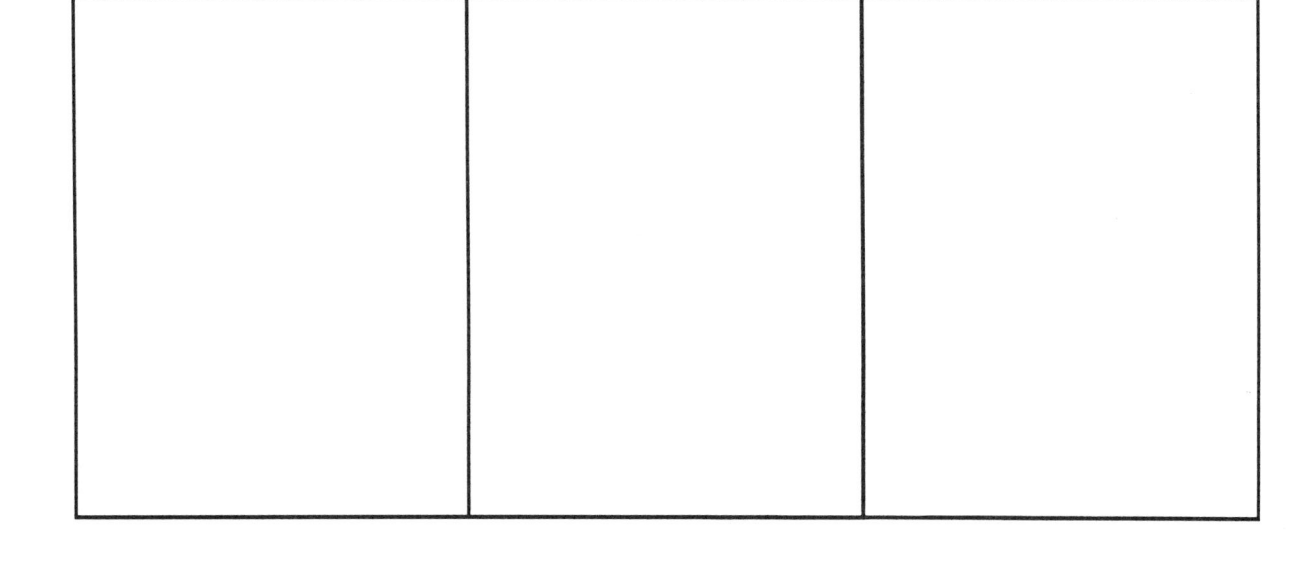

|  |  |  |
|---|---|---|
|  |  |  |

# Activity 1-2. Growing Bigger

## DIRECTIONS TO THE TEACHER

**Objective**  (Cognitive Domain: Knowledge Level)

Students will label pictures by numbering them to indicate the life stages of living things.

## Materials

Student Activity Sheet (1)
Pencil
Crayons

## Prerequisite Skills

Sequencing
Numbering

## Procedure

1. Review the concept of growth. Explain that some growing things look very different at certain stages of development. For example, a butterfly was once a caterpillar.

2. Distribute the activity sheet and explain the directions.

## Supplementary Activities

1. Have students bring in baby pictures and talk about ways they have grown. Try to match the pictures with the students. You can do this with the faculty, too. Ask faculty members to bring in photographs of themselves when they were in the grade they are now teaching.

2. Read The Very Hungry Caterpillar by Eric Carle. (Published by William Collins and World Publishing Company, 1970.) Help children to see the relationship between eating and growing.

3. Have students choose a vegetable seed to plant (navy beans or peas sprout quickly). Discuss how water, soil, and sunlight are required for growth. What happens if a plant is kept in the shade? What happens if it does not get enough water? Will a seed sprout without soil?

4. Have students write a short story to explain the stages depicted on the worksheet. Students should write at least one sentence to accompany each picture.

Name _____ Date _____

## Activity 1-2. Growing Bigger

**Directions:** Number the pictures in each row to show how things grow. The first one has been done for you.

rooster __3__      chick __2__      egg __1__

frog ____      egg ____      tadpole ____

sprout ____      plant ____      seed ____

**Now draw pictures to show how you have grown!**

| baby | preschooler | today |

© 1991 by The Center for Applied Research in Education

# Activity 1-3. How Big Am I?

## DIRECTIONS TO THE TEACHER

**Objective** (Cognitive Domain: Application Level)

Students will use a piece of string or tape measure to measure parts of his/her body.

**Materials**

Student Activity Sheets (2)
Pencil
Tape measure or string and ruler

**Prerequisite Skills**

Measuring
Reading/writing

**Procedure**

1. Discuss how we can discover the length of an object. Students may suggest rulers, yardsticks, tape measures, and so on.

    • What are different body parts that can be measured on the body?
    • How do measurements change as we grow? Students may say longer or bigger around.

2. Distribute the activity sheets and explain the directions. Demonstrate how to take some measurements. Give students directions for completing the activity. If you use the string/ruler method for measuring, give each student at least a yard of string. On the neck, for instance, show them how they would place one end of the string under the chin at their throat and place the other end at the bottom of their throat or top of their chest bone. They may want to measure two or three times before they record. This may reduce error. Older students can take three measurements at each site and then average the three-for-one length.

3. Provide suggestions for how to measure each body part. For example, explain that to measure the hand, start at the tip of the longest finger and end at the wrist.

**Supplementary Activities**

1. Have the students measure an adult. How are the results different?

2. Using a tape measure, have students work in pairs to measure their arm spans and their heights. Collect and display the data to determine if a relationship exists between arm span and height.

3. Give each child two squares of construction paper. Have students trace both hands and both feet on construction paper, then cut out the hand and foot shapes. Print each child's name and date on one hand and foot and on the other write a nutrition growing word, such as nutrients, protein, vitamins, minerals, bigger, longer, and so on. Then attach the hands and feet cutouts to the bulletin board in the shape of a body to symbolize class unity and growth. Do this at the beginning and end of the school year so the students can see their growth.

4. Have students work in pairs. Using large rolls of paper, one student can trace the other. Individuals can then draw in details and color themselves. Finished portraits can be compared to show differences in individual growth patterns.

5. Have students work in groups of three to measure each other. How much difference is there between the tallest and the smallest?

Name _____ Date _____

## Activity 1-3. How Big Am I?

**Directions:** Use a tape measure to fill in the measurements below. Answer the questions on page 2.

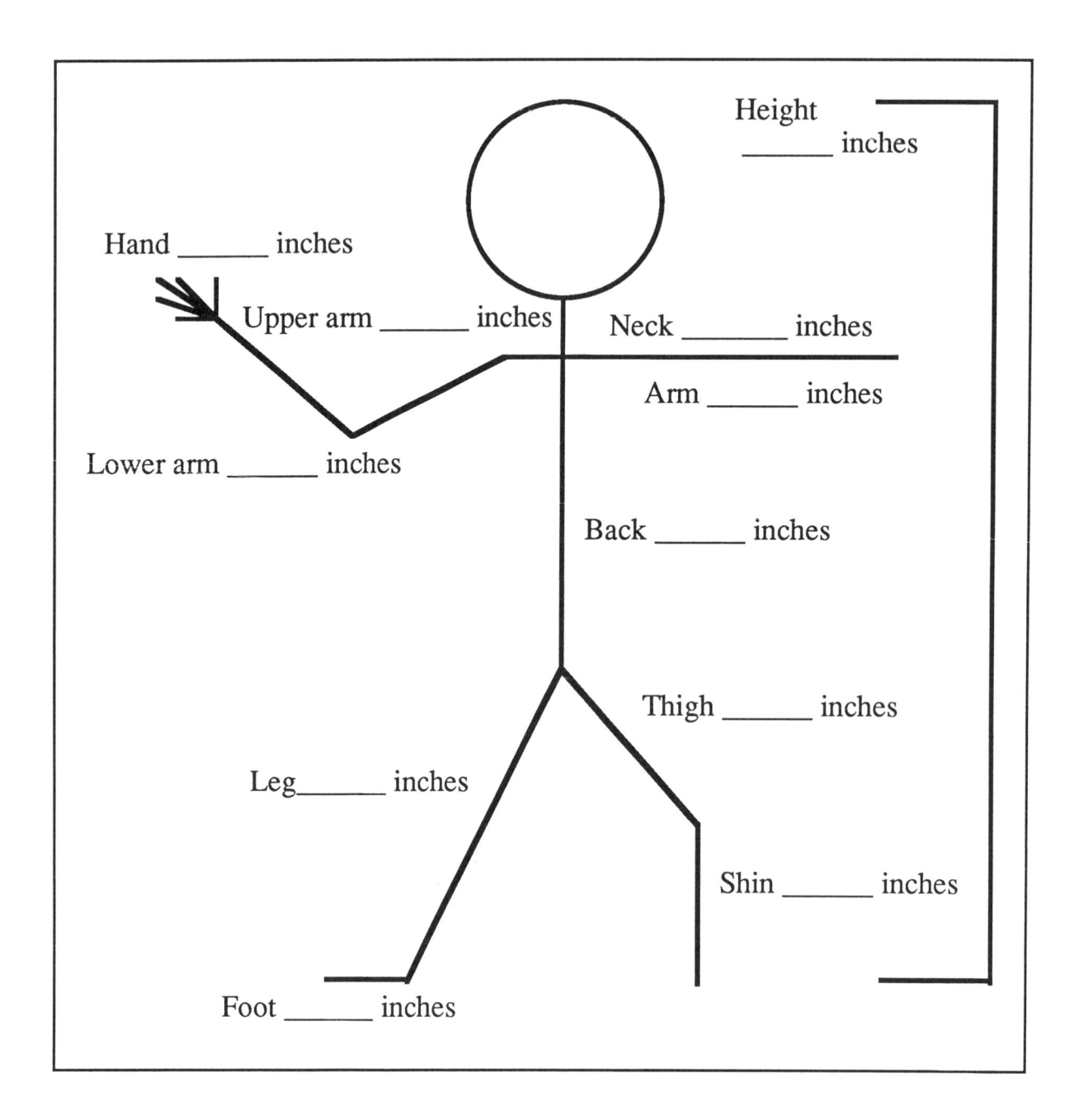

Height _____ inches

Hand _____ inches

Upper arm _____ inches

Neck _____ inches

Arm _____ inches

Lower arm _____ inches

Back _____ inches

Thigh _____ inches

Leg _____ inches

Shin _____ inches

Foot _____ inches

© 1991 by The Center for Applied Research in Education

Name _____ Date _____

## Activity 1-3. How Big Am I? *page 2*

1. Which is the longest part of your body? _____

2. How many inches tall are you? _____
   Most newborn babies are about 20 inches long.
   How much have you grown since you were born?

   _____

   (Hint: Height now in inches — 20 inches = growth)

3. How many inches long are your feet? _____
   Most newborn's feet are about 3 inches long.
   How much have your feet grown since you were born?

   _____

   (Hint: Foot now in inches — 3 inches = growth)

4. How many inches long is your hand? _____
   Most newborns' hands are about 2 inches long.
   How much have your hands grown?

   _____

   (Hint: Hand now in inches — 2 inches = growth)

© 1991 by The Center for Applied Research in Education

# Lesson 2. *Nutrients to Grow On*

## Things to Know About Nutrients

*Key Points:*

- There are six classes of nutrients.
- Only three nutrients give us energy.
- Over half of our food energy should come from carbohydrates.
- No one food contains all the nutrients needed.

*What are the major kinds of nutrients?*

There are over forty different nutrients required by the body for good health. These nutrients can be classified into six major groups:

| | | |
|---|---|---|
| carbohydrates | vitamins | protein |
| minerals | fat | water |

*What are the energy nutrients?*

There are three nutrients that provide energy. They are protein, carbohydrates, and fat. Both protein and carbohydrates provide four Calories per gram. Fat has more energy and provides nine Calories per gram. Besides providing energy, protein also has several important functions in the body and is used to build and repair tissue. However, most adults and children in America consume much more protein than their bodies need for these functions. Thus the excess protein is used for energy or stored as fat. Experts recommend that we reduce our intake of fat and eat more carbohydrates.

To increase your intake of carbohydrates, eat more:

| | |
|---|---|
| bread | pasta |
| cereal | fruit |
| starchy vegetables (potatoes, corn, lima beans) | rice |
| dried beans and peas | grains |

To decrease your intake of fats, eat less:

| | |
|---|---|
| butter and margarine | fried foods |
| fried snack foods (potato chips, nachos) | rich desserts ( pastries, pies) |
| fatty meats (sausage, hamburger, lunch meats) | cheese |
| | whole milk products |

Foods high in protein include:

- meat, fish, poultry
- milk
- eggs
- dried beans and peas (tofu, peanut butter, lentils)

*What about vitamins?*

There are two kinds of vitamins -- fat-soluble and water-soluble. Vitamins A, D, E, and K are fat-soluble and can be stored by the body. So, you don't need to have them every day. If you take high doses of fat-soluble vitamins in the form of a vitamin pill or supplement, you might experience toxic effects and become ill. You don't need to worry about toxicity if you meet your vitamin needs by consuming a varied diet. The water-soluble vitamins are all the B vitamins and vitamin C. These vitamins help the body use carbohydrates, protein, and fat for energy. These vitamins are needed every day because the body can only store a small amount of them. Most schoolchildren can meet all of their vitamin needs by eating a varied diet. Vitamin supplements are only needed in special circumstances. Parents who are concerned about their child's vitamin intake should speak to their pediatrician or dietitian.

*What about minerals?*

Many different minerals are needed by the body. Some of the minerals that are needed in the largest amounts include: calcium, phosphorus, magnesium, iron, iodine, zinc, and fluoride.

Calcium is a mineral that has received a lot of media attention. Most of the calcium in the body is used to build bones and teeth. When there is too little calcium in the diet, the bones and teeth become soft. As one ages this leads to a condition called osteoporosis. People who have osteoporosis tend to have a stooped back and are more likely to break their bones. To help prevent osteoporosis you should include adequate calcium in your diet over your lifetime. Milk and milk products are the richest sources of calcium in the diet. One cup of milk has about 300 milligrams of calcium. The Recommended Dietary Allowance (RDA) for calcium for children is 800 milligrams a day.

Iron is the nutrient that is most commonly deficient in the American diet. When iron deficiency is severe, a child will become anemic. The best sources of iron in the diet are organ meats, shellfish, and meats. These foods contain heme iron. Heme iron is well absorbed by the body. Non-heme iron is less well absorbed by the body. Good sources of non-heme iron include: nuts, green vegetables, and fortified breads and cereals. To increase the absorption of non-heme iron, these foods could be consumed with sources of heme iron or vitamin C. The RDA for iron for children is 10 milligrams a day.

*What about water?*

Water is a very important nutrient. A man could live for two months without food, but would die in about six days if deprived of water. Daily, we need to ingest a little more than eight cups of water. We obtain water from fluids and from solid foods. Many solid foods contain a large amount of water. For example, lettuce is 96% water, oranges 86%, and potatoes 80%.

All tissues in the body are made of water. Growth would be impossible without water. Water is also necessary for the process of digestion. It helps break complex nutrients into simpler components.

Water is an especially important nutrient for athletes since they lose large amounts of fluids in perspiration and exhalation. Children who participate in sports should drink before, during, and after exercising. Special sports drinks are not necessary for child athletes. Plain water is best. Since thirst is not always an accurate indicator of fluid needs, athletes need to make a conscious effort to replace fluids.

# Activity 2-1. Riddle

## DIRECTIONS TO THE TEACHER

**Objective** (Cognitive Domain: Knowledge Level)

Students will list water as a nutrition-smart drink.

**Materials**

Student Activity Sheet (1)
Pencils, pens, or crayons

**Prerequisite Skills**

Following directions
Reading/writing

**Procedure**

1. Distribute the activity sheet and explain the directions.

2. Follow up with a discussion on water. Reinforce the importance of drinking water every day. Ask the students: How do you know when your body needs water? When are you most thirsty?

**Supplementary Activities**

1. Food can have from a 0% to 96% water content. White granulated sugar has no water but lettuce has 96% water. Offer your students a variety of foods from the basic food groups and ask them to rank them according to water content. Foods within groups will vary, but typically vegetables, fruit, milk, meat, cheese, bread, butter, and sugar would be the order from most to least percent water content. (Bread is 36% water and butter is 20% water.) Conclude by reminding students that even though water is in the foods we eat, we still need other fluids or beverages throughout the day. Water needs increase as temperature and activity increase.

2. Demonstrate the water content of lettuce. Place lettuce leaves in the sun to dry. Explain that the water evaporates.

3. Provide a bag of oranges for the class or ask each student to bring in an orange and make orange juice. How many oranges does it take to make a cup of orange juice? Point out that oranges contain a lot of water. That is why we are able to make juice from them.

4. Ask groups of students to develop a television commercial to promote water and act out their commercial for their classmates.

5. Visit a bottled water facility. Facts about the amount of drinking water sold daily could help students recognize that water is becoming a more popular beverage choice.

Name _____ Date _____

## Activity 2-1. Riddle

**Directions:** Look at the two words in each row. Find the letter that is in the first word but not in the second word. Write the letter in the box on the right. When you are finished, you will spell the name of the nutrient. Here is an example:

| What letter is in | Box | but not in | Fox | B |

| What letter is in | SWARM | But not in | RAMPS | |
|---|---|---|---|---|
| What letter is in | CARE | But not in | CLEVER | |
| What letter is in | CREATE | But not in | RACE | |
| What letter is in | TEETH | But not in | THAT | |
| What letter is in | BARK | But not in | BAKE | |

Now write the name of the nutrition-smart word on the girl's sign.

Ice Cold
_ _ _ _ _ for sale!
5¢ a glass

© 1991 by The Center for Applied Research in Education

# Activity 2-2. Food Energy

## DIRECTIONS TO THE TEACHER

**Objective** (Cognitive Domain: Knowledge Level)

Given a list of foods and nutrient information, students will select the appropriate foods to answer a variety of nutrition questions.

### Materials

Student Activity Sheets (2)
Pencil

### Prerequisite Skills

Chart reading

### Procedure

1. Explain that energy makes things grow. For example, electricity is a form of energy that makes a lamp work. Gas produces energy to make a car go.

2. Ask the students what provides energy to make people go.

3. Discuss energy with students. Some sample questions are:

    • How do you feel when you have energy?
    • How do you feel when you don't have energy?
    • How do you get energy?
    • Do any foods give you energy?
    • How do you know how much energy is in a food?
    • What nutrients in foods give you energy?

4. Distribute both activity sheets and explain the directions.

### Supplementary Activities

1. Ask students to collect some food labels with nutrition information. Examine the food labels by answering the questions found on The Food Energy Worksheet.

2. Experts recommend that we get the majority of our energy from carbohydrates like fruits, vegetables, and grain products. Make a collage of foods that are high in carbohydrates (and low in fat). Present some high carbohydrate, lowfat snacks in class.

Name _____ Date _____

## Activity 2-2. Food Energy

**Directions:** Use the charts below to complete page 2.

**Whole wheat bread (1 slice)**

| | |
|---|---|
| Food energy | 70 Calories |
| Carbohydrates | 12 grams |
| Protein | 3 grams |
| Fat | 1 gram |

**Apple (1 apple)**

| | |
|---|---|
| Food energy | 80 Calories |
| Carbohydrates | 20 grams |
| Protein | 0 grams |
| Fat | 0 grams |

**Chicken leg (1 leg)**

| | |
|---|---|
| Food energy | 75 Calories |
| Carbohydrates | 2 grams |
| Protein | 12 grams |
| Fat | 2 grams |

**Cheddar Cheese (1 ounce)**

| | |
|---|---|
| Food energy | 115 Calories |
| Carbohydrates | 2 grams |
| Protein | 7 grams |
| Fat | 9 grams |

**Green pepper (1 pepper)**

| | |
|---|---|
| Food energy | 20 Calories |
| Carbohydrates | 4 grams |
| Protein | 1 gram |
| Fat | 0 grams |

© 1991 by The Center for Applied Research in Education

Name _____ Date _____

# Activity 2-2. Food Energy, *page 2*

1) Circle the food that has the most calories.

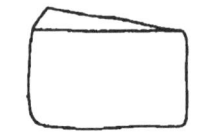

2) Circle the food that has the least calories.

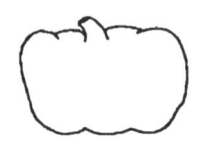

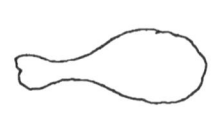

3) Circle the food that has the most carbohydrates.

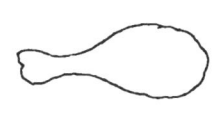

4) Circle the food that has the most protein.

5) Circle the food that has the most fat.

6) Circle the two foods that have no fat.

# Activity 2-3. Nutrient Words

## DIRECTIONS TO THE TEACHER

**Objective**  (Cognitive Domain: Knowledge Level)

Students will list the six major nutrients found in foods.

**Materials**

Student Activity Sheet (1)
Pencil

**Prerequisite Skills**

Letter finding skills
Letter formation

**Procedure**

1. Define nutrients. (*Refer to background information*)

2. Introduce the six major classes of nutrients. Provide students with one example (carbohydrates) and initial consonants for the remaining five nutrients. Can students list any from prior knowledge or experience? Give clues to help students as needed.

3. Distribute the student activity sheet and explain the directions.

**Supplementary Activities**

1. Contact your local Dairy Council and request that one of their nutrition educators speak to the class on nutrients.

2. Write the word "carbohydrates" on the chalkboard and ask students to arrange the letters to make as many different words as possible. Follow through with the other five classes of nutrients.

3. Look at the nutrition information on a food product label. Identify the nutrient classes. Have the students determine which nutrient class is missing. Explain that water content is not listed but this is no reflection of its importance as an essential nutrient. Point out that only some vitamins and minerals needed for health are actually listed.

Name _____ Date _____

## Activity 2-3. Nutrient Words

**Directions:** There are six major nutrients hidden in the puzzle below. Can you find them all?

*carbohydrate	vitamin*
*fat	mineral*
*protein	water*

```
c a r b o h y d r a t e x
w o x g k m v i t a m i n
a i l e m i s g l e p m h
t a n d w n d i l i r s n
e d j x g e o t y e o f y
r h u l r r y a e s t d w
a p q i j a e u o r e y z
p y r m w l r g e o i a z
s o t f a t o i r y n l o
```

Below you will see the word protein. Spaces are provided to write the other five nutrients using the letters in protein. Write them.

```
              P
              R
 _ _          O _ _ _ _ _ _ _ _
              
              
      _ _     T
    _ _ _     E _
              I _ _ _ _ _
        _ _   N _ _ _ _
```

# Lesson 3. *What's Inside Me?*

## Things to Know About What's Inside Me

*Key Points:*

- Body systems work together.

- Nutrients are necessary for all body systems to function properly.

*What's underneath our skin?*

Inside and outside, our bodies are composed entirely of cells. Cells are the structural units of the body from which all larger parts are formed. Not all these cells are exactly alike. They function differently and vary in shape and size. For example, muscle cells both function differently and look different than bone cells. They also use nutrients in different ways.

Underneath the skin, body systems are constantly at work. These include the skeletal, muscular, nervous, endocrine, digestive, respiratory, circulatory or cardiovascular, lymphatic, urinary, and reproductive systems. For this unit we will discuss only the skeletal, muscular, and circulatory systems.

*What is the muscular system?*

Muscles account for half the body weight. There are more than six hundred muscle groups in the human body. Muscle cells are unique in that they can contract and relax. When muscle cells contract, they pull on the parts to which they are attached. This results in movement, as when the joints of the leg are flexed and extended during walking. Sometimes muscles contract to resist movement, as when standing. Muscles are also responsible for the circulation of blood, and aid in maintaining body temperature, such as in heat production.

As children grow in body size so does the muscular system. No powders or special potions will make muscles bigger or stronger. Children need to learn that muscle strength comes from eating a variety of foods and exercising muscles.

Children perceive muscles differently than the physiologist. Children see muscles as strength and possibly even power. Muscles go beyond the "He-man" stereotype. Muscles are important for other things than just physical strength. Since the heart is a muscle and must be strong and conditioned, an explanation of how a muscle grows based on exercise and conditioning should also include the heart as a muscle. Aerobic exercise should be taught as the best way to condition the heart muscle.

*What nutrients support the muscular system?*

Protein, fat, zinc, potassium, and fourteen vitamins are just a few of the many nutrients needed during tissue growth.

*How does the muscular system work with the circulatory system?*

The blood, heart, and blood vessels make up the circulatory system. The heart muscle and blood vessels move blood throughout the body. To do this, the heart acts as a pump that forces blood through the vessels. The heart and blood vessels make up the cardiovascular system. The blood vessels transport the blood and allow an exchange of nutrients, gases, and wastes between the blood and the body cells.

*What nutrients support the circulatory system?*

Iron, protein, vitamin C, copper, and several B vitamins play major roles in blood formation and function. The average adult body contains only about one-half teaspoon of iron. Iron carries and releases oxygen to body cells for energy. During growth, when blood volume increases, iron requirements also increase.

*What is the skeletal system?*

The bones represent the skeletal system. There are 206 bones in the human body. Bones are hard on the outer surface and soft inside. Thirty percent of bone is living tissue, cells, and blood vessels. Forty-five percent is mineral deposits, mostly calcium phosphate. Twenty-five percent is water. Bones support and protect softer tissues in the body. Together, bones and skeletal muscles make movement possible. Bones move with other bones at joints. Bones lengthen and thicken during growth, and adapt to the changing weight of the body throughout life.

*What nutrients support the skeletal system?*

Bone growth requires protein, calcium, phosphorus, fluorine, boron, and vitamins D, A, and C. The skeleton serves as a calcium bank to maintain a constant level of calcium in the blood. Calcium can be "deposited" in the bones from the food we eat. Calcium can be "withdrawn" from the skeleton when blood levels are low. Calcium deposits and withdrawals are continually being made, keeping bones in a state of constant flux of formation and dissolution.

Calcium requirements vary throughout life. For children twelve and under, the recommended daily fluid milk intake is three cups or its equivalent in milk products. See Unit 2, Milk and Milk Products, for more information.

# Activity 3-1. Bone Smart

## DIRECTIONS TO THE TEACHER

**Objective** (Cognitive Domain: Application Level)

Students will demonstrate how joints work on a model and on themselves.

## Materials

Student Activity Sheets (4)
Scissors
Paper clasps (13 per student) - May substitute clasps with pipe cleaners, twist ties, or string
Hole punch

## Preparation

Students will each need two copies of arm/leg patterns and one copy of other pages. Complete a model

## Prerequisite Skills

Cutting

## Procedure

1. Have the students play "Simon Says" with commands that emphasize joint movements. For example, if Simon says, "Touch your toes," or "bend your elbows," the joints are emphasized.

2. Present a model of the Bone Smart Skeleton.

3. Explain that there are 206 bones in the human body. Half the bones are in the hands and feet. For this activity we are just looking at how large bones move at the joints.

4. Explain that the biggest bones (longest too) are the bones in the leg. If a person grows to be 6 feet tall each thigh bone will be almost 20 inches long. Show the students 20 inches on a yardstick.

5. Distribute the activity sheets and explain the directions. Young children just developing cutting skills may need to do this activity in groups to reduce the number of pieces needed to be cut and assembled.

6. Talk about and show how the joints work on the model. Explain that bones do not bend. Arms, legs, and other parts of the body bend at the places where two bones join together (the joints).

7. Have students stand with arms at their sides. From head to toe, what body parts can be moved by joints? How many movements can students generate?

8. Raise the hand with the glass of milk to show the skeleton drinking milk. Reinforce milk as a source of calcium. Explain that calcium is a nutrient used to make strong bones.

9. You may want to go a step further and explain that bones are hard and strong on the outside and inside they are soft and spongy.

**Supplementary Activities**

1. Demonstrate how the mineral *calcium* is needed to keep bones strong and healthy. Conduct an experiment to show students what bones would be like if some of the calcium were taken out. Show the children a healthy bone (such as a chicken bone or turkey bone) and ask them to describe how it looks and feels. Soak three or four chicken or turkey bones in two cups of white vinegar for two weeks. Check them every three or four days and change the vinegar if needed. (The acid of the vinegar will cause the bones to decalcify.) When the bones have softened, rinse them off with water and pass them around for the students to feel.

Compare the bones soaked in vinegar with the healthy bones. How are the bones that were soaked in vinegar different from the healthy bones? What has happened to the bones soaked in vinegar? Why do we need calcium in our bones?

NOTE: Under these experimental conditions, decalcifying the bones leaves them soft, flexible, and rubberlike. The acid environment we expose the bones to in the experiment is much different from what the bones experience in the body. When bones decalcify in the body, as with the disease osteoporosis, they become porous and brittle and can easily be broken. Point out these differences to your students.

2. Explain bone development. We were all born with soft bones. They are made of cartilage. Explain to your students this is a rubberlike substance. The tip of the nose is cartilage. Ask your students to use their fingers to wiggle around their noses to get an idea of what bones feel like before they harden. After birth bones become coated with layers of minerals, mostly calcium phosphate. As a result, they harden. Calcium phosphate comes from milk. It deposits on the bone from the center and builds outward in a process called calcification. In soaking the bone, you are reducing the bone to its underlying cartilage material.

3. Thinking of joints, introduce the words bend, swivel, stretch, snap, clench, pivot, and point. See if the children can perform these different kinds of motion.

4. Call or visit your local hospital and ask for some old X-rays you can display in the classroom. If a student (or teacher) breaks a bone, ask them to ask the doctor if the class could have the X-ray.

5. Bones are hidden behind layers of fat and muscle. However, there are places on our bodies where we can see some bones. Ask the students to name them. (They are the jaw bone, collar bone, elbow, pelvis, sternum, knee cap, and shin bone.)

6. Ask your butcher for bones. Try to get a cylindrical bone like the shin. Ask the butcher to saw it lengthwise so that your students can study its structure. You can do a joint dissection with beef knuckles. The outer layer of bone is calcified, followed by spongy bone, and the center is marrow. The marrow is the factory for red blood cell formation.

Name _____ Date _____

## Activity 3-1. Bone Smart

**Directions:**

1) Draw and color your face on the head pattern. Make sure the hole is at the bottom.

2) Cut out all pattern pieces.

3) Use a hole punch to punch holes where marked on each pattern piece.

4) Fasten joints together with clasps so it looks like your teacher's model.

Calcium helps make my bones strong

© 1991 by The Center for Applied Research in Education

**3-1. Bone Smart,** *page 2*

**Arm bone pattern**

**Leg bone pattern**

© 1991 by The Center for Applied Research in Education

**3-1. Bone Smart,** *page 3*

**Head Pattern**

**Foot Pattern**

© 1991 by The Center for Applied Research in Education

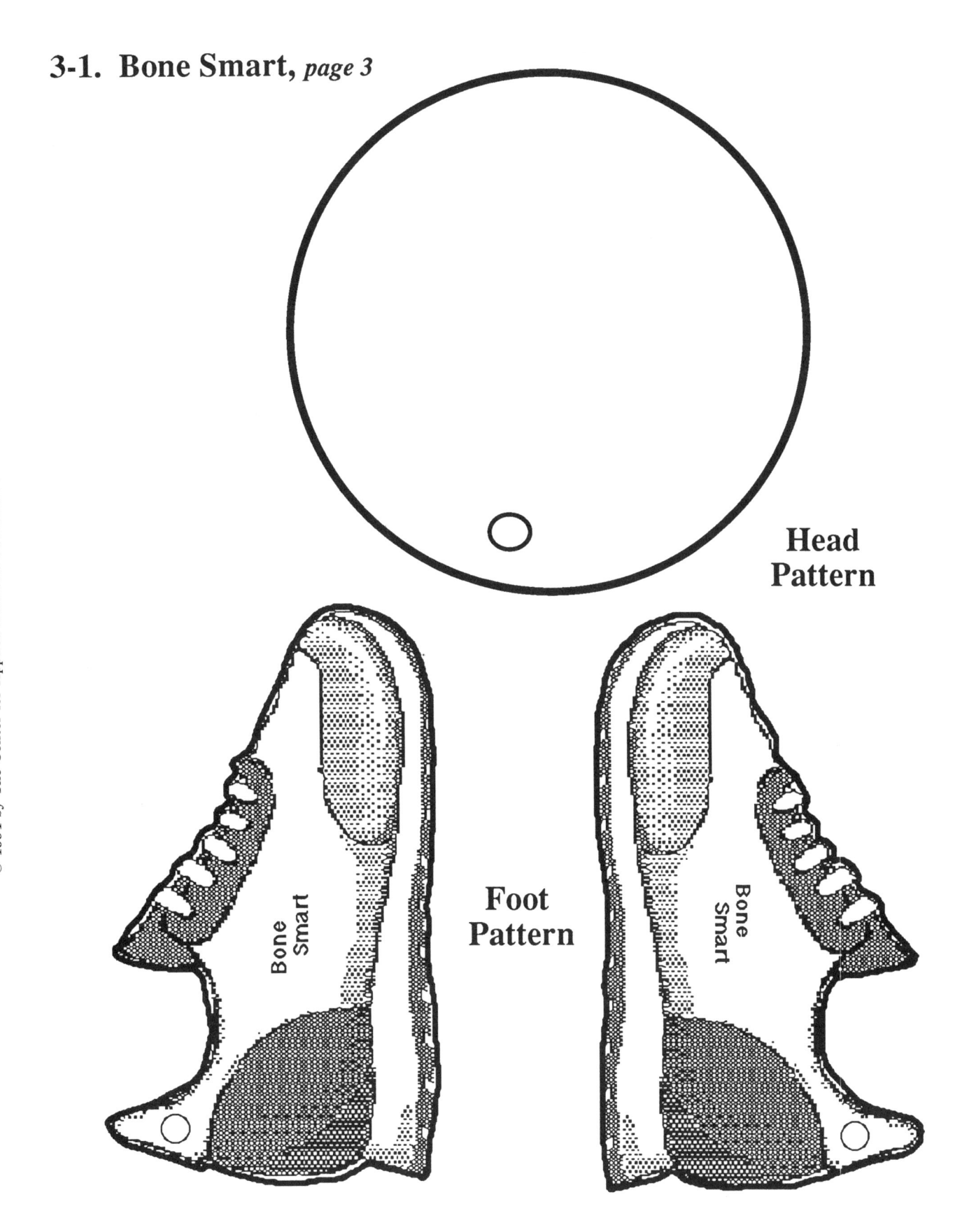

Bone Smart

**3-1. Bone Smart**, *page 4*

**Hand Pattern**

**Calcium helps make my bones strong**

**Body Pattern**

© 1991 by The Center for Applied Research in Education

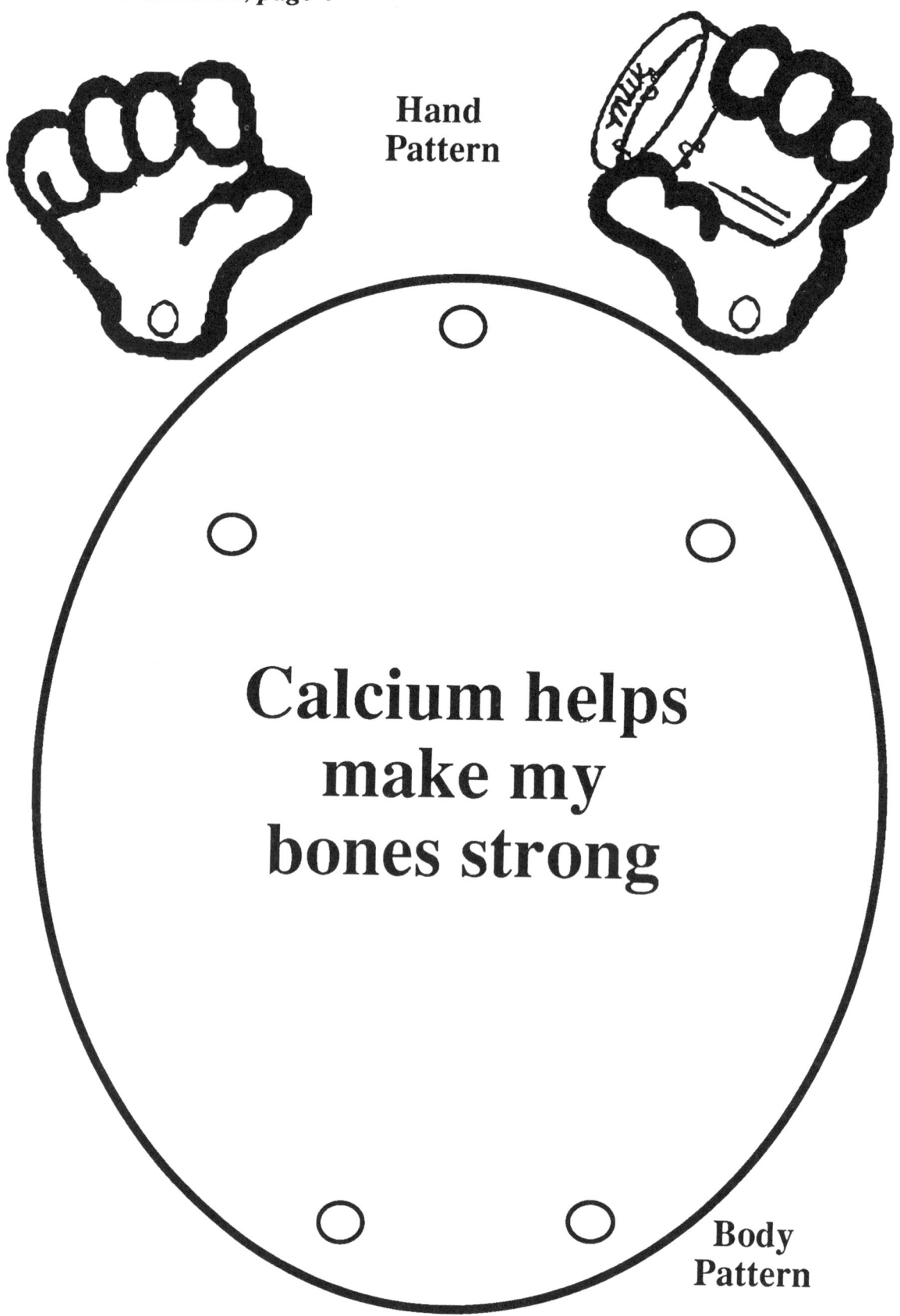

# Activity 3-2. Muscle Smart

### DIRECTIONS TO THE TEACHER

**Objective** (Cognitive Domain: Analysis Level)

Students will discriminate between gross motor (muscle building) activities and fine motor activities.

### Materials

Student Activity Sheet (1)
Pencil
Crayons or markers, if they choose to color the pictures

### Prerequisite Skills

Reading and writing are not required.

### Procedure

1. Introduce the muscular system and these words: bend, reach, twist, lift, flip, and leap. Ask students to demonstrate these words using muscles.

2. Inform your students that muscles make up about half the weight of the whole body. The size of the muscle depends on how much it is used and how big you are.

3. Explain that when you sit, lie down, or eat you use a small part of each muscle. On the other hand, when you run, play games, dance, or swim you make your muscles work hard. Hard work done often makes a muscle become stronger and bigger.

4. Discuss the importance of moving and working large muscles for strength conditioning and for building the heart muscle. You may need to remind your students that the heart is a major muscle. They may not see it working, but as they move large muscles the heart is also working. This can be experienced by placing their hand over their hearts before and after exercise. They should feel the heart pounding faster and harder.

5. Distribute the activity sheet and explain the directions.

6. Children may want to color the pictures.

### Supplementary Activities

1. Use the activities pictured on the activity sheet. Ask the students to act each one out. For example, say "While sitting in your chair, pretend you are riding a bicycle. What muscles do you use?" and so on.

2. Ask your students to keep a record of the activities they do for one or more days. Then categorize them into activities that work large muscles and those that work small muscles in the fingers, toes, and face. Look for a balance of both types of activities.

3. Ask your students to flex their biceps. Watch your students mimic the he-man concept. Let them feel their muscles contract and relax. Explain that muscles are made of long skinny cells that form a muscle bundle. Many bundles make a muscle group, like the biceps. Explain that a muscle fiber can either contract or relax -- there is nothing in between. When a child lifts a carton of milk to drink only a few fibers contract. However, when he or she lifts a younger brother or sister, every fiber may contract.

4. Let your students give their faces a workout. Using their face muscles, ask them to open and shut their nostrils, pull their scalp back, pull their ears back, raise their ears, raise their eyebrows, wink, open their mouth wide and pull their top lip down, and turn the corners of their mouths up and down.

5. Invite your school's physical education teacher to your classroom to discuss the muscular system. Ask the teacher to explain why exercise and the regular movement of the large muscles is important in health and well-being. Reinforce the necessity for regular exercise throughout life.

6. Do some stretching exercises. Ask your students to stretch -- mimicking a cat -- using both arms, legs, back, neck, and tail. Explain that stretching is important for muscle health. Any time you exercise the large muscles you should stretch before and after. This helps prevent injury to the muscle and gives you more flexibility.

Name _____  Date _____

## Activity 3-2. Muscle Smart

**Directions:** Activities like running and playing ball make muscles work hard. When muscles work hard, they become bigger and stronger. Some of the activities pictured below make muscles work hard. Circle them.

© 1991 by The Center for Applied Research in Education

# Activity 3-3. Body Smart

## DIRECTIONS TO THE TEACHER

**Objective** (Cognitive Domain: Knowledge Level)

Given information regarding organ functions, students will label statements as true or false.

## Materials

Student Activity Sheet (1)
Pencil

## Prerequisite Skills

Reading
An understanding of true/false concepts

## Procedure

1. Write two definitions for "organ" on the board. One definition should describe an organ as a musical instrument while the other should describe organs within the body. Explain that you will be discussing organs as part of the day's nutrition lesson. Have students vote on which definition seems to apply to the day's lesson.

2. Have students generate a list of organs found in the body. Are students aware of specific organ functions?

3. Distribute the activity sheet. Read and discuss the information presented in the box. Elaborate as appropriate for your students. Explain the directions.

## Supplementary Activities

1. Your students may enjoy watching the Live-Action Sesame Street video, *Parts of the Body: All About You.* Video catalog - Guidance Associates, Communications Park, Box 3000, Mount Kisco, NY 10549-9989, 800-431-1242. Songs, games, and exercises actively involve children as they learn to identify basic parts of their bodies.

2. Make students more aware of key organs in the body by demonstrating or discussing activities like: reacting to a movement or sound, taking your pulse, holding your breath, listening to your stomach growl, or feeling gas in your intestines.

3. An "invisible man" model might help students gain an awareness of organ location. If such a model is not available, overlays such as those often found in encyclopedias may serve the same purpose. Students may wish to make their own models with overlays made from clear plastic transparencies.

Name _____ Date _____

# Activity 3-3. Body Smart

| ORGAN | FUNCTION |
|---|---|
| Brain | control center |
| Kidneys | help get rid of waste |
| Heart | pumps blood |
| Lungs | help you breathe |
| Stomach | holds food |

**Directions:** Answer the sentence true or false. Circle the letter in the correct column. Copy the circled letters onto the blanks below to reveal the special message.

|  | True | or | False |
|---|---|---|---|
| 1. Your stomach is central control. | N |  | Y |
| 2. Your intestines help you breathe. | J |  | D |
| 3. Your lungs work with your stomach. | M |  | K |
| 4. Your brain controls your thoughts and actions. | N |  | U |
| 5. Your heart holds food. | S |  | T |
| 6. Your kidneys remove waste. | S |  | A |

_M_ _ _            _B_ _O_ _ _ _
    1                    2  1

_W_ _ _O_ _ _R_ _ _S_         _O_ _
        3                    4

_ _U_ _ _R_I_E_ _ _ _
4    5            4 5 6

© 1991 by The Center for Applied Research in Education

# Lesson 4. *After I Swallow, What Happens?*

## Things to Know About Digestion

*Key Points:*

- Digestion breaks down food into nutrients that can be used by the body.

- The small intestine is the major organ of digestion, but the mouth, esophagus, stomach, and large intestine all play a role in digesting foods.

*What are the organs of the digestive system?*

The major organs of the digestive system tract include the mouth, throat (esophagus), stomach, and intestines (large and small). The organs are listed in the sequence in which food passes through them.

*What is digestion?*

Digestion is a major physiological process involved in the utilization of food. Before cells can receive nourishment from ingested foods, the complex molecules contained in the food must first be broken down by digestion into molecules small enough to travel in the circulatory system to the cells.

A simple way to explain digestion to children may be to first explain that in their food there are things the body can use and things it cannot use. Digestion is the process of eating food which is chopped and churned and changed into tiny bits by special juices. Then the useful things can be sorted out and sent where they are needed.

Once food is swallowed, the food must be broken down into nutrients. These nutrients circulate to body parts and are incorporated into body cells. These three phases are termed digestion, absorption, and metabolism. Digestion is the process that breaks food down into its component nutrients. Absorption is the process by which the nutrients leave the digestive tract and move into the circulatory system. Finally, metabolism is the process in which the cells utilize the nutrients. The nutrients can be metabolized, or used, for energy, growth, or for the maintenance and repair of cells.

*How do the organs in the digestive system work?*

The mouth is the first organ of digestion. Chewing breaks the food into small particles and mixes the food with saliva. Just the anticipation or presence of food can stimulate the release of saliva in the mouth. Saliva plays several roles, including moistening the food so swallowing is easier. Saliva also contains enzymes that begin breaking down starchy foods, such as potatoes, carrots, corn, bread, pasta, and grains. The tongue rolls the food to the back of the mouth.

From the back of the mouth, the food is directed into the esophagus. The esophagus is a ten-inch pipe that connects the mouth to the stomach. The muscles of the esophagus contract in waves to propel the food along to the stomach.

The stomach is like a stewing pot, mixing up to two quarts of food particles and fluid for six to eight hours in preparation for digestion. Some digestive juices are added to begin breaking down proteins, and the food mixture is called chyme. The chyme is mostly liquid by the time it leaves the stomach and enters the small intestine.

The small intestine is the major organ of digestion and is twenty feet in length. The "small" refers to the diameter of the intestine, not the length, as the small intestine is longer but narrower than the large intestine. The presence of the liquidy chyme stimulates the release of bile, enzymes, and enzyme-activating hormones. Here all carbohydrates, proteins, and fats are finally broken down to their smallest components (i.e., monosaccharides, amino acids, fatty acids, and glycerol). These simple components, along with the vitamins and minerals, can then be absorbed into the bloodstream and carried to all parts of the body. The walls of the small intestine control absorption by regulating the amount of nutrients taken up from the intestine and the amount released to the bloodstream.

Individual cells pick up nutrients from the blood. At this point, the nutrients begin to perform their important functions, such as providing energy and building blocks for the cells. Excess nutrients are either stored for later use or excreted in the urine, depending on the nutrient.

The final stage of the digestive process takes place in the large intestine. Waste products, fiber, water, and undigested food travels through the large intestine. Within a few hours or days the waste products leave the body as fecal matter. Fiber and water are two important nutrients that help keep this process moving smoothly.

*How is digestion accomplished?*

Digestion of food is accomplished by two main types of processes: mechanical and chemical. Both mechanical and chemical digestion occur simultaneously as the food moves through the digestive organs. Breaking foods into smaller pieces by grinding them up with the teeth and by the muscular action of the digestive tract is essentially the job of mechanical digestion. On the other hand, chemical digestion refers to the breakdown of foods by the action of enzymes and other substances that are secreted into the digestive tract.

*Why does the body need food every few hours?*

The body needs food at regular intervals to keep offering nutrients to the body. Just as a car needs gasoline to run,' the body also needs fuel in the form of food to keep it running. Without fuel for an extended period of time (8-10 hours) the body will trigger hunger. Hunger pangs will often result, which are actually contractions in the stomach. When the stomach is not filled with food, it is filled mostly with gas. Contractions squeeze the gas against the stomach walls. You feel hunger pangs and hear growls as as result.

*Some facts about digestion:*

- The average person eats 3 pounds of food each day, or 1,095 pounds of groceries a year.

- Your mouth makes about 500 milliliters (1/2 quart) or saliva daily. In total, your body secretes more than 7 quarts of assorted digestive juices.

- Our appendix is a remnant of a longer intestine. Grazing animals use this organ for fermentation.

# Activity 4-1. Fun Facts

## DIRECTIONS TO THE TEACHER

**Objective** (Cognitive Domain: Comprehension Level)

Students will generalize measurements specific to the digestive system to more common concrete objects/activities.

### Materials

Student Activity Sheet (1)
Ruler, yardstick
Clock with a second hand
String
2 quart container or 8 - 1 cup milk cartons

### Prerequisite Skills

Measurement
Reading
Timing, using a second hand

### Procedure

1. Introduce the opportunity to experiment with measurements.

2. Describe specific procedures for sharing materials and present your behavioral expectations for the activity.

3. Distribute the activity sheet and explain the directions. Tell students there may be many correct answers to a given question.

### Supplementary Activities

1. Have students make a model of their own digestive systems. They can use rope or garden hose as the GI tract. It should measure 32 feet. Encourage creativity -- they can begin with teeth, a tube for the esophagus, a 2 quart capacity container for the stomach, a smaller rope or tube for the small intestine, and a different tube or rope with a larger diameter for the large intestine. Award prizes or have some kind of judging. This can be done individually or in groups, depending on the size of the class.

2. Read or tell the story What Happens to a Hamburger? by Paul Showers, illustrated by Anne Rockwell (New York: Thomas Y. Crowell Company, 1985). Talk about how the foods they eat are changed inside the body so that they can be used to give them energy and help them grow and stay healthy.

3. Compare the size of the adult digestive system organs to children ages 5 to 8 years old. For example, a child's small intestine is about 10 to 12 feet. To elaborate on this invite a pediatrician to class to discuss the growth of internal organs.

Name _____ Date _____

## Activity 4-1. Fun Facts

**Directions:**

The esophagus is 10 inches long. Use your ruler to find something in your classroom 10 inches long.
What is it? _____

Food travels down the esophagus in 7 seconds. Watch the clock and see how many times you can write your name in 7 seconds.

_____

The stomach holds 2 quarts of food and liquid. Two quarts are the same as 8 cups. Can you imagine 8 milk cartons inside you?

The small intestine is 22 feet long. Get a string and yardstick and cut the piece of string 22 feet. Now wrap it around your waist. How many times can you wrap it around your waist?

_____

The large intestine is 5 feet in length. It is shaped in an upside-down U. It is called large because it is wider than the small intestine. The passage of food and fluid from the stomach to the small intestine can take from 30 to 90 minutes. The passage through the large intestine may take 1 to 7 days.

What is something you do that takes 30 to 90 minutes?

_____

What is something you do that can take 1 to 7 days?

_____

# Activity 4-2. Where the Food Goes

## DIRECTIONS TO THE TEACHER

**Objective** (Cognitive Domain/Knowledge Level)

Given a diagram of the digestive system, students will label six major organs.

## Materials

Student Activity Sheets (2)
Scissors
Paste

## Prerequisite Skills

Cut and paste
Numerical order

## Procedure

1. Explain that the digestive system refers to the path through which food enters the body, is processed in the body, and exits the body. Food is not simply taken in and removed from the body. Various nutrients are taken from the food for the body's use. Only waste material is passed out of the body.

2. Introduce the path of food through the digestive system (e.g., mouth, esophagus, stomach, small intestine, large intestine, and anus). A model of the body may be helpful in allowing the students to see the path.

3. Define digestion. To digest is to break food down into pieces small enough to leave the digestive system and go out to enter body cells. Digestion begins in the mouth and ends in the small intestines. In the small intestine most food has become liquid and in small enough parts to be carried out to the cells. The parts of the food that can't be digested go to the large intestine and leave the body as waste.

4. Distribute the activity sheet and explain the directions.

## Supplementary Activities

1. Using the activity sheet, ask the students to trace the digestive path and color each organ.

2. Help your students find some of the digestive organs they cannot see. Demonstrate on your body and have them point on theirs: stomach is between the ribs and above the waist, esophagus can sometimes be felt when you take a swallow of cold water, small intestine sits under your belly button, and the large intestine is just below the waist.

3. Make digestive system tee-shirts using craft felt, fabric paints or permanent markers. Allow the students to wear the shirts and explain the digestive system.

Name _____ Date _____

## Activity 4-2. Where Food Goes

**Directions:** Cut out the words below. Paste the words over the same numbers by the body on page 2.

1. mouth

2. esophagus

3. stomach

4. small intestine

5. large intestine

6. anus

Name _____ Date _____

## Activity 4-2. Where the Food Goes, *page 2*

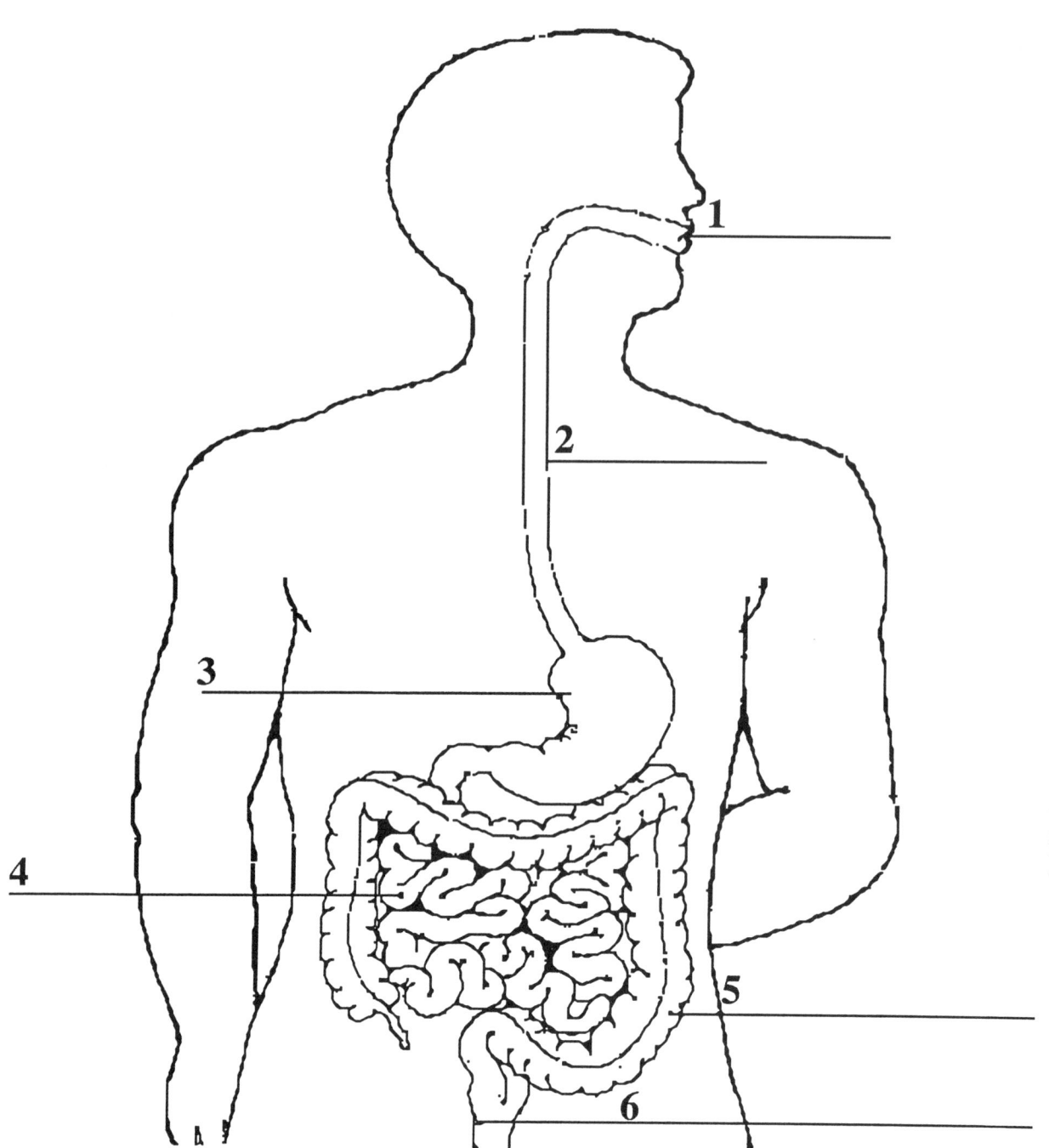

# Activity 4-3. Digestion Action

## DIRECTIONS TO THE TEACHER

**Objective** ( Cognitive Domain: Comprehension Level )

Students will demonstrate the mechanics of digestion by selecting an example of something that parallels the mechanical action of digestion.

## Materials

Student Activity Sheets (2)
Scissors
Paste

## Prerequisite Skills

Recognition of basic tools

## Procedure

1. Discuss the word *mechanical*. In order to digest food, our bodies act like a machine, breaking down food into small pieces that can be absorbed into the blood and carried into the cells. These small pieces are called *nutrients*.

2. Discuss action words that describe breaking down. Ask the students for examples of machines or tools that break things. Examples may be a hammer, jackhammer, coffee grinder, blender, or potato masher. If possible, show students examples and demonstrate how the tools work. Define action words using the vocabulary on the worksheets.

3. Distribute the activity sheet and explain the directions. All the organs except the intestines have one box for a machine or tool. The small intestine has one box split into two because the intestine has a dual role. It is the major site of digestion but also the major site for nutrients to leave the digestive tract and move into the blood. Nutrients leave the blood and go to the cells to provide energy and materials for growth and maintenance of body functions.

4. Conclude by asking the students to read aloud the statement at the bottom of the activity sheet. Discuss the mechanical role of digestion.

## Supplementary Activities

1. Bring to class some tools that represent the mechanical action of digestion. Ask the students to explain the analogy.

2. The other way we digest food is through chemical means. Talk with the students about chemical digestion. There are digestive juices that help break down foods. These digestive juices are specific for certain nutrients. Ask your students to use the library and look for books that explain how foods are changed to nutrients.

Name _____ Date _____

# Activity 4-3. Digestion Action

Digestion is how the body works to break the food you eat into pieces small enough to enter your cells. Your cells need these pieces (nutrients) for energy and to stay healthy.

**Directions:** Cut out the pictures below. Match the pictures with the digestion action words on page 2. Paste the pictures in the boxes on page 2. These pictures show the action of digestion.

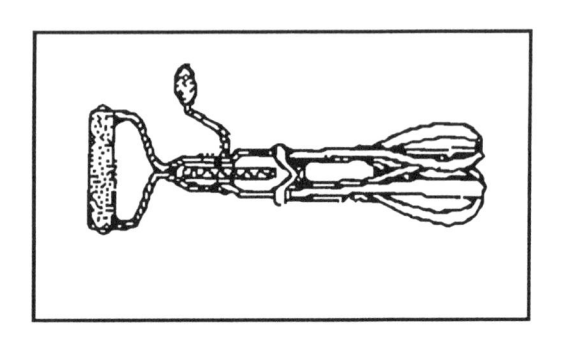

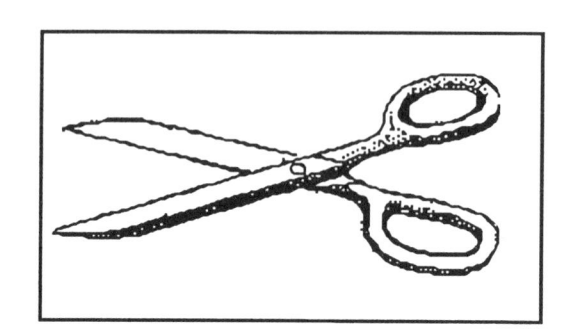

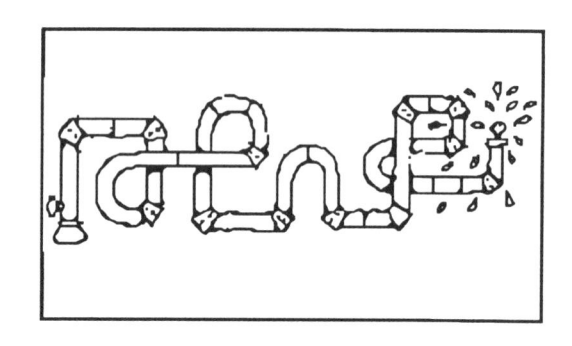

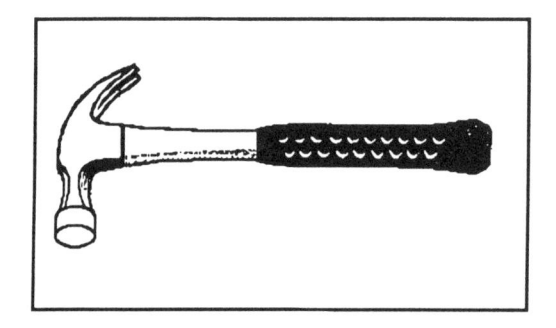

© 1991 by The Center for Applied Research in Education

Name _____ Date _____

## Activity 4-3. Digestion Action, *page 2*

**Body Parts**

mouth

esophagus

stomach

intestines

**Action Words**

breaks

slides

mixes

cuts apart

moves out or leaks

**Digestion works like a machine.**

© 1991 by The Center for Applied Research in Education

# Unit 2. EATING ALL KINDS OF FOODS

Lesson 5    <u>Introducing A Pattern for Daily Food Choices</u>
                 5-1. Beary-Good Eating
                 5-2. Eating Advice
                 5-3. Serving Numbers

Lesson 6    <u>The Meat Group</u>
                 6-1. Meat and Legume Scramble
                 6-2. Protein Smart
                 6-3. Green Eggs and Ham

Lesson 7    <u>Breads, Grains, and Cereals</u>
                 7-1. Grain Word Search
                 7-2. What <u>is</u> Enriched?
                 7-3. Pockets for Eating

Lesson 8    <u>Fruits</u>
                 8-1. Try It! You'll Like It!
                 8-2. Fruit Smart
                 8-3. How Fruits Grow

Lesson 9    <u>Vegetables</u>
                 9-1. Vegetable Taste Test
                 9-2. Pizza Smart
                 9-3. Vegetable Colors

Lesson 10    <u>Milk, Cheese and Yogurt</u>
                 10-1. Milk Product Maze
                 10-2. Milk Sorting
                 10-3. Milk Products

Lesson 11    <u>Fats and Sweets</u>
                 11-1. Food Group Smart
                 11-2. Smart Choices
                 11-3. Where's the Fat?

# Lesson 5. *Introducing a Pattern for Daily Food Choices*

## Things to Know About *A Pattern for Daily Food Choices*

*Key Points:*

- *A Pattern for Daily Food Choices* promotes a diet high in complex carbohydrates.

- *A Pattern for Daily Food Choices* promotes eating a variety of foods within each food group.

- *A Pattern for Daily Food Choices* recognizes fats, sweets, and alcohol in the diet.

*What is A Patern for Daily Food Choices?*

*A Pattern for Daily Food Choices* is a food guidance plan developed by the American Red Cross and the USDA. It is a comprehensive food guidance system to help people use the Dietary Guidelines (see Unit 3) in planning their food choices. Learning *A Pattern for Daily Food Choices* can be a fun way for children to discover the food groups. These foods are grouped according to the kinds of nutrients they contain, so that individuals can use the pattern to plan a total diet.

*Why teach A Pattern for Daily Food Choices over the Basic Four?*

*A Pattern for Daily Food Choices* is more realistic within today's food consumption patterns and food supply, and is an adaptation of the Basic Four. The Basic Four as a foundation diet emphasizes the types of foods to be included daily for nutrient needs, but, at the servings suggested, does not meet recommended levels of many nutrients. Also, the Basic Four provides little specific guidance on how to moderate fat and sugar in the diet.

*How does A Pattern for Daily Food Choices group foods?*

*A Pattern for Daily Food Choices* includes five major food groups and a sixth group -- alcohol, fats, and sweets -- to be used in moderation. It groups foods by the nutrients they provide. Food groups are not interchangeable. Fruits and vegetables are treated separately as two distinct groups. For a long time people considered fruits and vegetables as practically interchangeable. But fruits tend to be higher in sugar and often less nutrient-dense than vegetables. Each food group contributes significant nutrients to the diet.

*How does A Pattern for Daily Food Choices promote variety within each of the individual food groups?*

Within each group, individual foods vary in the specific kind and amount of nutrients they provide. For that reason, it is important not only to choose foods from each group each day but also to vary choices within each group. Variety is implied by dividing choices within a food group. For example, fruits are divided among citrus, melon, and berries, along with other fruits.

Vegetables are divided into three subgroups: dark-green leafy, deep-yellow vegetables, starchy vegetables, and others. *A Pattern for Daily Food Choices* recommends at least two servings of fruits and at least three servings of vegetables.

Whole grain products receive recognition in the breads and cereals group along with enriched grain products. Whole grains contribute fiber and trace minerals that tend to be low in refined grain products. *A Pattern for Daily Food Choices* suggests 6-11 servings a day, including several servings of whole grain products.

The meat group is important for protein, iron, and many other nutrients. Two to three servings are suggested for the meat group. The recommendations for the meat group focus on lean and lowfat alternatives. The meat group includes meat, fish, poultry, eggs, nuts, seeds, and dried beans and peas. The recommended number of servings a day is 2-3 servings or a total of 5 to 7 ounces.

The milk group includes milk, yogurt, and cheese. All are good sources of protein, calcium, and other minerals and vitamins. Two servings (or 2 cups) a day are recommended for children under 10 years of age.

Finally, *A Pattern for Daily Food Choices* suggests that fats, oils, and sweets be used in moderation. These foods can add flavor and appeal to other foods but contribute mainly calories.

| Food Group | Suggested servings |
|---|---|
| Vegetables | 3-5 servings |
| Fruits | 2-4 servings |
| Breads, cereals, rice and pasta | 6-11 servings |
| Milk, yogurt, and cheese | 2-3 servings |
| Meats, poultry, fish, dry beans and peas, eggs and nuts | 2-3 servings |
| Fats, oils and sweets | Used in Moderation |

Each of the individual food groups will be discussed in detail in the lessons that follow in Unit 2.

*How many servings do children need?*

Children's eating patterns are similar to adults but the serving sizes are smaller. Most of the groups in *A Pattern for Daily Food Choices* show a range in the number of servings recommended. Everyone should try daily to have at least the number of servings specified at the bottom of the range. Most people will need additional food. The additional amount needed depends on factors such as age, sex, physical condition, and physical activity. These people can select more or larger servings from the food groups with ranges. As more servings are added from these food groups, the level of nutrients in the diet is increased.

# Activity 5-1. Beary-Good Eating

## DIRECTIONS TO THE TEACHER

**Objective** (Cognitive Domain: Application Level)

Students will demonstrate understanding of the food groups by coloring foods according to a color chart.

**Materials**

Student Activity Sheet (1)
yellow, green, orange, blue, and red crayons

**Prerequisite Skills**

Recognition of color words
Recognition of food groups

**Procedure**

1. Review the basic food groups in *A Pattern for Daily Food Choices*. Have students generate foods for each group.

2. Distribute the activity sheet. As a group, have students color the items in the key. For example, the apple should be colored yellow and the vegetable should be colored green.

3. Explain the directions and allow the students to work independently.

**Supplementary Activities**

1. March is National Nutrition Month. Sponsored by the American Dietetic Association (ADA), this event is designed to help children and adults make informed nutrition food choices. The ADA makes available a wide selection of classroom aids to highlight this month's activities. For more information write to Nutrition Resources, the American Dietetic Association, 216 West Jackson Blvd., Suite 800, Chicago, IL 60606, or call (312) 899-4853.

2. Five of the six food groups in *A Pattern for Daily Food Choices* are made up of nutrient-dense foods. These five food groups are: meat, milk, bread, fruit and vegetables. When you have a few moments to fill before the bell rings or while waiting in line, play "Give me 5." To play, simply ask the students to:
   "Give me 5 food groups."
   "Give me 5 foods in the milk group."
   "Give me 5 foods in the meat group."
This quick thinking activity reinforces not only the food groups but the variety of foods within each group.

Name _____ Date _____

## Activity 5-1. Beary-Good Eating

**Directions:** Look at the food in each balloon. Color the balloons using the chart below.

fruit = yellow

vegetable = green

bread = orange

milk = blue

meat = red

Eat a rainbow of colors at every meal!

© 1991 by The Center for Applied Research in Education

# Activity 5-2. Eating Advice

## DIRECTIONS TO THE TEACHER

**Objective**  (Affective Domain: Knowledge Level)

Students will voluntarily follow directions to decode some nutrition-smart advice.

## Materials

Student Activity Sheet (1)
Pencil

## Prerequisite Skills

Letter recognition

## Procedure

1. Talk about how people are often given advice.  Define advice and have students give examples of advice they have been given.

2. Distribute the activity sheet, explain the directions, and explain that students will be decoding some advice.

3. After students complete the activity, discuss the rhyme.  Is it good advice or bad advice? Why?

## Supplementary Activities

1. The last week of April is National Library Week.  Challenge your students to read a book about foods or food groups.

2. Provide newspapers and magazines with food advertisements.  Ask the students to cut out the ads and put them into food groups.  Use food advertisements and have students "stop and think."  Evaluate foods by having students respond to a series of questions related to the food groups.

3. Make a poster or bulletin board with the "Eating Advice" rhyme -- "Before eating, keep repeating, stop and think, will this help me grow?"  Refer to this rhyme throughout your nutrition unit.

Name _____ Date _____

## Activity 5-2. Eating Advice

**Directions:** Cross out the letters E, C, B, M, L.

| E | S | C | T | B |
|---|---|---|---|---|
| O | P | B | M | C |
| C | L | A | L | N |
| D | M | E | B | T |
| B | H | C | I | N |
| E | L | K | M | E |

The letters left will spell a message.

Write the letters from left to right and row by row in the spaces below.

## Before eating, keep repeating,

__ __ __ __   __ __ __ __ __ __ !

## Will this help me grow?

Ask yourself... is it a fruit, a vegetable, a bread, a cereal, a meat, a nut, a seed, or a milk?

© 1991 by The Center for Applied Research in Education

# Activity 5-3. Serving Numbers

## DIRECTIONS TO THE TEACHER

**Objective**  (Cognitive Domain: Knowledge Level)

Students will list the suggested number of servings from each food group after completing a pictograph.

**Materials**

Student Activity Sheet (1)
brown, yellow, red, orange and green crayons

**Prerequisite Skills**

Word finding skills
Counting
Coloring

**Procedure**

1. Review the food groups. Students have been exposed to this information and should be able to do this easily. Explain that students also need to know how much of each food group to eat in order to eat healthfully.

2. Distribute the activity sheet and explain the directions.

**Supplementary Activities**

1. Make finger puppets with the cut-off fingers of old children's gloves. Ask each child to bring an old glove into class. You may even collect them from last year's "lost and found." Ideally, the gloves should be solid colored. Cut the fingers and thumb off. Have the children decorate all five. Each finger and the thumb will represent a different food group (milk, grain, meat, fruit, vegetable). The fats and sweets will not be represented. Remind children to look at their fingers and thumbs when they eat to check if they are eating a food from each food group at every meal.

2. Ask students to generate a list of typical foods eaten at breakfast. Then write one breakfast menu. Count the number of servings from the bread, fruit, vegetable, meat, and milk groups. Knowing how many servings of each food groups is recommended for a day, have the students subtract out the breakfast servings to determine the foods to eat the rest of the day.

3. After lunch, have students determine how many servings from each food group have been consumed. How many servings need to be consumed at supper in order to meet food requirements?

Name _____ Date _____

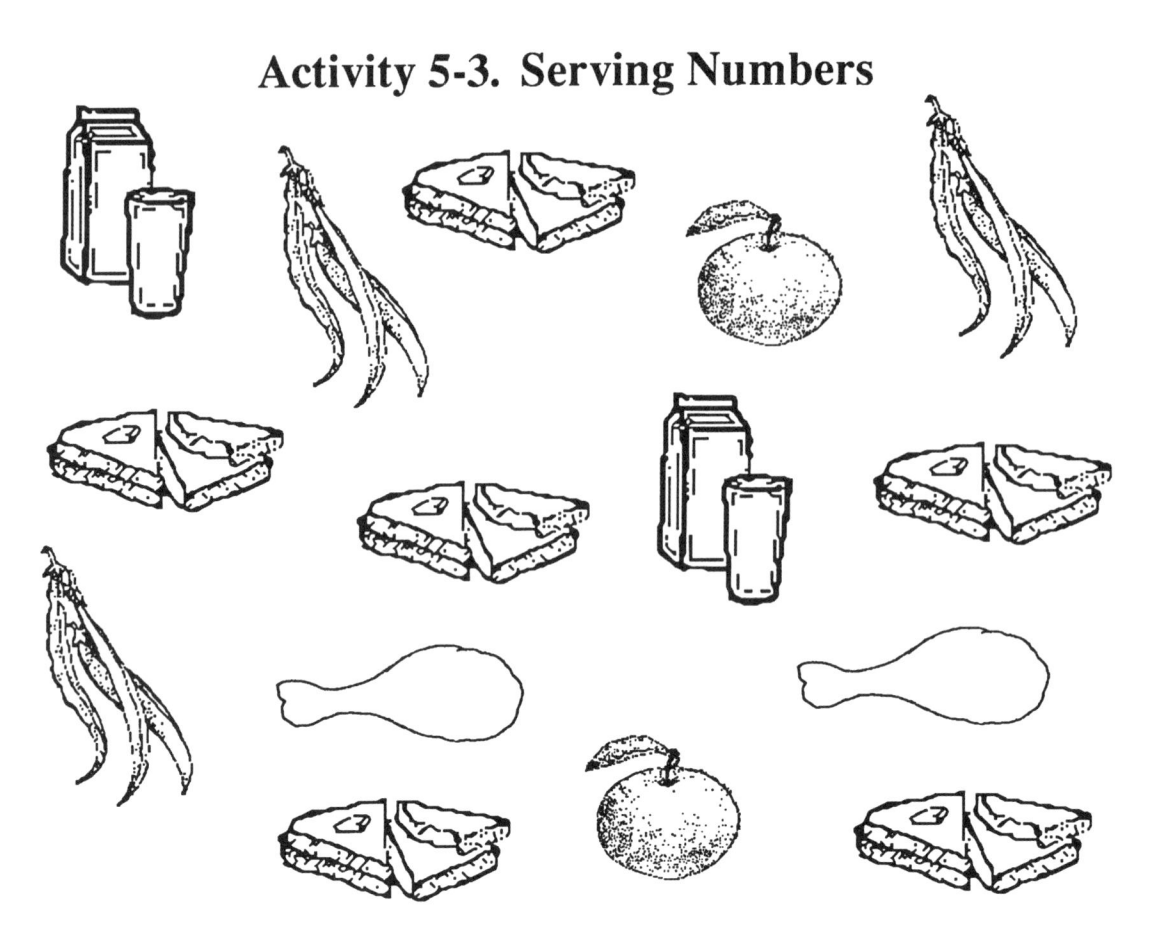

## Activity 5-3. Serving Numbers

**Directions:**
1) Color the foods using the chart below.
   - bread - brown
   - vegetable - green
   - milk - yellow
   - fruit - orange
   - meat - red

2) Count the number of times you find:
   - bread _____
   - milk _____
   - meat _____
   - fruit _____
   - vegetable _____

Try to eat this number of servings from each food group every day. It is also important to eat different foods within each group.

© 1991 by The Center for Applied Research in Education

# Lesson 6. *The Meat Group*

## Things to Know About the Meat Group

*Key Points:*

- Meat and meat alternatives are good sources of protein and iron.

- Some meats have more fat than others. When using the term "meat" add the word "lean" as a descriptor for healthy food choices.

- Eating fruits and vegetables high in vitamin C helps the body absorb iron.

*Why are there so many types of foods categorized as meats?*

Eggs, dried beans and peas, nuts, and seeds can be used as an alternative for meats. These foods provide protein and many other nutrients found in meat. Nutritionally, one egg, a half cup of dried beans or peas, 1/4 cup of seeds, or 1/3 cup of nuts can replace one ounce of meat.

*What are the nutritional benefits of meats and meat alternatives?*

All meats and the alternatives are good sources of protein, phosphorus, and niacin, and contribute iron, zinc, and vitamins B6 and B12. Meat, fish, and poultry are sources of the most absorbable form of iron, often referred to as heme iron. Cholesterol and vitamin B12 are found only in animal products. Plant products like dried beans and peas, nuts, and seeds contain the complex carbohydrates -- starch and fiber, which are not present in meat. Although dried beans and peas are low in fat, nuts and seeds are significantly higher in fat than lean meat.

Dietary fats have a bad reputation; however, they are essential to good health. Fat in meat provides a concentrated source of energy necessary for a growing child. The meat industry is making great strides in meeting consumer demands for leaner cuts of meat. Many processed meat products that combine lean meats with cereal and legume ingredients are available. Although a moderate dietary intake of fat and cholesterol is good advice, red meat need not be avoided and can actually be a valuable part of a balanced diet.

*What is the meat/iron-deficiency anemia connection?*

Meat is one of the most dependable sources of iron. Iron is a mineral that has been found to be low in children's diets, and iron-deficiency anemia is relatively common. It is difficult for a child to get all the iron needed without eating meat, fish, or poultry regularly. Without iron, oxygen cannot get to all the cells in the body. The result is decreased muscle function, fatigue, and poor attention span.

Even small amounts of meat, fish, or poultry eaten with a meal helps with the absorption of iron from all the other foods eaten in that meal. Including a vitamin C rich food (*see Unit 2, Vegetables and Fruit*) with the meat will enhance iron absorption. As you can see, teaching children to eat a variety of foods is important to achieve good nutrition.

*How many servings of meat or alternatives are recommended a day?*

The recommended number of servings a day is 2-3 servings, or a total of 5 to 7 ounces.

*What about lunch meats?*

Most packaged luncheon meats are relatively high in sodium and fat. Cold cuts, including the lower-salt products, contain between 200-300 milligrams of sodium per one ounce slice. This is one-tenth of the adult recommendation for a day (if just one slice is eaten). Similarly, when considering fat content, lunch meats tend to be high. One slice of beef bologna contains 90 Calories, 80% of which comes from fat. Several brands advertise reduced levels of fat. The claim is based on the total weight. So if a cold cut is 95% fat-free, it is 5% fat by weight, NOT calories. Even 80% fat-free turkey bologna can get 77% of its calories from fat.

*What are lean choices of beef?*

The leanest cuts are the parts that get the most exercise when an animal moves. The round, chuck, shank, and flank have more muscle and less fat than meat from the rib, loin, or sirloin. Color and general appearance of the beef can indicate fat content. The fewer the flecks of white or yellow marbling throughout the meat the better. Marbling is fat that cannot be trimmed. Beef grades are also a general guide to fat content. Prime contains the most marbling; choice has a relatively modest amount; and select, a comparatively small amount.

Hogs have also slimmed down. Many cuts of pork are 25% to 50% leaner than they were 25 years ago thanks to changes in breeding and feeding of hogs.

*How do poultry, chicken, turkey, duck, and goose stack up?*

Chicken and turkey provide high-quality protein and B-vitamins (especially B6 and niacin). However, they have less iron than red meat. Chicken and turkey are low in fat, particularly saturated fat, but turkey is the leanest poultry. On the average, skinned duck and goose have the same amount of fat as trimmed beef, lamb, or pork. Most poultry has as much cholesterol as red meat. But, remember, it is the saturated fat that tends to raise blood cholesterol.

*What about fish?*

Seafood is a good source of protein, B-vitamins, and minerals. It is also low in fat, sodium and cholesterol. Polyunsaturated oils found in fish (omega-3-fatty acids) have been shown to decrease blood triglycerides and cholesterol levels. They also have been shown to keep blood particles from sticking to blood vessel walls.

*What about eggs?*

Eggs are an excellent replacement for meat. One egg is equal in protein to one ounce of lean meat. The nutrients in eggs are important for the growth that occurs in childhood. Most dietary guidelines limit egg intake to four a week. The average large egg contains 213 mg cholesterol compared to the old value of 274 milligrams. The reasons for this difference are changes in feeding formulations, genetic differences in chicken, smaller egg yolks, and improved food analysis techniques.

*What about legumes?*

By definition, legumes are seeds that grow in pods. Over 20 legumes are used as food sources. Some common legumes are:

| | | | |
|---|---|---|---|
| great northern beans | navy beans | snap beans | peanuts |
| kidney beans | lima beans | soybeans (tofu) | black beans |
| mung beans | chick peas | split peas | |
| black-eyed peas | lentils | pinto beans | |

Legumes are an excellent source of B-vitamins, minerals, and complex carbohydrates including water-soluble fiber. Legumes contain no cholesterol and are low in sodium and fat (except peanuts which are high in fat). Children are familiar with eating legumes in chili, soups, stews, bean burritos, tacos, enchiladas, three-bean salad, baked beans, and peanut butter.

Although the amount of protein in legumes is high, the quality of the protein is lower than the protein quality of lean meat, fish, eggs, and dairy foods. But if legumes are combined with other grain products such as wheat, corn, rice, rye, barley, or oats they provide a higher quality protein with little or no fat. Many common foods combine legumes this way: corn tortillas and refried beans, peanut butter on wheat bread, beans and rice, baked beans and brown bread, pinto beans and cornbread, and so on.

*Is a meatless diet safe for children?*

Yes, if proper efforts are made to eat a variety of foods. Children who consume a well-planned vegetarian diet that includes milk and milk products can meet their nutritional requirements and achieve normal growth. Pure vegan children who choose no meat or animal products have been reported to have inadequate intakes of calories, protein, calcium, vitamin D, iron, riboflavin, and B12.

*Should children limit the amount of meat in their diets?*

Emphasis on lowering fat and cholesterol has triggered a decline in red meat consumption. However, evidence indicates reasonable consumption of meat is not only safe but beneficial to a long, healthy life. Meat contributes protein, iron, niacin, thiamin, zinc and other trace minerals. In addition, animal foods are the best food sources of vitamin B12.

# Activity 6-1. Meat and Legume Scramble

## DIRECTIONS TO THE TEACHER

**Objective** (Cognitive Domain: Knowledge Level)

Students will list foods that are members of the meat and legumes group.

**Materials**

Student Activity Sheet (1)
Pencil

**Prerequisite Skills**

Spelling

**Procedure**

1. Discuss the foods in the meat group. You may want to mention that the fat content of meats is variable, but all legumes are low in fat.

2. Introduce the word "lean." Lean meats have less fat. We don't always see the fat in meat since it is marbled throughout the meat. Explain that the word "lean" indicates lowfat meat with less marbling.

3. To connect "lean" meats back to beans, tell the students that the leanest meat is a bean. Ask them what this phrase means. Students should come up with the concept that meat and beans are in the same food group and therefore are similar in nutrients, but that beans have less fat than meats.

4. Children may not be familiar with the wide variety of beans. Write the list of legumes found in the "Things to Know" section of this unit on the chalkboard or on a poster. Review the words and leave the words visible while the students complete this activity.

5. Introduce protein as a nutrient needed to build body parts like muscles, and to repair skin and tissue when injury occurs.

6. Discuss that protein alone will not build bigger or stronger muscles. For added strength and muscle, the muscle must be worked, as in exercise.

7. Distribute the activity sheet and explain the directions. Students may enjoy doing this activity in pairs.

**Supplementary Activities**

1. Dry peas and lentils have been around since 9000 B.C. No one knows who discovered dry peas and lentils, but archaeologists say they were among the first plants to be domesticated. Ancient Egyptians, Hebrews, Greeks, and Romans cultivated them. You may want to tie this into history or geography.

2. Studying legumes can be a lesson in geography. The northwest region of the U.S. is the largest supplier of our nation's dry peas and lentils. One of the greatest areas where dry peas and lentils are grown is called the "Palouse" area (Spokane and Pullman, Washington and Moscow, Idaho) and covers both eastern Washington and northern Idaho. The unique combination of volcanic soil, mellow sunshine, and just enough moisture from snow, rain, and dew produces legumes. For more information and classroom ideas write to:

   American Dry Bean Board
   4502 Ave. I
   Scottsbluff, NE 69361

   Beans of the West
   California Dry Beans Advisory Board
   PO Box 943
   Denuba, CA 93618

   Colorado Dry Bean Administration Committee
   Commerce City, CO 80022

   Idaho Bean Commission
   PO Box 9433
   Boise, Idaho 83707

   Michigan Bean Commission
   Leslie, MI 49251

   Red River Edible Bean Growers Assoc.
   RR 3- Box 102
   Frazee, Minnesota 56544

   Washington and Idaho
   Dry Pea and Lentil Commissions
   State Line Office
   PO Box 8566
   Moscow, Idaho 83843

3. Put some dried beans and lentils in baby food jars. Label them. Hold a contest for children to guess the number per jar. Students will see it takes a lot more split peas than lima beans to fill a jar. Reinforce beans as a good source of protein, low in fat and high in fiber.

4. Soak dried beans overnight to see how they grow bigger.

5. At primary levels, sorting tasks using beans may be appropriate. Mix several different types of dried beans and have students sort by type. Provide a bowl for the mixture and small cups for the sorted beans.

Name _____ Date_____

# Activity 6-1. Meat and Legume Scramble

**Directions:** Unscramble the names and match the numbered letters to spell a message. Remember, meat and legumes are foods that give you protein.

n c h i e k c  _ h _ c k _ _
                          5

y r k t u e  _ t _ r _ e _
                      9

n a e l f e b e  _ l _ a _ _ _ e f
                           1

n a e l r o k p  _ _ e _ n _ _ p _ r _
                          11 10

t i n l e s l  _ l _ _ n _ _ l _
                  13    4

v y a n e n b a s  _ n _ _ y _ b _ a _ s
                             14 8

m a l i n a s b e  _ l _ _ m _ _ _ e _ n _
                       7

d n i y e k s b n a e  k _ _ n e _ _ _ e a _ s
                    6 12

l k a c b - y d e e s a e p  _ l _ c - _ y _ d _ _ a s
                          3     2

---

 _ _ _ _ _ _ _     _ _ _ _
 2 10 11 13 3 6 14     2 4 9 8

 _ X _ _ _ _ _ _     _ _ _ _ _ _
 3    3 10 5 6 8 3     1 9 6 4 12 8

 _ _ _ _ G _     _ _ _ _ _ _ _
 8 13 10 11 14     7 9 8 5 4 3 8

© 1991 by The Center for Applied Research in Education

# Activity 6-2. Protein Smart

## DIRECTIONS TO THE TEACHER

**Objective** (Cognitive Domain: Analysis Level)

Students will identify plant and animal foods.

### Materials

Student Activity Sheet (1)
Pencil

### Prerequisite Skills

Letter formation
Classification

### Procedure

1. Discuss the origin of foods. Foods come from plants or animals.

2. Ask students to give examples of animals we eat, such as cows, pigs, chicken, turkey, fish, deer, rabbit, buffalo, and quail.

3. Ask students to give examples of plants we eat such as fruits, vegetables, nuts, seeds, and grains.

4. Both plant and animal foods have protein, but not all plants do. For example, fruits, vegetables, and vegetable oils do not have protein, but grains, nuts, beans, and seeds do. Most animal foods contain protein. Explain that an animal is more like us than a plant, and therefore the protein in animals is more like the protein needs of the human.

5. Distribute the activity sheet and explain the directions.

### Supplementary Activities

1. Have students draw or cut out pictures to make a farm scene of plants and animals we eat. Then ask them to add some plants and animals we do not eat.

2. Ask students to think about the grocery store. Are products from plants and animals sold together in one department or are they in separate departments? Students should distinguish produce departments from meat/deli and dairy departments. Aisles in the middle of the stores are often combinations of plant and animal products.

3. Polyvinyl chloride (PVC) is a huge contributor to environmental pollution. Supermarkets package their meat, fish, and poultry in polystyrene trays and then wrap them in PVC wrap. But the deli counter will cut meat and wrap it in freezer wrap or molded pulp trays, which are better. Have students offer suggestions for alternative ways to buy and package meat.

Name _____ Date _____

## Activity 6-2. Protein Smart

**Directions:** Write **P** next to **Plant** foods.

Write **A** next to **Animal** foods.
The first one is done for you.

_A_     ___

___     ___

___     ___

___     ___

Protein can be found in foods that come from

P __ __ __ __ __ and A __ __ __ __ __ __.

## Protein helps my body grow.

© 1991 by The Center for Applied Research in Education

# Activity 6-3. Green Eggs And Ham

**DIRECTIONS TO THE TEACHER**

**Objectives**  (Cognitive Domain: Knowledge Level)

Students will select identical characteristics from two lists and combine them to form a new list. The new list will reflect characteristics of meat group members.

**Just For Fun!**  (Affective Domain: Responding Level)

Students will voluntarily report to the class after completing a nutrition-smart activity at home.

**Materials**

Student Activity Sheet (1)
Green Crayon

**Prerequisite Skills**

Comparing
Coloring

**Procedure**

1. Read Green Eggs and Ham by Dr. Seuss. Have the class try to state the moral of the story as succinctly as possible. The moral might be stated: "You never know if you'll like a new food until you try it" or "Try it, you'll like it."

2. Color is an important characteristic of foods that helps make food appealing before we even take a bite.

3. Distribute the activity sheet and explain the directions.

4. For food safety purposes clarify that eggs should be white and yellow. A green egg would not be safe to eat.

**Supplementary Activities**

1. Do *Just For Fun - Student Activity Sheet* that follows Green Eggs and Ham.

2. Discuss with your students purchasing environmentally sound egg cartons. Molded pulp cartons are generally made from 100% recycled paper. That makes these a better choice than polystyrene egg cartons. Polystyrene is not recycled, nor is it biodegradable.

3. Have students use their imaginations by drawing and coloring a picture of a food. Encourage students to color the picture so the the food looks interesting or fun to them. Older students may wish to write a paragraph to go with their pictures.

Name _____ Date _____

## Activity 6-3. Green Eggs and Ham

**Directions:** Color the pictures green. Read the lists below each picture. Fill in the blanks.

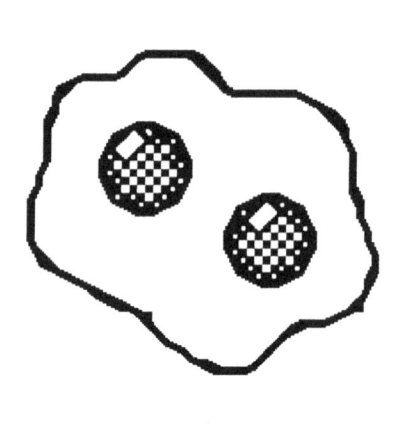

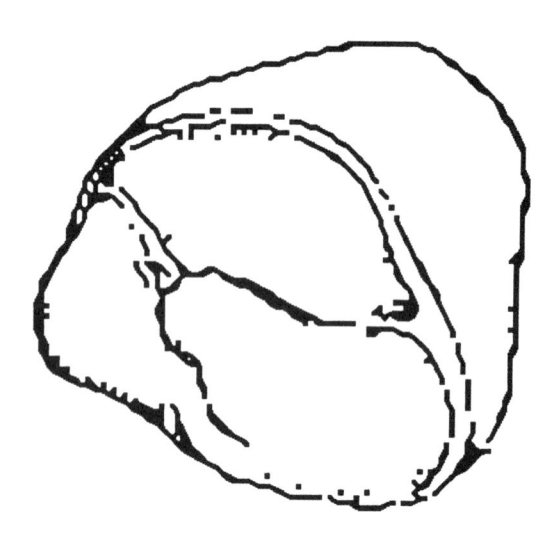

### Egg:

* has protein
* has iron
* is in the meat group
* is an animal product
* comes from a chicken
* can be eaten in many ways

### Ham:

* has protein
* has iron
* is in the meat group
* is an animal product
* comes from a pig
* can be eaten in many ways

What is the same about eggs and ham?

Eggs AND Ham BOTH:
1. have protein _____
2. _____
3. _____
4. _____
5. _____

© 1991 by The Center for Applied Research in Education

Name _____ Date _____

## Activity 6-3. Just for Fun!
## Green Eggs and Ham

**Directions:** Take this recipe home and try it out!

> **Warning!**
> This activity requires boiling water. Do not use boiling water unless you are with an adult.

### Green Eggs and Ham

1/2 inch thick slice of ham
2 eggs
2 cups water
30 drops green food coloring
1/2 teaspoon cooking oil

Put food coloring and water in a saucepan. Bring water to a boil. Dip ham in saucepan for a few seconds, move to oiled pan. Heat thoroughly. Return water to boil and remove from heat. Break eggs into a dish and gently slide eggs into water. Spoon water over eggs. Let stand for 4 minutes. Drain the eggs and serve with ham.

For a simpler recipe: Make scrambled eggs and add 3 drops of green food coloring before cooking.

Eggs and Ham both:

[✓] have protein and iron

[✓] are animal products

[✓] are in the meat group

# Lesson 7. *Breads, Grains, and Cereals*

## Things to Know About the Bread Group

*Key Points:*

- Grains, breads, and cereals are high in starch and fiber and low in fat.
- Children should eat at least six servings a day, including both whole grain and enriched products.

*What are grains and how do they end up on the table?*

Grains are the seeds or fruit of a cereal grass. All breads and cereals are made from a type of grain. Grain uses can be more easily understood using the following chart.

| Grains | Uses |  |  |
|---|---|---|---|
|  | **Bread** | **Cereal** | **Other** |
| **Rice** | Rice bran | Rice bran, puffed rice, Rice crispies | Rice pudding, cooked rice, rice cakes, rice flour, baby foods |
| **Rye** | Rye bread, biscuits, bagels | Rye flakes | Crackers, flour, pancakes |
| **Corn** | Tortilla, corn bread, tamales | Corn bran, flakes, grits, Farina | Hominy, cookies, corn-on-the-cob, succotash, chowder, pudding, popcorn, fritters, baked goods, polenta, flour, pancakes, oil, corn syrup |
| **Wheat** | Wheat bread, biscuits, muffins, rolls, "white" bread, bagels | Shredded wheat, flakes, puffed wheat, bran flakes | Flour, pasta, (noodles, spaghetti, macaroni), pancakes, waffles, crackers, baked goods, matzas, cracked wheat, bulgar, dumplings |
| **Barley** | Biscuits, muffins | Infant cereal, cooked cereal ready-to-eat-cereal | Soup, porridges, pancakes, flour |
| **Oat** | Oat bran, muffins, oat bread | Oat bran, oatmeal, oatmeal flakes, rolled oats | Flour, cookies, granola, oat cakes |

Reference: Foods and Nutrition Enclyclodedia (Vol. 1 and 2). (1983), Clovis, CA : Pegus Press.

*How do grains, breads, and cereals help children grow?*

Breads and cereals give children energy and nutrients to help them grow, and are one of the body's main sources of energy. Children must consume adequate amounts of breads and cereals at each meal in order to provide sufficient amounts of nutrients and energy to function throughout the day.

*What nutrients do grains, breads, and cereals provide?*

Whole grains, breads, and cereals contribute protein, complex carbohydrates such as starch and fiber, vitamins, and minerals. Enriched grain products are inexpensive sources of the B vitamins, thiamin, riboflavin, niacin, and iron. Compared to fat and protein, carbohydrates are the body's most efficient energy source. Fiber provides bulk. It is undigested, so it moves through the gastrointestinal track, absorbing water and helping to eliminate waste.

*How many servings of grains, breads, and cereals should children eat per day?*

*A Pattern for Daily Food Choices* recommends 6-11 servings a day. The range allows for differences in body size, sex, and age. Everyone should include a minimum of six servings of grain products each day. Children should eat six servings, including several servings of whole grain products. One serving would be equal to: 1 slice of bread, OR 2 large or 4 small crackers, OR 1/2 cup cooked cereal, rice, or pasta, OR 1 ounce of ready-to-eat cereal, OR 1 small roll or muffin. Whole grain English muffins, bagels, hamburger buns, and large rolls equal two servings.

*Why choose enriched breads and cereals?*

Enriched breads and cereals help children meet the U.S. Recommended Daily Allowances (RDA) for iron and other nutrients. Some examples of enriched grain products are:

| | | |
|---|---|---|
| Bagels | English muffins | Muffins |
| Biscuits | French bread | Noodles |
| Commercial breads | Grits | Pancakes |
| Corn bread | Hamburger and hot dog buns | Pasta |
| Corn muffins | Italian bread | Ready-to-eat cereal |
| Crackers | Macaroni | Rice |

*What are examples of whole grain products?*

Some examples are:

| | | |
|---|---|---|
| Barley | Granola | Whole wheat crackers |
| Brown rice | Oatmeal | Whole wheat pasta |
| Buckwheat groats | Pumpernickel bread | Other products made with |
| Bulgur | Rye crackers | whole grains |
| Graham crackers | Whole wheat bread and rolls | |

*Do all grains, breads, and cereals have fiber?*

No, not all breads, cereals, and grains contain fiber. Foods vary a great deal depending the type of grain and the type of processing used. Many families eat wheat bread and believe they are receiving all the fiber that whole wheat bread provides. To provide substantial amounts of fiber a label must say "whole" grain or "whole" wheat. Most wheat breads are white bread with cornmeal coloring. They contain almost no fiber.

# Activity 7-1. Grain Word Search

### DIRECTIONS TO THE TEACHER

**Objective**   (Cognitive Domain: Comprehension Level)

Given a list of grains, breads, and cereals, students will deduce which grain is in each bread and cereal.

### Materials

Student Activity Sheet (1)

### Prerequisite Skills

Word recognition skills
Word finding skills

### Procedure

1. Explain that breads and cereals are made from grains. List wheat as an example of a grain and ask students to generate a list of other grains.

2. Distribute the activity sheet and explain the directions.

3. Some children may finish this activity faster than others. You may want to suggest that the students turn the activity over to the back side and draw a picture of their favorite "grain" foods. They may also want to develop a new package design for this grain.

### Supplementary Activities

1. Grains provide an opportunity to apply agriculture and geography to nutrition. Using a map of the United States, point out some of the states that grow grains.

    The greatest corn production is in the area of the Midwest called the Corn Belt. It consists of seven states: Iowa, Illinois, Indiana, Kansas, Missouri, Nebraska, and Ohio. Other leading corn growing states are Wisconsin, Michigan, and Minnesota.

    The Soviet Union is the leading wheat-producing nation in the world. However, it does not grow enough wheat for its own needs. The United States is ranked second among wheat-producing countries of the world. Wheat is grown in every state, although production in New England is minor. The ten leading wheat-producing states are Kansas, North Dakota, Oklahoma, Texas, Washington, Montana, Minnesota, Nebraska, Idaho, and Missouri.

    The Soviet Union is also the leading oat-producing country, but the United States and Canada are also leaders. The ten leading oat-producing states are South Dakota, Minnesota, Iowa, Wisconsin, North Dakota, Ohio, Nebraska, Pennsylvania, New York, and Texas.

Rye production in the United States has steadily declined since World War I. The Soviet Union, Poland, Germany, and Turkey grow more rye than the U.S. The leading states that grow rye are South Dakota, North Dakota, Georgia, Minnesota, Nebraska, Oklahoma, South Carolina, Michigan, Texas, and North Carolina.

Rice is an inexpensive and abundant crop that can grow easily on little land. Asia produces most of the world's rice crop. The U.S. produces just a little more than one percent of the world crop. Rice production is largely concentrated in Arkansas, Texas, California, Louisiana, Mississippi, and Missouri.

Barley is grown throughout the world. In the United States the leading states are North Dakota, Idaho, California, Minnesota, Montana, Colorado, South Dakota, Washington, Utah, and Wyoming.

2. If you live in an area where grains are grown and processed, try to take your students on a few field trips. The first trip would be the farm. The second would be a bakery or cereal manufacturer. Your students may find it interesting to know that commercial bakeries mix dough in 2,000 pound batches to produce more than 3,000 loaves of bread an hour.

3. Provide your students with the packages from a variety of grain products. Read the labels to determine the different types of grains. Ask your students to go home and look at the grain products in their kitchen. Make a list of all the different kinds of grains they find at home. Ask if any types of grains were missing. They may want to ask their parents to buy a new grain next time they go to the store. For example, barley or rye are two grains that are less commonly found in most households. Yet children may really like the taste of both. All they need is to be exposed to the new food.

4. Ask the school food service to serve a new grain, such as barley, instead of rice.

Name_____ Date_____

## Activity 7-1. Grain Word Search

**Directions:** In the word search below, find the six major grains we use to make our breads and cereals.

| B | O | C | O | R | N |
|---|---|---|---|---|---|
| O | A | T | S | M | E |
| P | P | R | I | W | R |
| J | Q | U | L | H | A |
| K | D | F | C | E | R |
| M | A | L | H | A | Y |
| R | I | C | E | T | E |

### 6 Major Grains

CORN

WHEAT

OATS

RYE

RICE

BARLEY

Circle the grains in the foods below. Follow the example.

oatmeal        rye bread       rice bran cereal

corn flakes    rice cakes      whole wheat bread

cream of wheat cornbread       puffed rice cereal

oatmeal bread  oat bran cereal puffed wheat cereal

wheat bread    wheat squares   rye crackers

© 1991 by The Center for Applied Research in Education

# Activity 7-2. What Is Enriched?

## DIRECTIONS TO THE TEACHER

**Objective** (Cognitive Domain: Comprehension Level)

Students will demonstrate an understanding of enriched products by correctly defining the term.

**Materials**

Student Activity Sheet (1)
Dictionary

**Prerequisite Skills**

Dictionary skills

**Procedure**

1. Introduce the concepts of prefix, root word, and suffix. Use several examples to demonstrate how the meaning of a longer word can be inferred by the meanings of word parts. Some examples might include unlovable: un - prefix meaning "not"; love- root word "love"; able- suffix meaning "able to be" therefore unlovable means "not able to be loved." Another example is "indestructible": in- prefix meaning "not"; destruct- from the root word "destroy"; ible- suffix meaning "able to be" therefore indestructible means "not able to be destroyed."

2. Distribute the activity sheet and explain the directions.

**Supplementary Activities**

1. Bring to class an assortment of cereal boxes. Ask students to find the percent of U.S.RDA for iron under the nutrition information. Encourage children to choose enriched cereals with 25% or more of the U.S. RDA for iron per serving.

2. The next time the students go to the grocery store, have them check how many cereal boxes they find with the "Recycled" logo on the front or bottom of the box. Bring in an example to show the class to help them identify the circled continuous triangle of arrows that represents recycling.

3. Ask your students if they have heard the slogan "Gray is Beautiful." This is the slogan the American Paper Institute uses to promote packages that use recycled paper. Cereal boxes that are gray or tan on the inside are recycled. The inside of nonrecycled boxes are white. Ask your students to go home tonight and look into their cereal boxes. Report back which companies used recycled boxes. Write letters to cereal companies thanking those who recycle and suggesting to those that don't that they begin recycling. You'll find the cereal company address on the cereal box. You may want to tell your students that labeling laws require that the address of the manufacturer be listed on the box.

Name _____ Date _____

## Activity 7-2. What Is Enriched?

> The prefix <u>en</u> means to put into.
> The root word <u>rich</u> means well-supplied.
> The suffix <u>ed</u> means past.

Grain products such as cereal and bread are enriched with vitamins and minerals. These nutrients are added to the food because during processing some nutrients are destroyed. For example, when you make cornflakes from corn, some vitamins and minerals are lost.

**Directions:** Look up <u>enriched</u> in the dictionary. Write the meaning here.

_____

_____

What nutrients are usually added to an enriched food?

V __ __ __ __ __ __ __

and

M __ __ __ __ __ __ __ .

Circle the words that show the food is enriched.

**Bread**
Ingredients: Enriched flour, water, brown sugar, oil...

**Enriched Breakfast Cereal** provides 8 essential vitamins and minerals

**Enriched Rice**

DO NOT RINSE BEFORE COOKING

© 1991 by The Center for Applied Research in Education

# Activity 7-3. Pockets for Eating

## DIRECTIONS TO THE TEACHER

**Objective** (Affective Domain: Responding Level)

Students will voluntarily choose to fill a model pocket bread with a variety of stuffings.

## Materials

Student Activity Sheets (2)
Scissors
Crayons
Paste

## Prerequisite Skills

Cutting
Following directions

## Procedure

1. Discuss ways to add variety to sandwiches. Answers might include using different breads and stuffings.

2. Discuss the differences in breads. For example, some are puffy and round, like rolls, while some are flat and round, like tortillas and pita pockets.

3. Brainstorm foods that can be put in a pita pocket.

4. Distribute the activity sheet and explain the directions.

5. Follow up by asking your students to look for pita pockets in the bread section of the grocery store.

## Supplementary Activities

1. Pocket bread is a Middle Eastern bread. The pocket is made by baking two circles of twice-risen dough for a short time in a hot oven. Traditionally it is to filled with broiled lamb, onions, green peppers, tomatoes, chickpeas, lettuce, or cheese. Make pita bread in class or go to a bakery in your area that makes pita pockets.

2. Classify uses for pockets and different types of pockets. Students may think of clothes, carrying cases, animals (kangaroo) as well as food.

3. Talk about other variations of the bread/dough pocket. Examples might include stromboli, pierogies, burritos, corn dog, and pot pie.

Name _____ Date _____

## Activity 7-3. Pockets for Eating

**Directions:** Follow these directions using the form on the next page.

1) Fold your paper along the line marked fold.
2) Cut out the pita pocket. Do not cut the fold line.
3) Paste the right and left sides together. Leave the center and top open (or without paste). You should be able to get your hand inside. This is your pita bread pocket.
4) Using colored construction paper, cut out shapes to represent food (example, a red circle can be a tomato).
5) Fill the bread with foods you like to stuff into a sandwich.

## How many colors did you use?

_____ colors

## What food groups did you use?

_____

© 1991 by The Center for Applied Research in Education

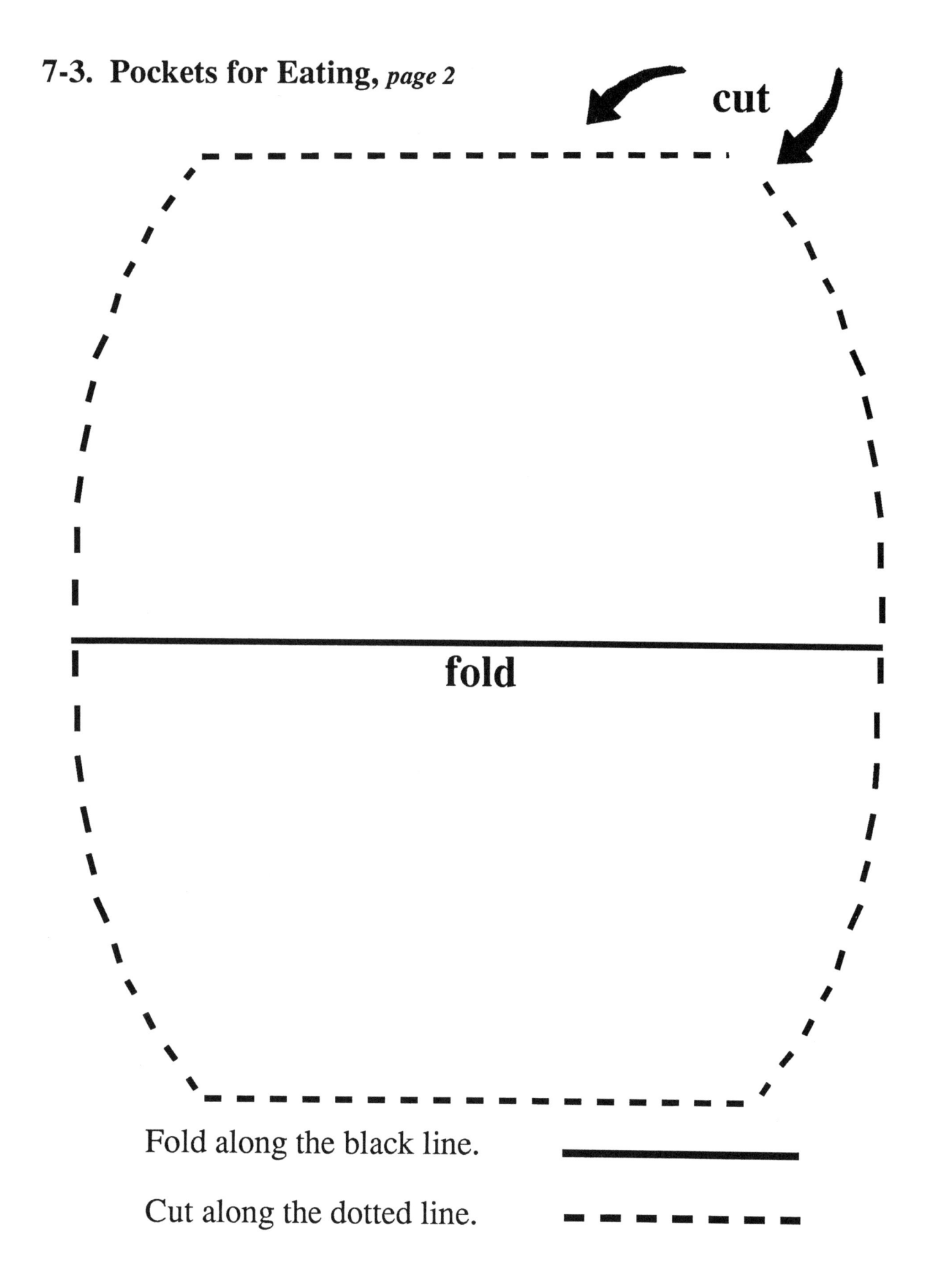

## 7-3. Pockets for Eating, *page 2*

**cut**

**fold**

Fold along the black line. ―――

Cut along the dotted line. - - - - -

# Lesson 8. *Fruits*

## Things to Know About Fruit

*Key Points:*

- Fruits are an acceptable substitute for sweet desserts and high fat snacks.

- Fruits provide carbohydrates, fiber, vitamin C and vitamin A, minerals, and water.

- Fruits are low in fat and sodium and have no cholesterol.

- Children should eat 2-4 servings of fruit a day.

- Children should eat citrus fruits, melons, and berries along with other fruits.

*How do you "sell" fruits to children?*

Typically you don't have to "sell" fruits to children. Fruits are naturally sweet, colorful, and juicy. They make an acceptable substitute for sweet desserts and snacks. They also help in avoiding too much (added) sugar. As a bonus, fruits also provide dietary fiber.

*Are all fruits equally rich in nutrients?*

Citrus fruits, melons, and berries are all excellent sources of vitamin C and provide other vitamins, such as folic acid, and minerals, such as potassium. Generally, other fruits contribute smaller amounts of the same nutrients that citrus fruit, melon, and berries do. Deep yellow fruits such as peaches and apricots are excellent sources of vitamin A.

### Fruits
### Sources of Vitamin C

| Citrus | Melon | Berries | Others | |
|---|---|---|---|---|
| grapefruit | cantaloupe* | blackberries | apple | nectarine |
| pink grapefruit* | honeydew | blueberries | apricot * | papaya* |
| kumquats | watermelon* | raspberries | avocado | passion fruit |
| lemon | | strawberries | banana | peach* |
| lime | | | carambola* | pear |
| orange | | | cherries | persimmon* |
| tangelo | | | fig | pineapple |
| tangerine | | | grapes | plum |
| ugli fruit | | | guava* | pomegranate |
| | | | kiwi | prune |
| * sources of vitamin A | | | mango* | raisins |
| | | | | tomato |

*Does processing change the nutrient contribution of fruits?*

The processing of fruits can change the nutrient content. Freezing, canning, or drying can cause loss of vitamins A and C, although canning depletes more of their nutrients than freezing. Also, canned and frozen fruit are often packed in heavy syrup, which adds sugar and extra calories to the product. Fruits are usually also available packed in water, juice, or light syrup, and these are better choices.

*Are all fruits equally rich in fiber?*

Even though all fruits contain fiber, some fruits contain more than others. Whole raw fruits, particularly those with edible skins or seeds, are good sources of dietary fiber. Per serving, bananas, kiwis, pears, and raspberries are the fruits richest in fiber.

*How many servings of fruits should children eat per day?*

*A Pattern for Daily Food Choices* recommends 2 to 4 servings. Children should eat at least 2. An average size piece of whole fruit is a serving, as is a wedge of melon; 6 ounces of fruit juice; a half cup of berries, or sliced or cooked fruit; or a quarter cup of dried fruit.

*Are dried fruits a good substitute for raw fruits?*

Dried fruits have the vitamins, minerals, and fiber of raw fruit. But the removal of the water means the nutrients and calories are more concentrated in the dried fruit. For example, a half cup of raisins provides more than 10 times the iron and number of calories than a half cup of grapes. Dried fruit may contain up to 70% sugar by weight, more than many cookies and as much as some candies. Dried fruits tend to stick to teeth. Therefore, children should be reminded to brush their teeth or rinse their mouths after eating these.

*What about the dried fruit snacks and frozen fruit bars? Are they the same as eating fruit?*

While dried fruits are nutritious (although high in calories and sugar), fruit snacks such as fruit rolls and bars are not very nutritious. They usually provide fewer nutrients at a higher cost than fresh fruits, and so should be considered less preferable than fruits for a snack.

*Are juice drinks the same as juice?*

No. Fruit juices retain nearly all the nutrients but have lost the fiber from the whole fruits. Orange juice is the major source of vitamin C in the American diet, with an 8 ounce glass providing nearly 3 times the RDA for children. Most red and orange-colored juices are rich in beta-carotene (vitamin A).

Many times children see the word "fruit" on a beverage label and assume it is pure juice. However, the word "juice" must appear to guarantee that it is 100% fruit juice. Labels with the words fruit drink, beverage, punch, juice blend, ade, or cocktail usually contain very little fruit juice. What these beverages do contain are water, fruit flavorings, and added sugars.

*Fascinating Fruit Facts*

- There are pear trees more than 100 years old still producing edible fruit.
- Strawberries were named by children. After picking the berries, the children would string them on grass straws and sell them "by the straw."
- Americans consume about 22 pounds of bananas per person each year. Since 3 bananas weigh 1 pound, that's 66 bananas a year!
- Cranberries were once known as "bouncing berries" because the good ones bounced.
- There are 7,500 varieties of apples grown worldwide. In the United States, 2,500 of these varieties are available.
- Avocados, although a fruit, contain 31 grams of fat per fruit!

# Activity 8-1. Try It! You'll Like It!

## DIRECTIONS TO THE TEACHER

**Objective**  (Affective Domain: Responding Level)

After tasting a new fruit, students will voluntarily share one positive comment with the class.

## Materials

Student Activity Sheet (1)
Fruit for taste test (suggested fruits include star fruit, pineapple, coconut, pomegranate)
Knife and other preparation tools as needed, depending on the fruit chosen.

## Prerequisite Skills

Drawing
Color recognition
Letter formation

## Procedure

1. Display the taste-test fruit in its natural state (don't use canned pineapple, etc.) Prepare the fruit by peeling it (if needed) and cutting it. If coconut was chosen, "milk" it.

2. Talk about the characteristics of fruits and identify the stem, skin, seeds, and so on.

3. Tell students that they will be participating in a taste test.

4. Distribute the activity sheet and explain the directions.

5. Clean up the taste area.

## Supplementary Activities

1. Find out how berries keep fresh the longest. Put a few berries in each of three containers. Put one container in the refrigerator covered, one in the refrigerator uncovered and one on a table top. Watch each day. What happens?

2. Discuss environmentally sound ways to buy produce.
   1) Bring back to the store your plastic bags to fill with apples, pears, potatoes, etc.
   2) Avoid buying vegetables or fruit on a polystyrene tray wrapped in plastic.
   3) Produce rule of thumb: Just about any packaging is overpackaging.

   Discuss with your students why polystyrene is environmentally unsound. Explain that polystyrene is a toxic and possibly cancer-causing chemical, and the process by which it is produced results in hazardous waste. Ask your students to offer suggestions for packaging produce in a manner safe for our environment.

3. For information, recipes, and teaching aids, contact any or all of the following.

California Apricot Advisory Board
1280 Boulevard Way
Walnut Creek, CA 94595

California Avocado Commission
17620 Fitch
Irvine, CA 92714

California Date Administrative Committee
PO Box 1736
Indio, CA 92202-1736

California Fig Advisory Board
PO Box 709
Fresno, CA 93712

California Fresh Peach Committee
PO Box 255627
Sacramento, CA 95825

California Fresh Tomatoes
690 Fifth Street
San Francisco, CA 94107

California Kiwi Fruit Commission
1540 River Park Drive, Suite 120
Sacramento, CA 95815

California Strawberry Advisory Board
PO box 269
Watsonville, CA 95077

California Table Grape Commission
PO Box 5498
Fresno, CA 93755

California Tree Fruit Agreement
PO Box 255383
Sacramento, CA 95865

Consumer Affairs Dept.
Del Monte Corporation
PO Box 3575
San Francisco, CA 94119

Consumer Services
Castle and Cooke Foods
PO Box 7758
San Francisco, CA 94120

International Banana Association
1101 Vermont Ave., Suite 306
Washington, DC 20005

Oregon Washington California Pear Bureau
813 SW Alder, Suite 601
Portland, OR 97205

Sun-Diamond Growers of California
PO Box 1547, Dept. F
Stockton, CA 95201

Sunkist Growers, Inc.
Consumer Services
PO Box 7888
Van Nuys, CA 91409

Texas Fresh Promotional Board
PO Box 730
Harlingen, TX 78551

United Fresh Fruit/Vegetable Association
727 N. Washington Street
Alexandria, VA 22314

Washington Apple Commission
PO Box 18, 229 S. Wenatchee Ave,
Wenatchee, WA 98801

Name _____ Date _____

## Activity 8-1. Try It! You'll Like It!

Today I tasted a new fruit called _____.

It looked like this. ⇦

I looked like this. ⇨

Draw a picture of the fruit here.

Draw a ☺ ☻ or ☹ here.

The skin was _____ and the
(color)
inside of the fruit was _____.
(color)
The thing I liked best about the fruit was

_____.

It's fun to taste new foods!

© 1991 by The Center for Applied Research in Education

# Activity 8-2. Fruit Smart

## DIRECTIONS TO THE TEACHER

**Objective**    (Cognitive Domain: Analysis Level)

Given a dictionary, students will classify fruits as citrus, melons, or berries.

**Materials**

Student Activity Sheet (1)
Pencil
Dictionary

**Prerequisite Skills**

Dictionary skills

**Procedure**

1. Distribute the activity sheet and explain the directions.

2. Allow students to work independently or in small groups.

3. After completing the activity, have students generate identifying characteristics shared by berries, melons, and citrus fruits.

**Supplementary Activities**

1. Using the school lunch menu, classify the fruits as citrus, melons, berries, and others.

2. Have a citrus tasting party. Discuss the taste difference between sweet and sour. Have the students rank the four major citrus fruits from sweetest to most sour. They'll probably rank them as orange, grapefruit, lime, and lemon, respectively. Then you may want to follow up with a discussion of why sugar is added to lemonade and limeade and not to orange juice.

3. Melons are often out of season during the school year, but if you plan ahead you can save the seeds and rind and set up a melon display in your classroom. You'll need seeds in a jar from watermelon, honeydew, and cantaloupe, rinds in a jar, and squares of construction paper in light green, light orange, and red. See if the children can match the seeds to the rind. Then ask them to select the color of construction paper that matches each melon. Older students, using the library, can investigate why melons are more available in the summer.

Name _____ Date _____

## Activity 8-2. Fruit Smart

All fruits are not the same. Some have vitamin C, some have vitamin A, and some have both. That's why it is important to eat different kinds of fruit.

**Directions**: Use your dictionary to decide to which group each fruit belongs. Draw a line from the fruit to its group.

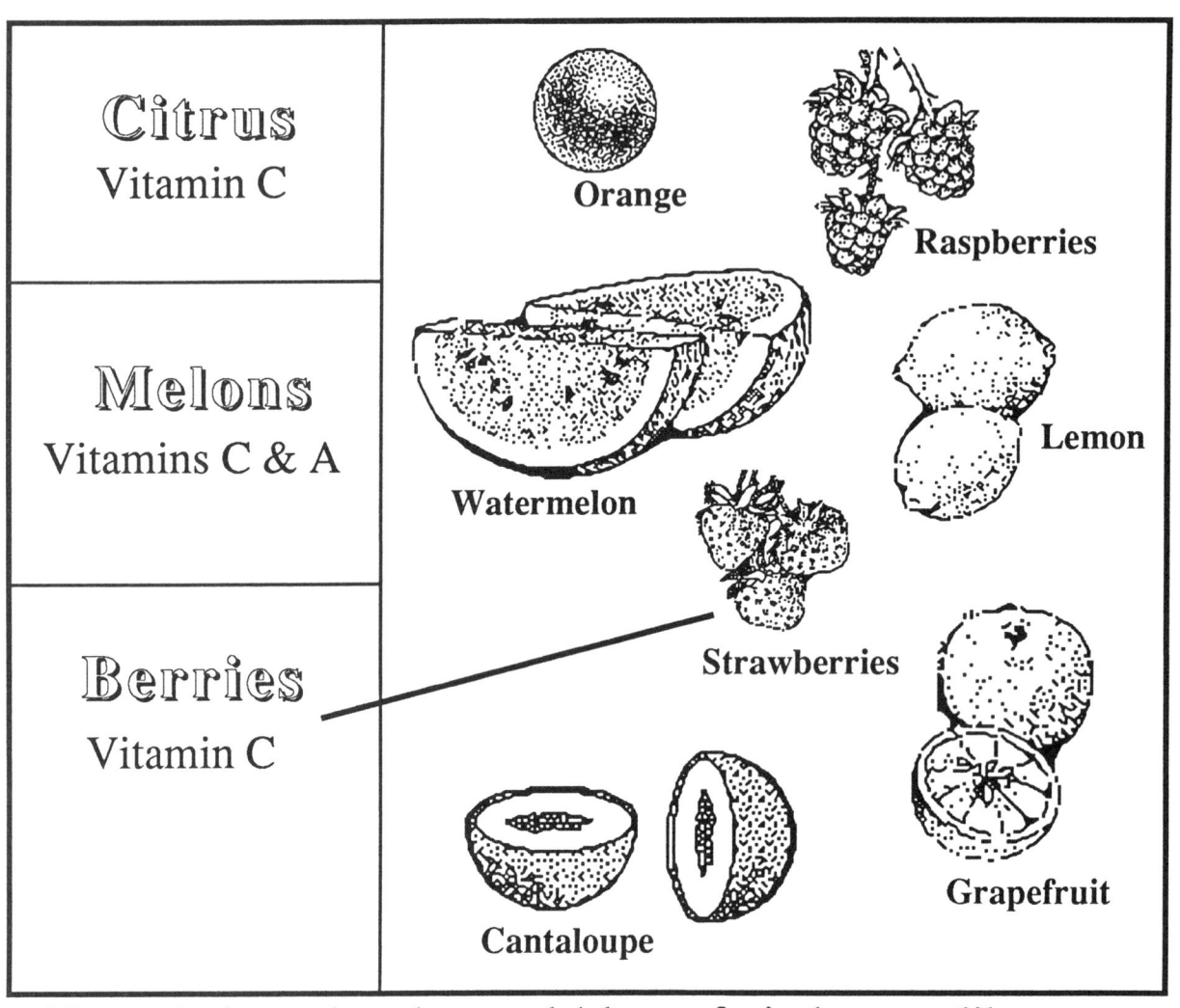

| | |
|---|---|
| **Citrus** Vitamin C | Orange, Raspberries |
| **Melons** Vitamins C & A | Watermelon, Lemon |
| **Berries** Vitamin C | Strawberries, Cantaloupe, Grapefruit |

Name 1 citrus, 1 melon, and 1 berry fruit that you like to eat.

_____        _____        _____
citrus                         melon                          berry

© 1991 by The Center for Applied Research in Education

# Activity 8-3. How Fruits Grow

## DIRECTIONS TO THE TEACHER

**Objective** (Cognitive Domain: Knowledge Level)

Students will select which fruits grow on a tree by drawing a line from the fruit to the tree.

**Materials**

Student Activity Sheet (1)
Crayons
Pencil

**Prerequisite Skills**

Coloring

**Procedure**

1. Review the concept of fruit by giving an example and having students generate additional examples.

2. Ask students how fruits grow. (If they don't know, ask them how they could find out.)

3. Distribute the activity sheet and explain the directions.

4. After completing the activity sheet, have students try to identify how "non-tree" fruits grow.

**Supplementary Activities**

1. Take a field trip to a produce farm and observe the fruits that grow from trees, vines, and bushes.

2. Discuss how fruits grow from seeds. Many fruits we eat have seeds that we do not eat, such as watermelon, apple, pears, oranges, or grapefruits. Have the students generate a list. As they eat these fruits with seeds, ask the students to bring the seeds into class. Set up a learning station with seeds in jars <u>or</u> have the children use the seeds for art.

3. Discuss how fruits differ from vegetables (growth from seeds). Discuss how many fruits are commonly classified as vegetables (tomato, green pepper).

Name_____ Date_____

## Activity 8-3. How Fruits Grow

**Directions:**

Fruits can grow on trees, vines or bushes.
Look at the fruits around the tree.
Color all the fruits.
Draw a line from the tree to the fruits that grow on a tree.

© 1991 by The Center for Applied Research in Education

# Lesson 9. *Vegetables*

## Things to Know About Vegetables

*Key Points:*

- Raw vegetables with dip are often more popular with children than cooked vegetables with strong odors.

- Vegetables are low in fat, high in fiber, starch, vitamins, and minerals.

- Vegetables should not be forced on children but offered in a positive social situation.

*Why do so many children dislike eating vegetables?*

Vegetables may be unpopular with children because of the ways in which they are prepared. Raw vegetables tend to be more popular than cooked ones, and to many children raw vegetables with dip they have prepared themselves are even better yet. When a child's parents and other adult role models view vegetables as a "necessary evil," that negative perception is passed on to the child. Children develop an attitude that vegetables are good for you, but not enjoyable.

In our society, vegetables need to be more effectively promoted. They need to be presented as a dietary opportunity, not a dietary obligation. Children naturally dislike new foods. To promote the acceptance of vegetables, they need to be repeatedly offered to the child. Children should not be coaxed or manipulated. They simply need to be offered the vegetable on more than one occasion.

*How many vegetables should children eat a day?*

*A Pattern for Daily Food Choices* recommends 3-5 servings of vegetables per day. Children should eat at least three. One serving is 1/2 cup of cooked or chopped raw vegetables. To insure optimal nutrient intake, all five types of vegetables should be eaten regularly.

**Dark Green**

| | |
|---|---|
| Beet greens | Kale |
| Belgium endive | Kolrabi |
| Broccoli | Mustard greens |
| Chard | Radiccio |
| Chicory | Seaweed |
| Collard greens | Spinach |
| Dandelion greens | Turnip greens |
| Jicama | |

**Starchy Vegetables**

| | |
|---|---|
| Breadfruit | Lima beans |
| Corn | Potatoes |
| Green peas | Rutabaga |
| Hominy | Taro |
| | Yucca |

**Yellow/Orange**

Acorn squash
Butternut squash
Carrots
Hubbard squash
Pumpkin
Sweet potato

**Other Vegetables**

| | |
|---|---|
| Artichokes | Green beans |
| Asparagus | Green peppers |
| Bamboo shoots | Lettuce |
| Bean and alfalfa | Mushrooms |
|   sprouts | Okra |
| Beets | Onions |
| Bok choy | Radishes |
| Brussels sprouts | Summer squash |
| Cabbage | Turnips |
| Cauliflower | Vegetable juices |
| Celery | Water chestnuts |
| Chinese cabbage | Zucchini |
| Cucumbers | |
| Eggplant | |

*What are the benefits of eating vegetables?*

Vegetables are lowfat, cholesterol free, and high in carbohydrates, starch, and fiber, and high in vitamins and minerals. Dietary patterns high in fats and low in starch and fiber have been associated with a high incidence of health problems, such as heart disease, obesity and cancer.

*What is the connection between eating vegetables and reducing the risk of cancer?*

Guidelines for reducing the risk of cancer include the following dietary recommendations:

1. Increase dietary fiber
2. Reduce fat
3. Increase cruciferous vegetables
4. Increase vitamins A and C

Since some vegetables can help you meet all of these recommendations, vegetables are an important part of a diet to reduce cancer risk.

*What are cruciferous vegetables?*

These vegetables are from the cabbage family. Cruciferous vegetables have been shown to reduce cancer risk. They include:

| Bok choy | Cabbage | Kale | Rutabagas |
| Broccoli | Cauliflower | Kohlrabi | Turnips |
| Brussels sprouts | Collards | Mustard greens | Turnip greens |

*Which vegetables contain vitamin A?*

The vitamin A value of vegetables is generally proportional to the color of the food. The deeper orange, yellow, or green the vegetables, the higher the vitamin A content. The same holds true for fruits. Fruits and vegetables don't really contain vitamin A. They contain beta-carotene, a substance that can be converted in the body to vitamin A. Since vitamin A is a fat-soluble vitamin (and the body stores fat-soluble vitamins), an excessive intake can lead to undesirable toxic effects as the vitamin A accumulates. Beta-carotene, however, does not have those toxic effects. So an individual doesn't need to worry about overdoing on vitamin A by eating too many vegetables. (The only food-related vitamin A overdoses that have been reported have been for individuals who consumed polar bear liver.) However, overeating beta-carotene foods may cause the skin color to turn yellow.

*Which vegetables contain vitamin C?*

Although citrus fruits are the predominant source of vitamin C in children's diets, some vegetables also contribute significant amounts of this vitamin. The following vegetables provide vitamin C.

| Bok choy | Brussels sprouts | Green pepper |
| Broccoli | Cauliflower | Tomato |

*How can teachers promote vegetables at school?*

Offer raw vegetables as party food with dips. Invite the produce person from your local supermarket to come to class and promote vegetables. Describe vegetables in a delicious manner using words such as crunchy, crisp, refreshing, smooth, warm, or colorful. Do not force vegetables on children but present them in a friendly social situation with an approving and supportive attitude. Let your students see you enjoying and eating vegetables.

# Activity 9-1. Vegetable Taste Test

## DIRECTIONS TO THE TECHER

**Objective** (Affective Domain: Responding Level)

After tasting a new vegetable, students will voluntarily answer all items on the taste test data card.

## Materials

Student Activity Sheet (1)
4 plates
4 tables (one vegetable per table)
4 raw vegetables (for example, spinach, cauliflower, snow peas, green beans, summer squash, green pepper, broccoli, sweet potato, and mushrooms)
4 vegetable identification cards
Pencils or crayons

## Preparation

Duplicate Student Activity Sheet (two per student if four vegetables are tested)
Cut up vegetables in bite size pieces (one piece of each vegetable per student)
Display each vegetable with its identification card on a table

## Prerequisite Skills

Copying skills

## Procedure

1. Discuss vegetables with students. Some example questions are:
    - What vegetables do you like?
    - What colors are the vegetables you like?
    - How do they taste?
    - Do you like vegetables that are crunchy?

2. Distribute two activity sheets per student and explain the directions.

3. Divide the class into four groups. Assign each group to a different table. Have the students try one piece of the vegetable at that table and fill out the activity sheet.

4. Rotate groups so each group can evaluate each vegetable.

## Supplementary Activities

1. Organize a salad bar luncheon. Ask each student to bring in an item to be included in the salad bar. For optimal nutrition, be sure to include foods from each food group in the *Pattern for Daily Food Choices*.

2. Ask students to keep a record of all the different vegetables they consume in a three-day period. Evaluate the records by considering frequency of consumption of vegetables, variety of vegetables eaten, and number of new vegetables tasted.

3. Discuss environmentally sound ways of packaging vegetables. Cans can be recycled; however, the nutritional drawback is fewer vitamins and possibly more sodium than in frozen vegetables. But if you choose frozen foods you have choices. A pound of frozen corn in a plastic bag will generate less waste than two 8-ounce boxes of corn that come in paper wrappers. A rule of thumb: The most food in the least packaging is best.

    When discussing recycled paper that has been used in wrapping foods, inform your students that recyclers don't like paper that's been contaminated with food. This is one technological problem that needs to be solved in the future.

4. For information, recipes, and teaching aids to supplement your unit on vegetables have your students contact any or all of the following:

Broccoli Hall of Fame
Mann Packing Co., Inc.
P.O. Box 908
Salinas, CA 93902

California Fresh Tomatoes
690 Fifth Street
San Francisco, CA 94107

California Iceberg Lettuce Commission
P.O. Box 3354
Monterey, CA 93940

Nutrition and Cancer Prevention Program
California Department of Health Services
P.O. Box 942732
Sacramento, CA 94234-7320

The Potato Board
P.O. Box 16111
Denver, CO 80216

Produce Marketing Association
1500 Casho Mill Road
Newark, Delaware 19711-3598

United Fresh Fruit and Vegetable Association
North Washington at Madison
Alexandria, VA 22314

Washington Asparagus Growers Association
P.O. Box 150
Sunnyside, WA 98944

Washington State Potato Commission
108 Interlake Road
Moses Lake, WA 98837

Name _____ Date _____

## Activity 9-1. Vegetable Taste Test

**Directions:** 1) Write the name of the vegetable. 2) Taste the vegetable. 3) Answer the questions about that vegetable. 4) Repeat steps 1 through 3 for each vegetable.

===

Vegetable Taste Test

Name of vegetable _____

What color is it? _____

Is the vegetable crunchy?    YES    NO

I think this vegetable tastes    ☺    or    ☹

Would you eat this vegetable again?    YES    NO

===

Vegetable Taste Test

Name of vegetable _____

What color is it? _____

Is the vegetable crunchy?    YES    NO

I think this vegetable tastes    ☺    or    ☹

Would you eat this vegetable again?    YES    NO

# Activity 9-2. Pizza Smart

## DIRECTIONS TO THE TEACHER

**Objective**   (Cognitive Domain: Knowledge Level)

Given a selection of pizza toppings, students will select the lowfat toppings by circling them.

**Materials**

Student Activity Sheet (1)
Pencil

**Prerequisite Skills**

Identifying initial consonants and vowels
Letter formation

**Procedure**

1. Explain that the fat content in some foods varies depending on how it is prepared and the selection of ingredients. For example, pizza can be lowfat or high fat, depending on the toppings used.

2. Distribute the activity sheet and explain the directions.

## Supplementary Activities

1. Plan a pizza party. Serve only lowfat vegetable toppings, such as mushrooms, onions, green pepper, broccoli, tomatoes, and so on. Have older students cut up the vegetables to prepare the toppings.

2. Pizza represents a single food item made up of several food groups (i.e., bread, meat, milk, and vegetable.) Ask your students to name the different food groups in various types of pizza. Be creative. Some pizzas may have pineapple and ham toppings. Ask the students to generate a list of other foods that are combinations of food groups. Some examples are tacos, tuna casserole, chili with beans, soups, and spaghetti with meatballs. Have your students name the different groups in these dishes. The answers may vary depending on how the foods are served at home. If this occurs, point out how this adds variety and cultural differences from one family to another.

3. Obtain a menu from a pizza shop and classify toppings by food groups. Reclassify them by high fat and low fat.

Name _____ Date _____

**Activity 9-2. Pizza Smart. Directions:** Write the first letter of the picture on the blank. Each line will spell the name of a pizza topping that is low in fat.

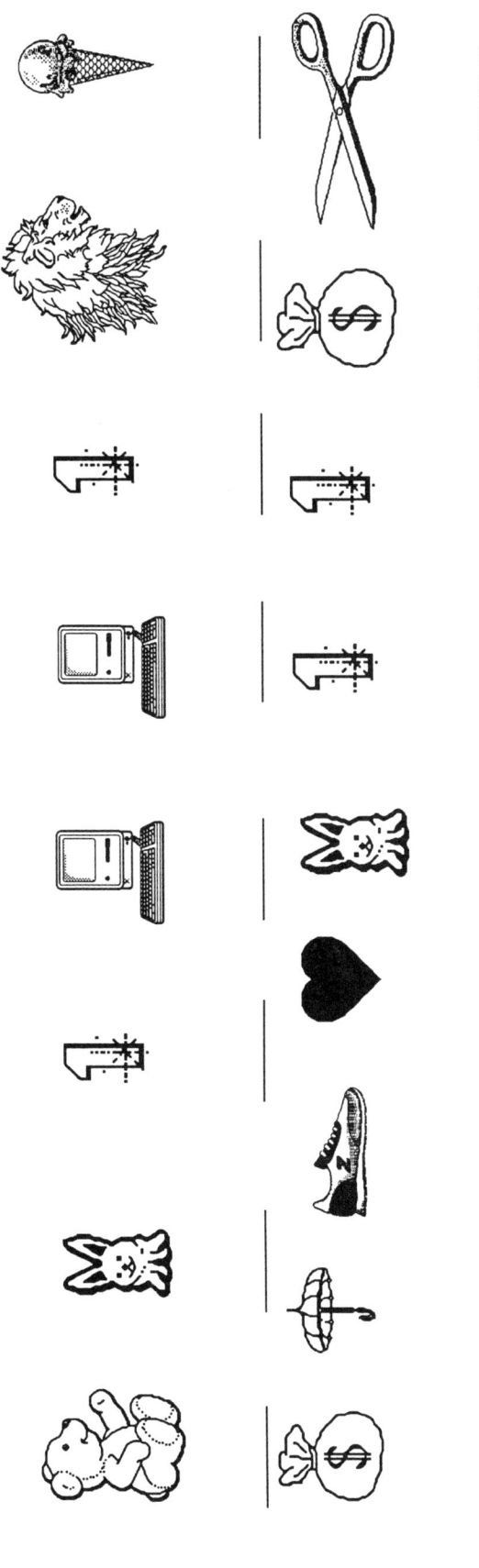

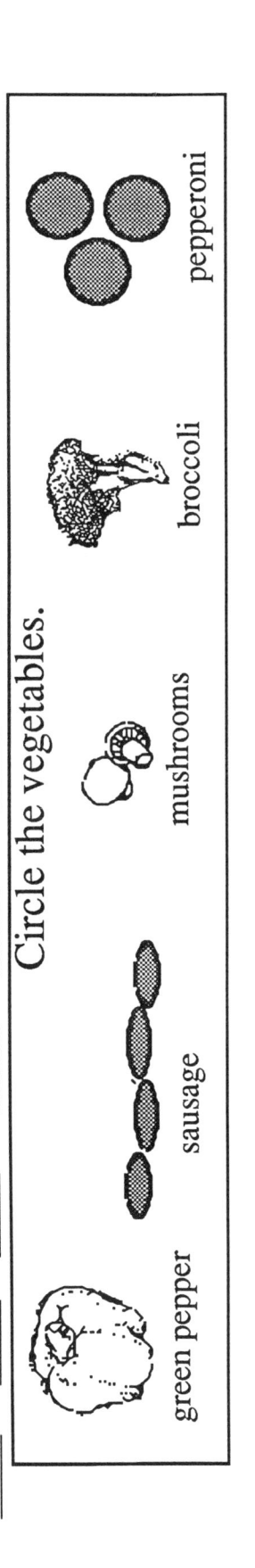

Circle the vegetables.

green pepper   sausage   mushrooms   broccoli   pepperoni

# Activity 9-3. Vegetable Colors

## DIRECTIONS TO THE TEACHER

**Objective**   (Cognitive Domain: Analysis Level)

Students will recognize that vegetables come in many colors.

## Materials

Student Activity Sheet (1)
Crayons, colored pencils  (green, red, blue, yellow, brown)

## Prerequisite Skills

Color words
Coloring

## Procedure

1. Discuss colors of vegetables with students. Some sample questions are:

    - What are your favorite vegetables?
    - What colors are your favorite vegetables?
    - What are your least favorite vegetables?
    - What colors are your least favorite vegetables?

2. Distribute the activity sheet and explain the directions.

## Supplementary Activities

1. Collect an assortment of vegetables. Sort the vegetables by color. Which vegetables are high in vitamin A?

2. Make a collage of vegetables that are high in vitamin A.

3. Provide students with a color classification chart. The chart can be divided into six boxes headed with colors: brown, white, red, green, yellow, and orange. Have students cut out magazine pictures of vegetables, and place appropriately on the chart.

Name _____ Date _____

## Activity 9-3. Vegetable Colors

**Directions:** Color by number to find the vegetables. Circle the vegetable that is a good source of vitamin A.

1 - green    2 - red    3 - blue    4 - yellow    5 - brown

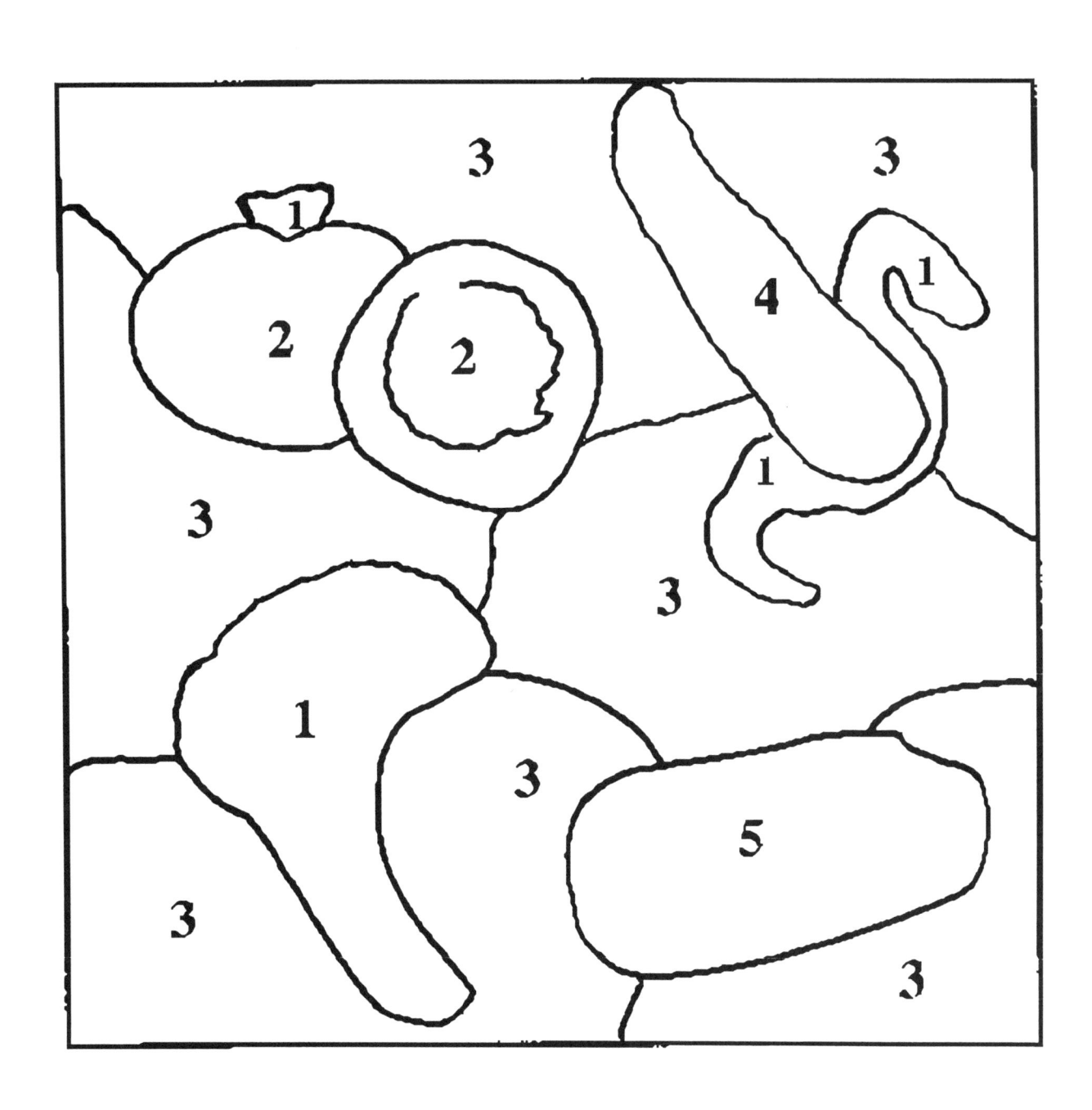

# Lesson 10. *Milk, Cheese, and Yogurt*

## Things to Know About the Dairy Group

*Key Points:*

- Milk and milk products are sources of calcium, protein, riboflavin, vitamin B12, phosphorous, potassium, and vitamin A.

- Children's caloric and fat needs vary from child to child. Milk products with fat and those with no fat can be part of a healthful diet.

- Chocolate milk is an acceptable alternative to white milk.

- If a child cannot drink milk or eat milk products, there are other foods that offer calcium for bone growth and maintenance.

*Is milk the perfect food?*

There is no perfect food. After six months of life humans cannot live on milk alone. Milk products provide a variety of nutrients such as calcium, protein, riboflavin, vitamin B12, phosphorus, potassium, and Vitamin A. Fortified milk is also an important source of Vitamin D. However, milk is not a perfect food since it lacks iron, vitamin C, fiber, and zinc.

*Are some milks, cheeses, and yogurts lower in fat than others?*

Yes. Lowfat milk products are:
buttermilk
lowfat milk (1% and 2%)
lowfat plain yogurt
skim milk

Milk products that contain fat and sugar are:
| American cheese | flavored yogurt | Swiss cheese |
| cheddar cheese | fruit yogurt | whole milk |
| chocolate milk | ice cream | other cheeses |

Cottage cheese contains less calcium than other cheeses. One-half cup of cottage cheese contains only as much calcium as found in one-quarter cup of milk.

*What is a serving size and how many do children need a day?*

Examples of a serving are: one cup of milk or yogurt, one and one-half ounces of natural cheese, and two ounces of processed cheese. Children ages 10 and under need two servings a day.

*Why are milk products needed daily?*

Milk products are our major food source of calcium, which gives bones strength. Calcium is constantly deposited and withdrawn from our bones; 99% of the calcium in the body is in bones, 1% is in the blood. This blood calcium is vitally important for normal nerve transmission, muscle contraction, heart function, and blood clotting. When this small but critical amount falls below a certain level the bones must release some of their calcium. Over time a low intake of calcium-rich foods may compromise bone health.

*Is chocolate milk an acceptable alternative to white milk?*

Many schools offer both chocolate and white milk. If a child does not drink white milk, chocolate milk may be offered as an acceptable alternative. Chocolate milk consumed by a child provides more calcium, protein, vitamins A and D and riboflavin than white milk left in the carton! Whole chocolate milk provides 60 more Calories per cup than whole white milk, but chocolate milk is often sold in the lowfat form. If a child replaces whole milk with lowfat chocolate milk, this difference is reduced to 20 Calories. In addition, the caffeine content is minimal, and chocolate milk contains the same valuable nutrients as white milk. The availability of lowfat chocolate milk may help to ensure that both youngsters and adults take in the daily recommended amount of calcium.

*What if a child doesn't like to drink milk?*

If a child does not like to drink milk, that's okay. There are plenty of other milk products to serve them or for them to choose. Cheese and yogurt are good substitutes for a glass of milk. Ice cream and ice milk are good sources of calcium, but be careful of the fat!

Children sometimes complain that the milk at school is warm or tastes funny. If this complaint is well-founded perhaps taking steps to improve milk handling practices are necessary. This is where teachers can work with students and food service personnel in addressing the issue. Paying closer attention to milk temperatures and code dates may be simple solutions to the problem.

# Figure 10-1. Food Sources of Calcium

**Milligrams of Calcium**

**300-350**
- White or chocolate milk, 1 cup
- Yogurt, 8 oz. container
- Milkshake, 10 oz.

**200-275**
- Calcium fortified orange juice (Citrus Hill), 6 oz.
- Canned sardines or salmon (with bones), 3 oz.
- Tofu, raw, firm, 1/2 cup
- Cheddar, Mozzarella, Swiss, 1 ounce
- Pizza, 1 piece
- Burrito, 1
- Egg McMuffin, 1

**150-175**
- Rhubarb, cooked & sweetened, 1/2 cup
- Instant oatmeal, 1 pkt.
- Cheese spread, 1 oz.
- Jello cheesecake, 1/8 cheesecake
- Pudding, regular or instant (prepared w/milk), 1/2 cup
- Macaroni & cheese, 3/4 cup
- Canned cream of tomato & mushroom soups (prepared with milk), 1 cup

**100-125**
- Broccoli w/cheese sauce, 1/2 cup
- Broccoli, 1/2 cup cooked
- Au Gratin potatoes, from mix or homemade, 1/2 cup
- Wax beans, 1/2 cup
- Hershey kisses, 9 pieces
- Maypo, cooked, 3/4 cup
- American cheese, 1 ounce
- Vanilla ice cream or ice milk, 1/2 cup
- Custard pie, 1/8 pie
- Taco
- Cheeseburger
- Pancakes (fast food), 1 serving
- Cornbread, 1 piece
- Frozen french toast, 2 slices
- Pancakes & waffles from mix
- English muffin, 1

**50-75**
- Corn pudding, 1/2 cup
- Navy beans, 1/2 cup cooked
- Okra, 1/2 cup
- Instant mashed potatoes, 1/2 cup
- Total cereal, 1 cup
- Wheaties, 1 cup
- Pumpkin pie, 1/8 pie
- Gingerbread cake, 1 piece
- Pudding pops, 1 pop
- Orange sherbet, 1/2 cup
- Baked beans, 1/2 cup
- Turkey frank, 1
- Cottage cheese, lowfat, 1/2 cup
- Devils food cake, 1/12 cake

**Below 50**
- Soy milk, 1 cup
- Kidney Beans, 1/2 cup cooked

**Children ages 1-10 need 800 milligrams (mg.) of calcium per day.**

All figures are rounded to the nearest 25 mg.

Dark green leafy vegetables (spinach, kale, etc.) have been excluded because the calcium cannot be absorbed.

Source: Pennington, J. (1989). <u>Food Values of Portions Commonly Used</u>. Philadelphia: J.B. Lippincott.

# Activity 10-1. Milk Product Maze

## DIRECTIONS TO THE TEACHER

**Objective**     (Cognitive Domain: Knowledge Level)

Students will list milk products.

**Materials**

Student Activity Sheet (1)
Pencil

**Prerequisite Skills**

Identify milk products

**Procedure**

1. Define product: A product is something that is produced or made.

2. Define milk product: A milk product is something that is produced or made from milk.

3. Distribute the activity sheet and explain the directions.

4. Students may have fun racing with the clock to complete the maze. Depending on the grade level the race may be completed in one minute or less.

**Supplementary Activities**

1. Discuss with your students the environmentally sound way to purchase milk. They may be surprised to know that buying milk in plastic jugs is environmentally better than cardboard cartons. That is if your municipality recycles the plastic jugs. (Most recyclers recycle soda bottles first, then plastic milk jugs.) Explain that cartons are made of paperboard which has been coated with polyethylene. As a result the two materials must be separated before they can be recycled. This sounds easy but is too costly. Recyclers don't bother, so the carton goes to a landfill and stays there forever.

2. As far as recycling polystyrene or polypropylene yogurt containers goes, no one is recycling them, as of 1990. Children can save and use yogurt containers. Have children generate fun ways to use yogurt containers, for example, to hold their marble collection, plant their orange seeds, carry parts of their lunch, make sand castles, store food in the refrigerator, or collect bugs if holes are poked in the top.

3. Decorated plastic yogurt lids make great classroom achievement awards. Wash and dry the lids, then cover both sides with self-sticking adhesive paper. Attach cutout stars and other symbols to the front of the lids, or print statements such as a "good job" or "you're a star" on them. Then poke two small holes just inside the rim of each lid. Thread a 24-inch piece of thin cord, rug yarn, or ribbon through the holes and tie the two ends together. The awards are ready for students to wear around their necks.

Name _____ Date _____

# Activity 10-1. Milk Product Maze

**Directions:** Follow the MILK products to get out of the maze.

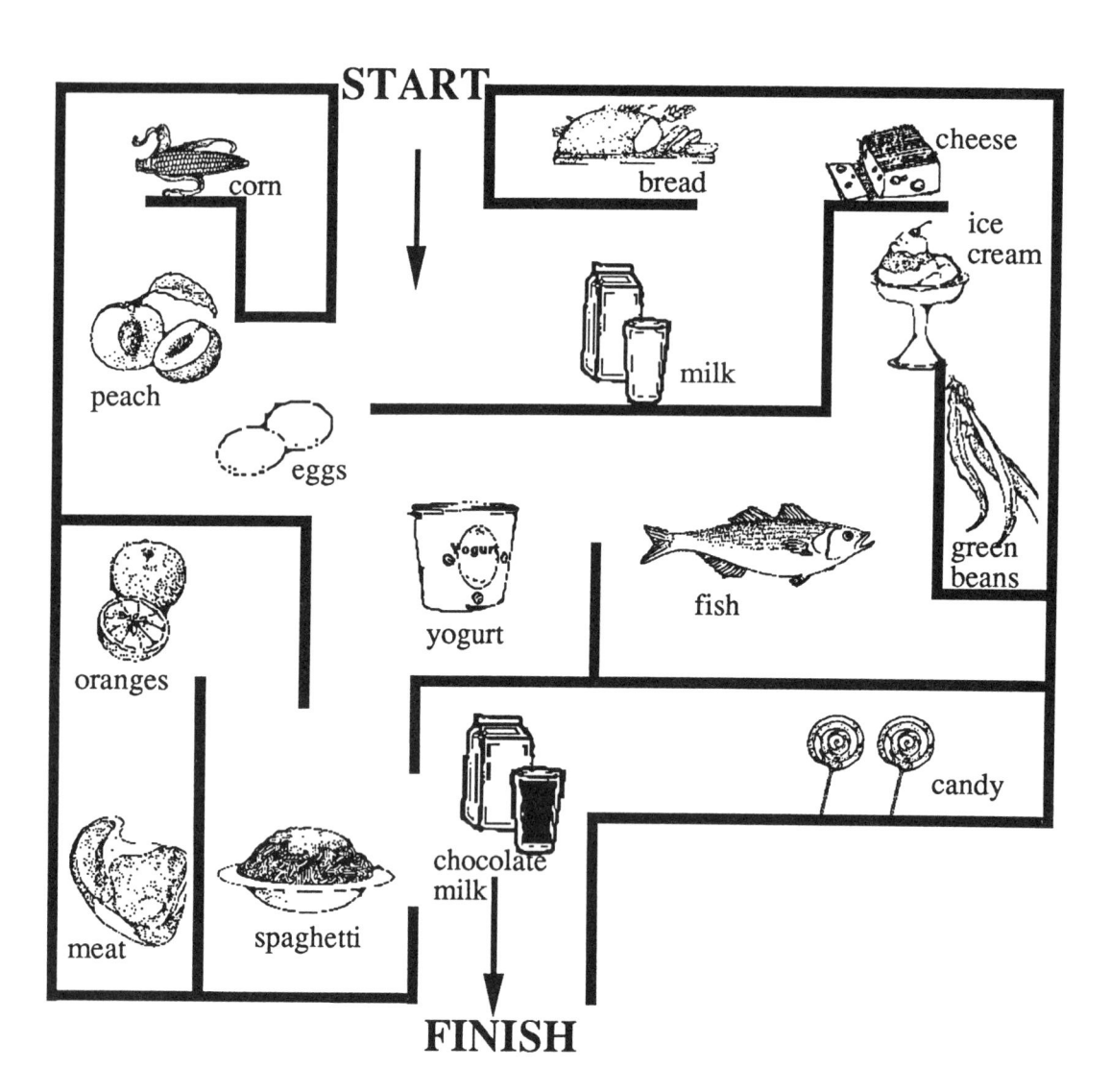

Now rewrite the milk products on the spaces below.

_____   _____

_____   _____

_____

# Activity 10-2. Milk Sorting

## DIRECTIONS TO THE TEACHER

**Objective** (Cognitive Domain: Analysis Level)

Students will categorize milk products by completing a classification chart framework.

### Materials

Student Activity Sheet (1)
Pencil

### Prerequisite Skills

Classification skills

### Procedure

1. Review the concept that milk is an animal product. Explain that there are a variety of milk products. Can students generate a list?

2. Explain how classification charts help to organize information.

3. If necessary, demonstrate the difference between solid and liquid. Although milk products can be in a solid or liquid form, they are still originally made from the liquid milk.

4. Distribute the activity sheet and explain the directions. Explain the subdivisions. Allow students to work independently or in small groups to complete the activity.

5. Follow up with further classification of these milk products by classifying them as white or yellow, hot or cold.

### Supplementary Activities

1. Ask students to consider other food groups and generate appropriate classifications, for example, meat products from various animals or fruits that grow on vines or trees. Have the students name the products.

2. Students can make mobiles out of classifications. Use hangers and string to connect words and pictures of different classes of milk products.

3. Using similar frameworks, have students subdivide other food groups. For example, the meat group can be divided into meat, poultry, fish, eggs, dried beans, nuts, and seeds. Further subdivisions are possible. How many can your students come up with?

Name _____ Date_____

# Activity 10-2. Milk Sorting

**Directions:** Cut out the pictures of the milk products and paste them on the chart where they belong.

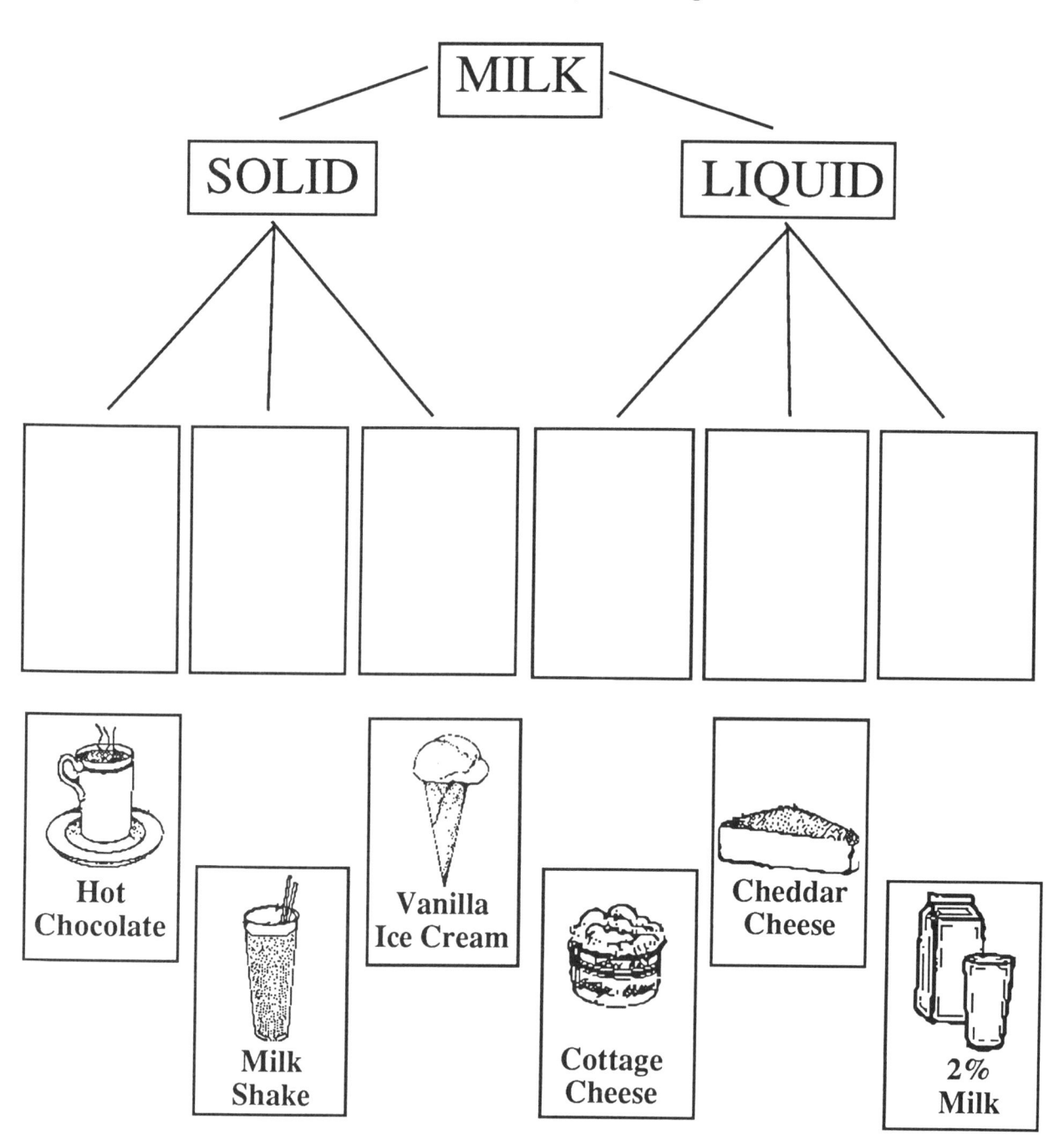

```
              MILK
           /        \
        SOLID      LIQUID
       / | \       / | \
      □ □ □      □ □ □
```

Hot Chocolate

Milk Shake

Vanilla Ice Cream

Cottage Cheese

Cheddar Cheese

2% Milk

© 1991 by The Center for Applied Research in Education

# Activity 10-3. Milk Products

## DIRECTIONS TO THE TEACHER

**Objective** (Cognitive Domain: Analysis Level)

Given a variety of products that come from cows, students will separate them into meat products and milk products.

## Materials

Student Activity Sheet (1)
Crayons or markers

## Prerequisite Skills

Coloring

## Procedure

1. Explain what is meant by the term "animal product." Differentiate between milk products and meat products. Have students think of animals that could provide both milk and meat products.

2. Distribute the activity sheet and explain the directions.

## Supplementary Activities

1. Take a field trip to a dairy farm.

2. Make milk products in the classroom. Yogurt makers, ice cream makers, and butter churns are available in easily portable sizes.

Name _____ Date_____

## Activity 10-3. Milk Products

**Directions:** All of these products come from a cow. Color the milk products. Do not color the meat products.

© 1991 by The Center for Applied Research in Education

# Lesson 11. *Fats and Sweets*

## Things to Know About Fats and Sweets

*Key Points:*

- Foods high in fats and sweeteners add flavor to the diet but contribute few vitamins and minerals.

- Foods high in fats and sweets should be used in moderation.

- Fats have more than twice the calories of carbohydrates and protein.

- There are no bad foods, but there can be bad diets.

- Children's caloric needs vary, so there are no recommended number of servings for fats and sweets.

*Why is there a fats and sweets food group?*

A group called "fats and sweets" was created to represent the foods that nutritionally do not fit into any of the other food groups. These foods can add flavor and appeal to other foods but contribute few vitamins and minerals themselves.

*What foods are in the fat and sweet group?*

Fats refer to:
| | | |
|---|---|---|
| bacon | cream cheese | salad dressing |
| butter | margarine | sour cream |
| cream | mayonnaise | vegetable oil |

Fats do provide essential fatty acids to the diet and some vitamin E. Gram for gram fats have more than twice the calories of either protein or carbohydrates.

Sweets and sugar refer to:
| | | |
|---|---|---|
| candy (may contain fat) | ices | sherbet |
| corn syrup | jam | soft drinks or colas |
| fruit drinks, ades | jelly | sugar (white or brown) |
| frosting | maple syrup | sugar syrup (such as in canned |
| gelatin desserts | marmalade | or frozen fruits) |
| honey | molasses | |

Refined sugar, such as in those foods listed above, contribute few nutrients along with their calories. Although sweeteners such as honey and molasses contain traces of some vitamins and minerals, the amount of these nutrients they contribute to the diet is insignificant.

Many desserts and snack foods contain a mixture of ingredients that offer nutrients, but at a high cost for calories. For example, a slice of peach pie has the nutrients of one third of a peach and two slices of bread, but it also has six teaspoons of sugar and three teaspoons of fat. Or a slice of cake with frosting has the nutrients of one piece of enriched bread, but also six teaspoons of sugar and three teaspoons of fat. A potato has starch, fiber, and vitamins, while potato chips have an additional three teaspoons of fat for one third of the potato. Although these foods are appealing to children's taste buds, they do not add many nutrients that their bodies need to grow.

*Are foods high in fat and sugar bad for children?*

By consuming large quantities of these foods, children can acquire a taste for foods high in fats and sweets at a very young age. After developing a preference for these foods, habits may be very difficult to break.

There are no "bad" foods, but there can be "bad" diets. A diet high in fat and sugar may be related to certain degenerative diseases such as heart disease, some types of cancer, and tooth decay. Also, foods high in fat and sugar tend to replace more nutrient-dense foods.

Most children learn from adults to think of foods high in fat and sugar as "goodies," and also learn that these foods aren't good for them. In turn they may learn to feel guilty about choosing them. Children need to understand that these foods can be part of a healthy diet as long as they are chosen occasionally and eaten in moderation.

*How many fats and sweets should children consume?*

Because children's caloric needs vary widely, there is no recommended number of servings for fats and sweets. If a child is overweight, choices in this group should be decreased first.

*How can children cut down on their fat and sweet intake?*

Children need to be encouraged to make all their food choices wisely, and to consume fats and sweets in moderation. If changes need to be made, they should be made gradually. It may be best to occasionally substitute a hot fudge sundae with a fresh fruit sundae. If a rich dessert is chosen, cutting down on the portion size may be a viable alternative. Another suggestion may be to start by adding desirable foods lower in fat and sugar and letting them crowd out the high fat, high sugar ones.

# Activity 11-1. Food Group Smart

## DIRECTIONS TO THE TEACHER

**Objective** (Cognitive Domain: Analysis Level)

Given three foods, students will identify which two foods are in the same food groups.

**Materials**

Activity Sheet (1)
Pencil

**Prerequisite Skills**

Food group recognition

**Procedure**

1. Reinforce the idea that there are a variety of foods to choose from in each of the food groups.

2. Reinforce that foods are grouped together according to nutritional value.

3. Distribute the activity sheet and explain the directions.

4. Follow up with a reminder that foods in the Fat and Sweet group are often high in calories, fat, and sugar, and low in nutrients. Therefore, these foods should be used in moderation.

5. Reinforce the idea that all the other food groups offer more nutrients to help the body grow and be healthy.

**Supplementary Activities**

1. Using the Food Group Smart activity sheet, ask the students to name the food groups remaining on each line across.

2. Using the Food Group Smart activity sheet, ask each student to identify each food and comment on how often they personally eat them, using descriptors such as daily, occasionally, never. In summary, ask the students if they choose fats and sweets only occasionally and in moderate amounts.

3. Ask the students to draw pictures of their favorite foods in each food group. Ask each student to fold a blank sheet of paper into six squares. Label each square a food group (i.e., milk, meat, fruit, vegetable, bread and cereal, fats and sweets). In each square the students will draw their favorite food. As a follow up, tabulate how many students named the same foods. The results could be graphed. You may even send a list to the school food service director.

Name _____ Date _____

# Activity 11-1. Food Group Smart

**Directions:** Each box below has three rows of foods with three foods in each row. Two of these three foods are in the same food group. Circle the food that is in a different group. Do this for each row. Draw a line through the three circled foods in each box. On the line below the box write the food group to which these circled foods belong. The first one has been done for you.

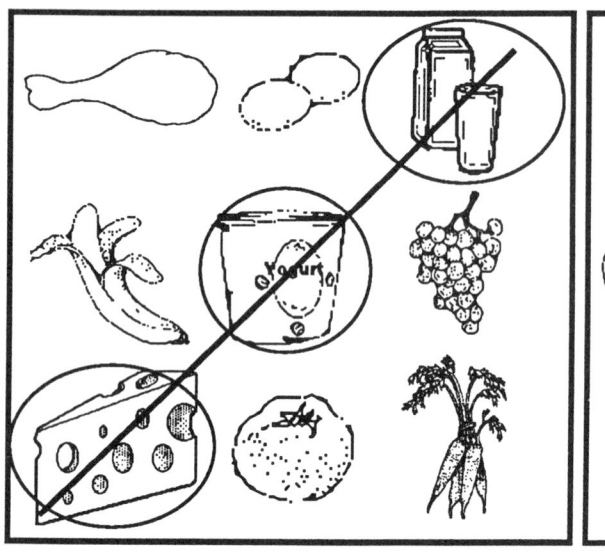

Food group __milk__                Food group _____

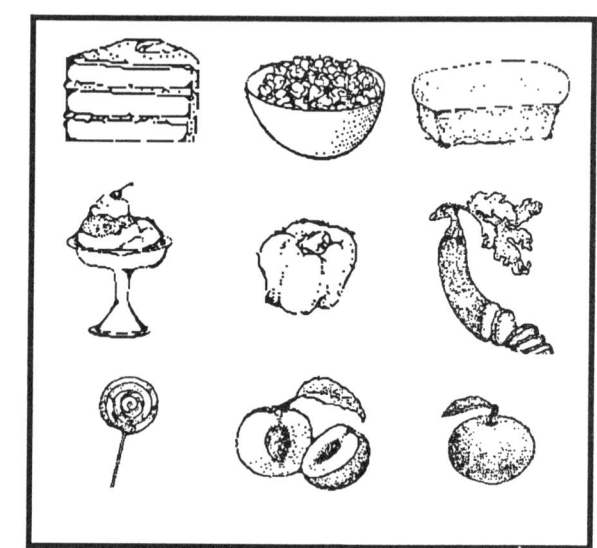

Food group _____          Food group _____

# Activity 11-2. Smart Choices

## DIRECTIONS TO THE TEACHER

**Objective** (Cognitive Domain: Analysis Level)

Given two alternatives, students will identify the food lower in fat and sugar content.

**Materials**

Student Activity Sheet (1)
Pencil

**Prerequisite Skills**

Recognize foods in the Fats and Sweets Group

**Procedure**

1. Review the foods found in the fats and sweets group.

2. Explain that there is no recommended number of servings for foods from this group. This is because caloric needs for children vary considerably. Reinforce that this group of foods provides predominately calories from sugar and fat and very few nutrients.

3. Present the general rule that foods in this food group can be part of a healthy diet, but should be eaten in moderation and only occasionally.

4. Distribute the activity sheet and explain the directions.

5. Discuss the rewards the children choose. Reinforce the idea that non-food items are fun rewards. Ben has worked hard to eat less fat and sugar. A reward like a lollipop would not be appropriate since it is predominately sugar.

**Supplementary Activities**

1. Discuss other means to balance out high caloric foods. For example, increased exercise can "work off" a high calorie food. Explain how caloric needs differ depending on energy expenditures.

2. Generate a list of treats that students feel are appropriate for Halloween, Christmas or Easter. Make sure the list has non-food items and lowfat, low-sugar items. Send the list home to the parents.

Name _____ Date _____

## Activity 11-2. Smart Choices

**Directions:** Ben is trying to limit the number of fats and sweets in his diet. Draw a line from Ben to the food choice in each group that is nutrition smart and lower in fats or sugars. One is done for you.

Ben does a great job in choosing foods lower in fats and sugars. Ben deserves a reward. Circle a reward that you would like to give to Ben.

© 1991 by The Center for Applied Research in Education

# Activity 11-3. Where's the Fat?

## DIRECTIONS TO THE TEACHER

**Objectives**   (Cognitive Domain: Knowledge Level)

Students will recognize that fresh fruits and vegetables are fat free.

Students will recognize that processing of fruits and vegetables into other products usually adds fat.

## Materials

Student Activity Sheet (1)
Pencil
Yellow crayon or marker

## Prerequisite Skills

Understanding charts
Coloring

## Procedure

1. Introduce the idea that we sometimes take simple foods like fruits or vegetables and process them so that the nutritional quality of the food changes.

2. Explain that fat can be added to food. Many times processing a food will change its fat content. For example, potatoes have no fat. But when processed into French fries, potatoes are fried in oil and the potato takes in some of the fat. Sometimes, as in the example of the French fries, a food with no fat can change so that over half the calories come from fat.

3. Distribute the activity sheet and explain the directions.

## Supplementary Activities

1. Bring to class some food products made with fruits and vegetables. Ask the students to read the list of ingredients, looking for sources of fat such as butter, lard, margarine, and oils. Make a comprehensive list of common fats added to food. Discuss why fat is used. (It can enhance the flavor, the form, or the texture of the food.)

2. To illustrate the concept of processing food, bring an ice cream maker to school. Allow students to make ice cream and compare the beginning ingredients to the final product. You may want to make ice cream and sorbet. Sorbet is a great lowfat alternative to ice cream. The students will understand the fat comparison based on the starting ingredients.

Name _____ Date _____

## Activity 11-3. Where's the Fat?

**Directions:** Color the amount of fat in each pie graph yellow. Answer the questions below.

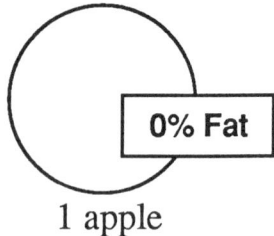

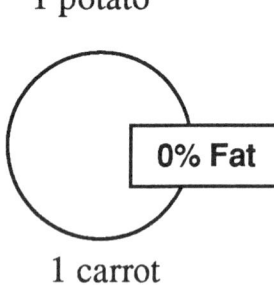

0% Fat
1 apple

40% Fat
1 slice apple pie

0% Fat
1 potato

61% Fat
10 potato chips

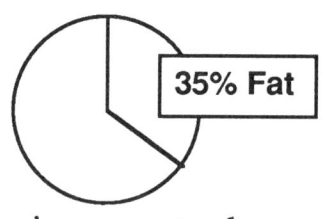

0% Fat
1 carrot

35% Fat
1 piece carrot cake

Pick the correct answer.

There is <u>no</u> fat in   a) fruits   b) fruit products

There <u>is</u> fat in   a) fruits   b) fruit products

There is <u>no</u> fat in   a) vegetables   b) vegetable products

There <u>is</u> fat in   a) vegetables   b) vegetable products

Fresh fruits and vegetables are fat free!!

© 1991 by The Center for Applied Research in Education

# Unit 3. EATING HEALTHY FOODS

Lesson 12    <u>Dietary Guidelines</u>
         12-1. NutritionSmart Guidelines Game
         12-2. Guidelines Code
         12-3. Keeping Score

Lesson 13    <u>Eating a Variety of Foods</u>
         13-1. Cheeseburger Smart
         13-2. Food Diary
         13-3. Varietarian

Lesson 14    <u>Maintaining Healthy Weight</u>
         14-1. Good Moves
         14-2. Using Energy
         14-3. Exercise Message

Lesson 15    <u>Eating Lowfat Foods</u>
         15-1. Milk Carton Cutouts
         15-2. Clogged Pipes
         15-3. Fat Finder

Lesson 16    <u>Eating Plenty of Vegetables, Fruits, and Grain Products</u>
         16-1. Starch and Fiber Chains
         16-2. Fiber Foods
         16-3. Fiber Count

Lesson 17    <u>Using Sugars in Moderation</u>
         17-1. Tooth Smart
         17-2. Ingredient Smart
         17-3. Sugar Decoder

Lesson 18    <u>Using Salt and Sodium in Moderation</u>
         18-1. Sodium Smart
         18-2. Sodium Inspector
         18-3. Sodium Vending

# Lesson 12. *Dietary Guidelines*

## Things to Know About the Dietary Guidelines

*Key Points:*

- The Dietary Guidelines provide a foundation for a healthy diet.
- Diet is just one factor that influences one's risk for chronic diseases.
- Healthy children two years and older are advised to follow the Dietary Guidelines.

*What are the Dietary Guidelines?*

There are seven Dietary Guidelines for Americans. They are:

> Eat a variety of foods.
> Maintain healthy weight.
> Choose a diet low in fat, saturated fat, and cholesterol.
> Choose a diet with plenty of vegetables, fruits, and grain products.
> Use sugars in moderation.
> Use salt and sodium in moderation.
> If you drink alcoholic beverages, do so in moderation.

These guidelines do not apply to a single food or meal but to the total diet over several days.

*Who Should Follow the Dietary Guidelines?*

The Dietary Guidelines were developed for all healthy Americans over the age of two. They may not apply to persons with special conditions such as diabetes, heart disease, or kidney disease. In these cases, special attention from a physician and/or dietitian is required.

*Why were the Dietary Guidelines developed?*

The Dietary Guidelines were developed to improve food habits and to attempt to reduce the incidence of diet-related diseases. Many of the most prevalent diseases, such as heart disease, cancer, stroke, diabetes, high blood pressure, and atherosclerosis, are related to diet. Although prevention of these diseases through dietary change is not guaranteed, it is believed that the chances of developing some diseases may be reduced by following these dietary guidelines.

*Can food alone make you healthy?*

No. Although the guidelines can serve as a basis for good health, food alone cannot make us healthy. Health is also influenced by factors other than diet, such as genetics, personality traits, mental health and attitudes, cigarette smoking, environment, and physical activity. However, good eating habits can help keep you healthy and even improve your health.

*How do the Dietary Guidelines apply to children?*

Children accustomed to choosing food low in sugar, sodium, and fat, along with foods providing adequate amounts of starch and fiber, are developing healthy habits. Children can be made aware of how a diet high in sodium, fat, and sugar relates to an increased risk for obesity, diabetes, heart disease, or cancer. If children are aware of degenerative diseases within their families it may personalize their diet and health. This knowledge can be beneficial in helping children become accountable for their health behaviors.

*How can the Dietary Guidelines benefit children?*

Although the benefits of following the Dietary Guidelines may not show up immediately, if followed they may improve each child's future health, lifestyle, and quality of life.

*What is the history behind food guidance?*

During the 1940s there was a high rejection rate among young service recruits due to deficiencies caused by suboptimal nutrition. For this reason the government developed the Recommended Daily Allowances (RDAs) for the public to address the various nutrients needed to maintain health. To make the RDAs applicable to the public, a general guideline was developed called the "Basic Four." This guideline was to aid the public in selecting a diet that would meet the RDAs.

The next twenty years brought about a more heightened awareness for nutrition as the recognition of nutritional deficiencies became a national concern. Prior to 1977 all dietary advice was based on the "Basic Four Food Groups" published by the United States Department of Agriculture (USDA). However a question arose concerning foods that do not fit into one of the "Basic Four Food Groups." Consequently a fifth group was added consisting of fats, sugars, and alcohol.

Another issue which arose in the 1970s was the relationship between food and chronic degenerative diseases. This concern had not been addressed by the "Basic Four." Because of this concern, the "Dietary Goals" were developed to address specific recommendations. The availability of the food supply in the American diet was taken into account when developing these goals as well as the possible hazards from an excessive intake. Specifically the "Dietary Goals" focused on the role of diet in chronic degenerative diseases, such as hypertension, coronary heart disease, obesity, diabetes, and cancer. The government perceived that these goals were too specific for many Americans, and felt there was a need for a more general approach.

The Dietary Guidelines were developed due to concern that the "Dietary Goals" were too specific. The guidelines were still based on the connection between food and disease; however, they were a more general list of guidelines to help Americans achieve variety and moderation. The first two guidelines form the basic framework for a healthy diet. "Eat a variety of foods" that provide enough of the essential nutrients and energy (calories) to "maintain desirable weight." The last five guidelines give special recommendations for a good diet. The recommendations suggest that you get adequate starch and fiber, choose a diet low in fat, and use sugar, sodium, and alcohol in moderation.

*What can teachers do?*

First and foremost, set an example. If you don't already, begin now to follow the Dietary Guidelines. Share the guidelines with other teachers, your students, and their parents. Write for copies of the <u>Nutrition and Your Health: Dietary Guidelines for Americans</u>, (third edition, 1990), Consumer Information Center, Pueblo, CO 81009. Send a copy home to parents. Letting parents know you and the school care about the health of the entire family can make a difference.

# Activity 12-1. Nutrition-Smart Guidelines Game

## DIRECTIONS TO THE TEACHER

**Objective** (Cognitive Domain: Application Level)

Students will demonstrate an understanding of nutrition guidelines by indicating whether or not given actions adhere to the guidelines.

## Materials

Student Activity Sheets (2)
List of nutrition-smart guidelines ( USDA Dietary Guidelines)
Playing piece
Dice

## Prerequisite Skills

Understanding of the Dietary Guidelines

## Procedure

1. Provide the students with a copy of the guidelines. Discuss the nutrition-smart guidelines. Ask students for examples of ways to apply these guidelines in daily food choices.

2. Distribute the activity sheets and explain the directions.

3. The correct responses for the game are as follows:

| Phrases | Follows the Guidelines |
|---|---|
| Snack on fresh fruit | YES (increases fruit consumption) (low fat) |
| Watch TV all afternoon and snack on chips and soda | NO (added fat and sugar) (not keeping my body fit) |
| Order pizza with mushrooms | YES (mushrooms are low fat) (pizza dough is a grain product) |
| Choose whole grain bread | YES (increases fiber consumption) |
| Eat a whole bag of cookies at once | NO (added fat and sugar) |
| Don't salt your French fries | YES (reduces sodium) |
| Choose soft drink over milk | NO (added sugar) |
| Choose mustard over mayonnaise | YES (low fat) |
| Don't eat your vegetables | NO (no starch) (missing variety) |

| | |
|---|---|
| Enjoy carrots as a snack | YES (increases vegetable consumption) (low fat) |
| Trade sandwich for candy | NO (added fat and sugar) |
| Order pizza with pepperoni and sausage | NO (high-fat toppings) |
| Eat the same foods for breakfast and lunch all week | NO (missing variety) |
| Eat salad at a fast-food restaurant | YES (increases vegetable consumption) (low fat) |
| Choose lowfat milk over whole milk | YES (low fat) |
| Put two pats of butter on a piece of bread | NO (too much added fat) |

## Supplementary Activities

1. Ask your students to keep a food record of when they follow the nutrition-smart guidelines; i.e., choose lowfat milk, eat fruit, and so on. Praise them for their efforts. Children will learn from their successes.

2. Ask students to list ten foods they eat often, being as specific as possible. When they have completed the list, assist them in categorizing each food as it fits into the Dietary Guidelines. Some questions you might ask are:

    • Does your list include a variety of foods?
    • What food groups are represented?
    • Do you eat many foods that are high in sugar?
    • Do you eat many foods that are salty?
    • Do you think the foods on your list are nutrition smart?

    Conclude by asking, "What changes could you make in your diet? Are there foods you should include more of? Are there foods you should include less of?"

3. Ask students to list all the foods they ate yesterday. Ask them to evaluate food choices according to the Dietary Guidelines. What changes do they have to make to conform to the Dietary Guidelines?

4. Have students generate a list of guidelines they follow in school. Sample guidelines might include: when you're writing a story and you can't fit a word on a line, write it on the next line instead of squeezing it in; or, unless absolutely necessary, use the restroom only during restroom breaks.

**Dietary Guidelines for Americans**

Eat a variety of foods.

Maintain healthy weight.

Choose a diet low in fat, saturated fat, and cholesterol.

Choose a diet with plenty of vegetables, fruits, and grain products.

Use sugars only in moderation.

Use salt and sodium only in moderation.

© 1991 by The Center for Applied Research in Education

Name _____ Date _____

## Activity 12-1. Nutrition-Smart Guidelines Game

The following game is about nutrition-smart guidelines.

**Directions:**

1) Pick a playing piece such as a coin, eraser, or paper clip.

2) Each player must roll the dice. The highest roll goes first. Play continues clockwise.

3) When it is your turn, roll the dice and move your playing piece to the appropriate space.

4) Read what is in the box. For each box with a message, tell the other players if this message follows the nutrition-smart guidelines. If it does, you get to move ahead the number of spaces indicated. If it doesn't follow the guidelines, you must move back the number of spaces indicated.

5) If you land on a box with a picture, stay there until your next turn. The first player to reach the "Winner's Block" wins the game.

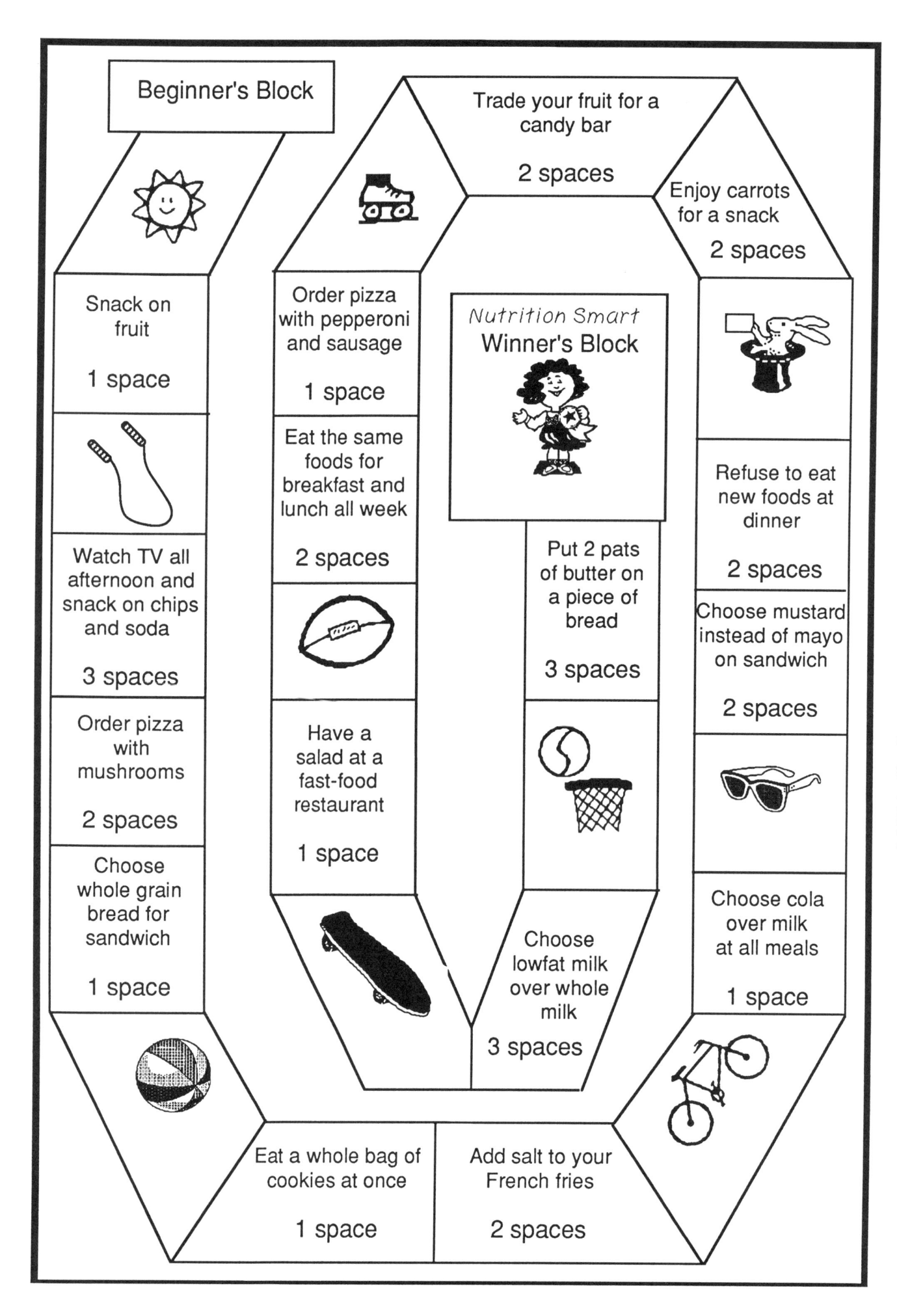

# Nutrition Smart Board Game

**Beginner's Block**

| Space | Instruction |
|---|---|
| Snack on fruit | 1 space |
| Watch TV all afternoon and snack on chips and soda | 3 spaces |
| Order pizza with mushrooms | 2 spaces |
| Choose whole grain bread for sandwich | 1 space |
| Eat a whole bag of cookies at once | 1 space |
| Add salt to your French fries | 2 spaces |
| Choose lowfat milk over whole milk | 3 spaces |
| Choose cola over milk at all meals | 1 space |
| Choose mustard instead of mayo on sandwich | 2 spaces |
| Refuse to eat new foods at dinner | 2 spaces |
| Enjoy carrots for a snack | 2 spaces |
| Trade your fruit for a candy bar | 2 spaces |
| Order pizza with pepperoni and sausage | 1 space |
| Eat the same foods for breakfast and lunch all week | 2 spaces |
| Have a salad at a fast-food restaurant | 1 space |
| Put 2 pats of butter on a piece of bread | 3 spaces |

**Nutrition Smart Winner's Block**

© 1991 by The Center for Applied Research in Education

# Activity 12-2. Guidelines Code

## DIRECTIONS TO THE TEACHER

**Objective** (Cognitive Domain: Knowledge Level)

Students will match symbols to letters to decode a message that will reveal six dietary guidelines.

**Materials**

Student Activity Sheet (1)
Pencil

**Prerequisite Skills**

Formation of letters

**Procedure**

1. Discuss guidelines with the students. Some sample questions are:

    • What does "guideline" mean?
    • What are examples of things people say about what to eat?
    • Ask students if they think about the guidelines when they choose food.

2. Distribute the activity sheet and explain the directions.

**Supplementary Activities**

1. Talk about guidelines derived by the government. Government functions for the well-being of all people. The Department of Agriculture (a watchdog on food safety) works to help keep Americans healthy. You may want to tie in the concept of democracy/democratic government which is aimed at the common good of all people.

2. Obtain copies of Nutrition and Your Health: Dietary Guidelines for Americans, (third edition, 1990), Home and Garden Bulletin No. 232 from USDA and US Health and Human Services. Write to Dietary Guidelines, Consumer Information Center, Pueblo, CO 81009. Have the students share these with their parents.

3. Have your students take the "Code" activity sheet home to discuss the guidelines with their parents. Instruct the students to explain what each guideline means and possible ways to eat according to the guidelines.

Name_____  Date_____

# Activity 12-2. Guidelines Code

**Directions:** Decode the messages below to find nutrition-smart eating habits. Each symbol represents a letter.

**Code**

a =
b =
c =
d =
e =
f =
g =
h =
i =
l =
m =
n =
o =
r =
s =
t =
u =
v =
w =
y =

1. Eat _____ kinds of foods.

2. Keep your body _____.

3. Choose foods low in _____.

4. Eat _____, _____ and _____.

5. Eat just a little _____.

6. Use just a little _____.

© 1991 by The Center for Applied Research in Education

# Activity 12-3. Keeping Score

## DIRECTIONS TO THE TEACHER

**Objective** (Affective Domain: Responding Level)

Students will voluntarily try to improve eating habits.

## Materials

Student Activity Sheet (1)
Pencil

## Prerequisite Skills

Reading
Addition

## Procedure

1. Discuss the comment "there's always room for improvement." How does this apply to eating habits?

2. Distribute the activity sheet and explain the directions.

## Supplementary Activities

1. Ask students to list the things they did yesterday that followed the Dietary Guidelines. Have them name three things they can do tomorrow to follow the Dietary Guidelines.

2. Discuss other healthy behaviors the students do that are not related to the Dietary Guidelines, such as getting plenty of rest, brushing their teeth, washing their hands when handling food, and so on.

3. As a class, select one Dietary Guideline that is difficult to meet. Discuss ways to make positive changes. Let each child set small individual goals that he or she can easily measure and attain. When the children are successful at one change, they'll find other changes easier. Working together as a class can support change and success.

Name _____ Date _____

## Activity 12-3. Keeping Score

**Directions:** Think of what you have done in the past three days and answer the questions. If you are doing what the ball says, draw a line from the ball to Ben's foot. If you haven't done what the ball says, cross out that ball.

---

I tried a new food this week. **5**

I ate three vegetables in the same day. **3**

I read a food label. **1**

I drank lowfat milk at school. **1**

I had a whole fruit with the skin on it. **1**

I ate pasta, rice, or beans. **2**

I played outside for at least a half hour. **2**

I rinsed my mouth or brushed my teeth after eating supper. **4**

Add the numbers on the soccer balls that are left. What is your score? _____

Try to score even more points next week!

© 1991 by The Center for Applied Research in Education

# Lesson 13. *Eating a Variety of Foods*

## Things to Know About Eating a Variety of Foods

*Key Points:*

- Eating a variety of foods means eating foods from all the food groups, and eating a variety of foods within that group.

- Exposing children to a variety of foods can promote acceptance in trying new foods.

*What does it mean to eat a variety of foods?*

A varied diet doesn't simply mean eating foods from each food group every day. It also means eating different foods within each group. For example, instead of eating white bread every day, eat whole wheat or rye bread, a bagel, or a pita pocket. Eating a variety of foods can be more pleasurable than eating the same foods day after day. These foods should fit each individual's personal, family, and cultural traditions, as well as lifestyle and budget restraints.

*Why eat a variety of foods?*

Children and adults need over forty different nutrients to stay healthy. These include carbohydrates, protein, fat, water, vitamins, and minerals. No one food supplies all the nutrients needed for growth and the maintenance of body cells. Therefore, it is important to eat several types of foods each day to get all the essential nutrients.

The more variety in the diet, the less likely one will develop either a deficiency or an excess of any single nutrient. For example, iceberg lettuce provides water and is low in fat, but lacks vitamin A. Vitamin A is found in deep orange and green vegetables. Eating iceberg lettuce exclusively, in place of a variety of vegetables, may result in a less than optimal intake of vitamin A.

Milk is an example of a food that contains many nutrients. Milk provides proteins, fats, sugars, riboflavin and other B vitamins, vitamin A, calcium, and phosphorus among other nutrients. However, it contains very little iron or vitamin C. To drink only milk would cause a deficiency in iron and vitamin C. Therefore, everyone should eat a variety of foods from all the food groups to assure an adequate diet.

Eating exactly the same food every day can become boring and may deliver dangerous amounts of undesirable food constituents, such as plant toxins or chemical contaminants. Each undesirable component is diluted by all the other foods eaten with it, and even further diluted if several days are skipped before it is eaten again.

*How can variety be integrated into children's meals?*

Exposure is the building block for variety. A teacher can promote variety by starting a discussion on new or different foods or by having tasting parties at school. When children recognize that new and different foods are acceptable by their peers, they may be more apt to try incorporating variety into their own diet.

When discussing bread, use the terms whole grain and enriched breads, cereals and pasta; when discussing fruits, talk about citrus, melons, berries as well as other fruits; when discussing vegetables, use the words dark green, deep yellow, or starchy; when talking about milk, don't forget products like yogurt and cheese; when discussing meat, mention eggs, legumes, nuts, and seeds. Hearing this variety of food names may promote acceptance in trying new foods and eating a variety of foods.

Variety also appeals to the senses. Different smells, colors, tastes, and textures can add to the pleasure of eating. To maximize taste appeal, something tart can be suggested to go with something sweet, something crisp to balance something soft, and something moist to go with something dry.

Trying new foods and teaching children to eat a variety of foods should be a slow and unstressful process, with no pressure. Start out with the goal of simply introducing one or two bites. Acceptance of new foods is age related. As children grow older, they are more likely to refuse new foods. Children show more acceptance to new foods when they don't feel pressured.

*What about food jags?*

Sometimes children go on food jags when they prefer one food over another. This is normal. Teachers and parents must be understanding about children's reactions to food.

# Activity 13-1. Cheeseburger Smart

## DIRECTIONS TO THE TEACHER

**Objective** (Cognitive Domain: Knowledge Level)

Students will identify food groups that are or are not represented in a cheeseburger.

### Materials

Student Activity Sheet (1)
Pencil

### Prerequisite Skills

Classification of foods in basic food groups

### Procedure

1. Discuss how one food item we eat may be a combination of a variety of food groups.

2. Distribute the activity sheet and explain the directions. Discuss other food combinations we eat that offer a variety of food groups, such as pizza, spaghetti, tacos, tuna casserole, and so on. Have your students generate more examples.

### Supplementary Activities

1. Have the students design a meal of favorite foods using all the food groups.

2. Have the students choose a favorite common food and invent an uncommon food combination to make with it. Have them pretend that they will open a specialty restaurant to sell this new food. What will they name it?

3. Have students "dissect" a pizza, taco, spaghetti, or other multi-food item. List individual foods that comprise the item and label them by food group.

Name _____ Date _____

## Activity 13-1. Cheeseburger Smart

American children report their favorite restaurant food to be cheeseburgers.

**Directions:** Write the names of the food groups in the foods found in a cheeseburger.

_____ group

_____ group

_____ group

_____ group

Draw a fruit you like to eat with a cheeseburger.

Draw a vegetable you like to eat with a cheeseburger.

© 1991 by The Center for Applied Research in Education

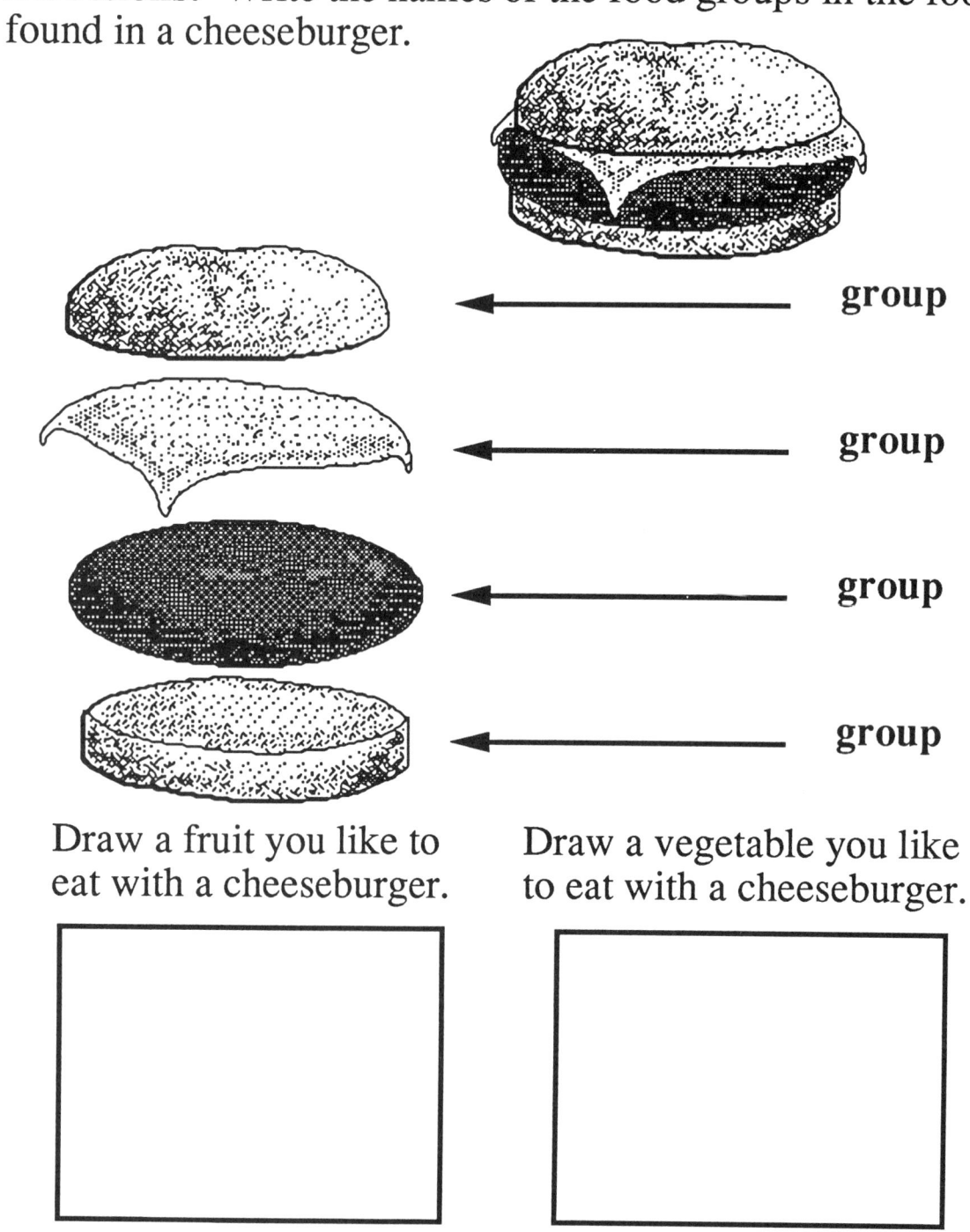

# Activity 13-2. Food Diary

## DIRECTIONS TO THE TEACHER

**Objective** (Cognitive Domain: Knowledge and Evaluate Levels)

Students will list foods eaten for a defined period of time and evaluate the diet to determine if a variety of foods are eaten.

**Materials**

Student Activity Sheets (2) - page 1 is homework, page 2 is in-class follow up

**Prerequisite Skills**

Classification of foods in basic food groups

**Procedure**

1. Explain that the purpose of a diary is to record daily events. Students will keep a food diary. All food eaten between school and going to bed should be recorded for one day.

2. Distribute the activity sheets and explain the directions. Go over the example as a group.

3. Follow up the next day by reviewing the purpose of a diary. Review the food groups.

4. Distribute page 2 questions and have the students work independently to complete questions 1-8.

5. Discuss results. Define variety. Reinforce the importance of eating a variety of foods to obtain all the nutrients needed for growth. Have students evaluate their personal eating habits by completing question 9.

**Supplementary Activities**

1. Introduce the concepts of variety and diet. First, ask the children to look for the word "variety" in the dictionary. One definition of variety is a collection of different things. Next, ask the children to look for the word "diet" in the dictionary. One definition of diet is food or drink regularly eaten. If the children think of the foods and drinks as a collection and then apply the word "different" from the definition of variety, they will begin to connect the two concepts.

2. What are some of the things students in your class collect? What do they look for when they add something new to their collection? Where do they store their collection? Connect the idea of a collection to food stored in various places in the kitchen.

3. For those students who respond "no" to question 9, dieting goals could be generated by each student to improve eating habits. The diary could be extended and progress monitored.

Name _____ Date _____

## Activity 13-2. Food Diary

**Directions:**

To keep a food diary, write down all foods that you eat and drink between coming home from school today and coming back to school tomorrow.

See the example.

## FOOD DIARY

<u>Example:</u>

   peanut butter sandwich
   2% milk
   banana

_____

_____

_____

_____

_____

_____

_____

© 1991 by The Center for Applied Research in Education

Name _____ Date _____

## Activity 13-2. Food Diary, *page 2*

1) How many different foods did you eat? _____

2) How many foods were fruits? _____ List them:
_____

3) How many foods were vegetables? _____ List them:
_____

4) How many were meats? _____ List them:
_____

5) How many were breads or cereals? _____ List them:
_____

6) How many were milk products? _____ List them:
_____

7) How many were fats or sweets? _____ List them:
_____

8) Did you miss a food group? Yes ____ No ____

   If so, which one(s)? _____

9) Do you eat a variety of foods? Yes ____ No ____
   Why or why not?
_____

_____

# Activity 13-3. Varietarian

## DIRECTIONS TO THE TEACHER

**Objective** (Affective Domain: Responding Level)

Students will voluntarily participate in a parade to celebrate food variety.

## Materials

Student Activity Sheet (1)
Crayons
Scissors
Tape
Pencil

## Prerequisite Skills

Cutting

## Procedure

1. Introduce your students to the idea of a class parade. They will be parading to celebrate that they are "varietarians." Varietarians eat a variety of foods that are good for them.

2. Distribute the activity sheet and explain the directions.

3. Ask students to draw and color their varietarian banner decorated with their favorite foods from all the food groups. Have students attach banners to pencils with tape.

4. While parading, have the leader list a food from a given food group. Have each student try to add a food to the list without repeating a food. Variations of the parade might include foods that start with a given letter or foods of a certain color.

## Supplementary Activities

1. Have students earn a variety badge (made from plastic yogurt lids, described in Activity 10-1 by trying every food in the school lunch.

2. Follow up with a discussion on variety by pointing out how varied banners were made. They vary in color, pattern, and food drawings.

Name _____     Date _____

**Activity 13-3. Varietarian**

**Directions:**
1. Color the banner.
2. Cut out the banner.
3. On the other side of the banner, draw and color a variety of your favorite foods.
4. Tape the banner to the ruler or pencil.
5. Get ready for the parade.

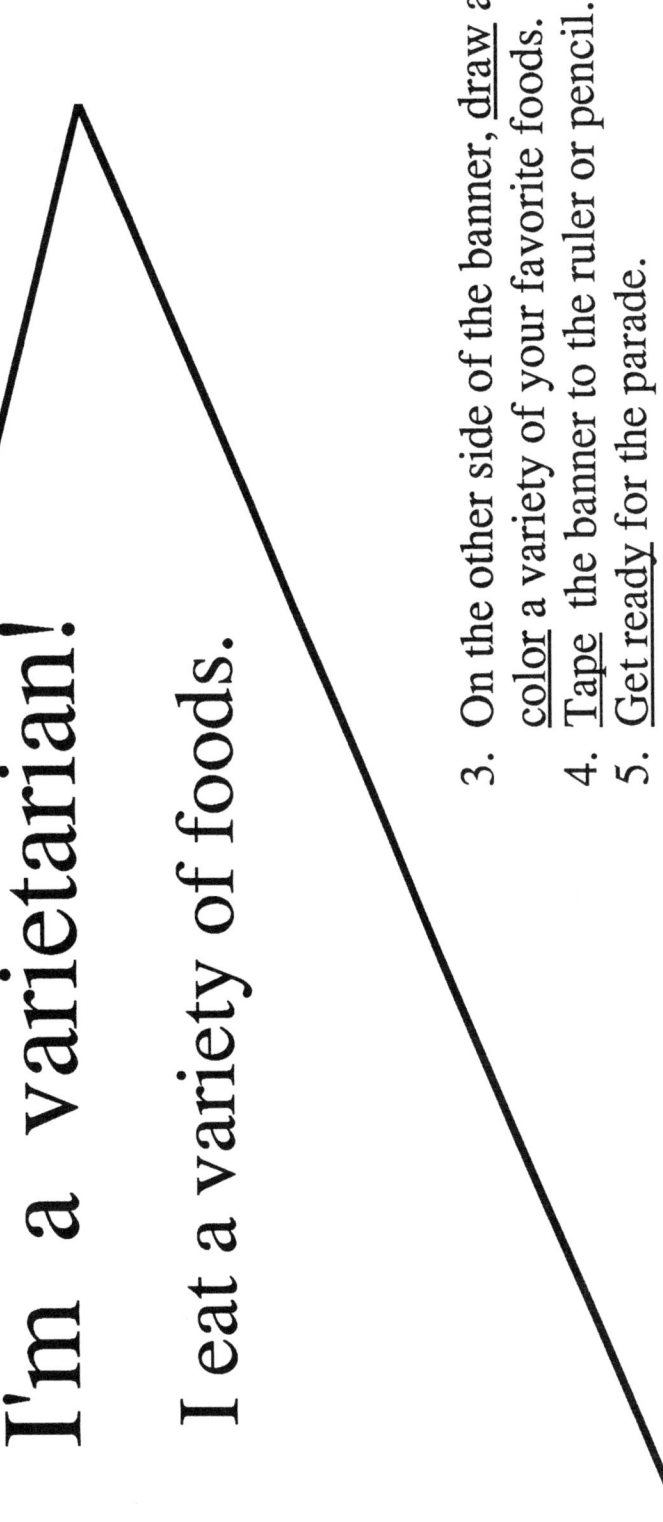

# I'm a varietarian!
# I eat a variety of foods.

# Lesson 14. *Maintaining Healthy Weight*

## Things to Know About Maintaining Healthy Weight

*Key Points:*

- Childhood obesity is on the rise in America, as is inactivity.

- Nutrient requirements are so great during childhood that calorie restriction is not recommended.

- Constant pressure on children to be thin and reduce calorie intake can lead to eating disorders.

- Behavior modification, nutrition education, and increased exercise are the keys to helping overweight children.

*What is the health/weight connection?*

Being too fat or too lean increases one's chances for health problems. Obesity is linked with high blood pressure, heart disease, stroke, diabetes and some types of cancer. Being too lean is a less common problem, but it is linked with bone disease in women and early death.

*What is healthy weight for children?*

A healthy weight for one child may be undesirable for another child. Healthy weight is solely dependent on the individual child. Children come in a wide variety of shapes and sizes. There are wide differences in the rate of growth and development among individual children during any age period. Variations between slow and rapid growth do not necessarily indicate abnormal growth.

Growth charts are used to track a child's weight and height at different ages. When a child fails to follow the pattern he or she normally follows, the doctor should notice it and assess the underlying cause. Although growth charts can be used to compare children to a standard, it is important to keep individuality in mind and not compare "Mary" to "Sue." Children vary enormously in the way that they gain weight and height.

*Why do children gain excess weight?*

Children gain excess weight for a variety of reasons. Before starting school, young children rarely sit still. Thus, they have no problem burning calories. In elementary school, however, children sit for five or six hours a day. Unfortunately, this requires fewer calories. Recess and physical education used to be a time to burn calories, but many schools have cut back physical education or even cut out recess. As a result, some children begin gaining excess weight at age seven or eight.

Some children turn to food to create a sense of security, warmth, or happiness. Life situations that may trigger overeating are: moving to a new town, having a working mother, divorced parents, or sickness in the family. Other children turn to food out of boredom. Many children are left at home after school with no one to encourage physical activity. For many children this may lead to long hours of television watching and snacking. As a teacher, helping an overweight child develop a positive self-image and encouraging exercise may be the most positive measures you can take.

*What is obesity and what is its prevalence among school-age children?*

Obesity is defined as excess body fat. An individual is considered obese when he or she is more than 20% above his/her expected body weight. It is estimated that 10-25% of grade school children are obese.

The level of concern about childhood obesity has heightened as a result of data indicating obesity in children is on the rise. Reasons for this have been attributed to the greater prevalence of calorie-dense snack foods as well as a more sedentary lifestyle. Instead of exercising or playing sports, many grade-school children average 24 hours a week in front of the television. Too often they eat high-calorie snacks while watching TV. Children who consume as little as 50 to 100 more calories a day than they need are likely to gain weight if there isn't a commitment to increase activity. Over the period of one year, this could be a gain of five to ten extra pounds. If this continues over time, obesity will most likely be the outcome.

Evidence supporting a trend toward a greater prevalence of obesity gives us reason for concern. Since children's habits are beginning to form for the future, the prevention of obesity is of greatest concern. Lack of exercise, poor eating habits, and inappropriate food choices are much easier to change at this age than later in life.

*What are the effects of being an obese child?*

The longer the child is obese, the more likely the child will remain obese later in life. Since the risks of the obese child becoming an obese adult increase with the degree and duration of obesity, the more quickly the problem is addressed, the better the chance of preventing a long-term problem. Obese adolescents who remain obese through adulthood run a greater risk of developing some chronic disorders, such as high blood pressure, heart disease, diabetes, respiratory disease, and orthopedic problems.

The way overweight children see themselves and the way they are treated by classmates can either make or break a lifetime weight problem. All children, no matter what their weight, should be encouraged to feel good about themselves and their capabilities. Children and adults should not be judged based on body size.

*How to encourage weight loss?*

The approach to weight loss in children is not the same as adults. Dieting is not the answer for children. Their energy and nutrient needs are high because they are growing. Rather than working on decreasing energy input, more emphasis should be placed on the other end of the scale -- energy output, or exercise. The goal is to decrease body fat without reducing muscle tissue.

The promotion of regular activity, not just team sports, should be emphasized. Suggest activities such as walking or bicycling that students can engage in alone. The overweight child may feel more comfortable with this type of physical activity and be able to do it for a lifetime. Regular activity not only burns calories, but it may also improve a child's self-confidence. The more enjoyable the exercise, the more likely the child will keep to the exercise over a long term.

*Is dieting a concern among school-age children?*

Yes, dieting is definitely a major concern among school-age children. In our society, a majority of children and adults feel pressured to control their weight. Girls, especially, need to be taught that fat gain is a normal part of maturation. Girls need encouragement to allow themselves to grow up. And growing up requires some fat accumulation. Concern about weight can lead to use of appetite inhibitors, low-calorie diets, and self-imposed dieting, including skipping meals and excessive exercise. Such practices are detrimental to children's health and could lead to serious eating disorders. A child that goes hungry may become preoccupied with food. Whenever food is available, the child may overeat out of fear of going hungry again. Inadequate calorie intake during childhood can also interfere with normal growth and even delay puberty. Therefore, dieting should be discouraged.

Behavior modification, nutrition education, and exercise can be the keys to helping overweight children. Programs for children should teach long-term behaviors to control weight gain rather than attempts to lose weight quickly. Overweight children may need only to hold weight constant while they grow in height. The focus should be on regulating food intake.

*What can teachers do?*

Teachers can be a positive influence on children in many ways. A teacher can and should promote both group and individual exercise. Feeling fit can help children feel better about themselves. Exercising large muscles can reduce the amount of excess body fat and increase lean muscle mass. Challenging students to engage in a contest in which they keep track of the exercise they prefer, such as walking, running, or bicycling, may be a simple solution to helping the overweight child.

Promoting nutrition education in the classroom can help in weight management. Children need to associate food as a necessity for healthy growth. Children need to learn how to make informed food choices. Understanding energy balance, or calories in and calories out, can help them see the importance of eating food, and can also help them understand what can happen if excess calories are eaten and not used in energy expenditure.

A teacher can also help children to like themselves for who they are, and to be accepting of each other. Teaching children that "everybody's different" and that everyone has feelings, can help children get past discrimination, and reinforce a sense of worth in individual differences. All children need love and support regardless of size and shape. A teacher can help a child achieve a sense of accomplishment and status regardless of fatness or thinness.

Last, but not least, setting a good example is another way to teach children the importance of good nutrition and regular exercise. A teacher can be an excellent role model.

# Activity 14-1. Good Moves

## DIRECTIONS TO THE TEACHER

**Objective** (Cognitive Domain: Knowledge Level)

Students will select activities he or she participates in by completing a physical movements chart.

**Materials**

Student Activity Sheet (1)
Pencil

**Prerequisite Skills**

Reading/writing not required
Recall

**Procedure**

1. Introduce the idea of record keeping and choose to record either in the morning or afternoon -- same time each day for one week. When working with younger children you may need to work daily on recording.

2. Review record keeping as an honest account of what has been done. Present familiar examples of record keeping such as lunch count, attendance, grade records, and so on.

3. Distribute the activity sheet and explain the directions.

4. Follow up with a Friday discussion of the importance of activity (e.g., exercise strengthens muscles and the heart, exercise helps build physical skills, team sports offer a time to be with friends and work together ).

**Supplementary Activities**

1. May is National Physical Fitness and Sports Month as well as American Bike Month. Although American Bike Month focuses on bicycle safety, you can discuss the health benefits of bicycling.

2. National Youth Fitness Week is the last week in April. To receive a free instructional packet that includes a teacher's guide, poster and reproducible activities, send your name and address to National Youth Fitness, Athletic X-Press, PO Box 307, Coventry, CT 06238.

3. Show "Fit to Be," available through Modern Talking Picture Service, 3520 Progress Dr., Suite C, Cornwells Heights, PA 19020. (1989) This is a fifteen minute video in which an apple comes to life and gives health and fitness advice to a ten-year-old boy who has poor eating and exercise habits.

Name _____ Date _____

# Activity 14-1. Good Moves

**Directions:** Draw a picture of yourself in the first box. Place a check (✓) in the right boxes to show what you did this week.

|  | Ride Bike | Walk | Team Games | Play in the Park |
|---|---|---|---|---|
| Monday |  |  |  |  |
| Tuesday |  |  |  |  |
| Wednesday |  |  |  |  |
| Thursday |  |  |  |  |
| Friday |  |  |  |  |

Moving your body helps use the energy you get from food.

1) Which activity above do you like best? _____

2) What activity do you spend the most time doing? _____

© 1991 by The Center for Applied Research in Education

# Activity 14-2. Using Energy

## DIRECTIONS TO THE TEACHER

### Objective (Cognitive Domain: Application Level)

Students will show which of two activities uses more energy by coloring the appropriate choice.

### Materials

Student Activity Sheets (2)
Crayons

### Prerequisite Skills

Reading not required

### Procedure

1. Introduce energy expenditure. Energy needed for body functions comes from food. The body uses energy even while at rest. It takes energy for our heart to beat and for blood to circulate. These are things we do without thinking (involuntary), but when the body is moving actively, it requires more energy to move muscles. How much energy an activity uses depends on how intense the exercise is and how long the exercise is performed.

2. Ask the students to sit at their desks, but find a quiet way to use more energy while sitting. Students may write, raise arms, wave hands, rotate neck, or flex feet. Ask the students to stand up. Ask them to find a quiet way to expend more energy while staying in one place. Students may touch toes, march, hop on one leg, and so on.

3. Discuss the concept that the more the body moves, the more energy is used.

4. Distribute the student activity sheets and explain the directions.

5. Follow up with the concept that food gives us energy. If we don't use the energy we take in, the energy is stored in our bodies as fat. Fat either accumulates, or gets used when we are active and use our muscles.

### Supplementary Activities

1. Play "Simon says" only use the words "Simon says use more energy" or "Simon says use less energy." Let the students decide what "more" and "less" activities are.

2. Using the two student activity sheets, ask your students how long they engage in any of these activities. For example, we sleep for eight to ten hours, watch TV two or more hours, play ball one hour, play piano a half hour, read a half hour, and so on. Discuss the concept that the longer they move muscles, the more energy they use.

Name _____ Date _____

## Activity 14-2. Using Energy

**Directions:** Circle the activity that uses more energy.

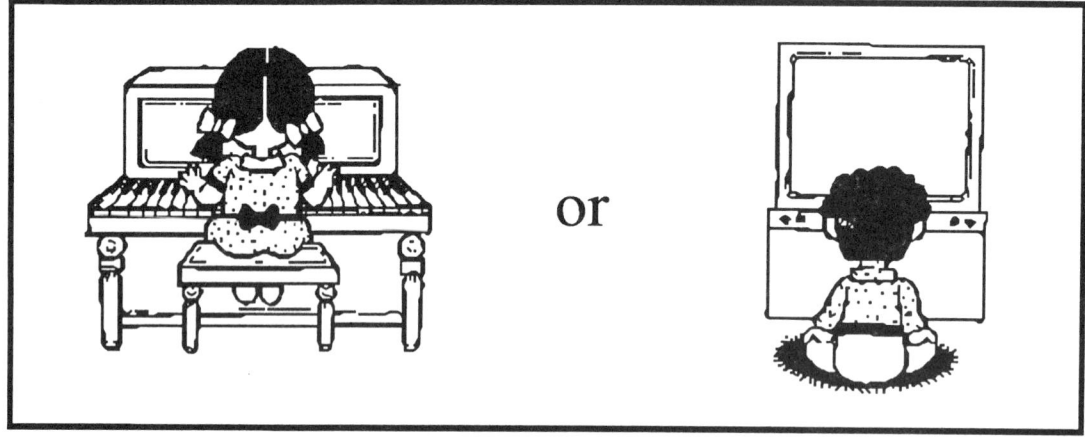

Movement uses energy. Energy comes from food.

© 1991 by The Center for Applied Research in Education

Name _____ Date _____

# Activity 14-2. Using Energy, *page 2*

or

or

or

Movement uses energy. Energy comes from food.

# Activity 14-3. Exercise Message

## DIRECTIONS TO THE TEACHER

**Objective** (Cognitive Domain: Application Level)

Students will discover how exercise makes a body fit by decoding phrases.

**Materials**

Student Activity Sheet (1)
Pencil

**Prerequisite Skills**

Symbol/letter representations

**Procedure**

1. Distribute the activity sheet and explain the directions.

2. Have students generate a list of possible benefits of exercise. Have students guess which ones will appear on the sheet. Then solve to find out.

3. Follow up with a discussion on the benefits of exercise. Some benefits to include are:

    •improves circulation
    •strengthens the heart
    •improves lung capacity
    •reduces body fat
    •increases lean muscle
    •helps strengthen bones
    •improves mental capacity
    •increases feeling of fun

**Supplementary Activities**

1. Invite a representative from your local chapter of the American Heart Association to come to your classroom to discuss the relationship between fitness and heart disease.

2. Ask your physical education teacher to visit the classroom and explain cardiovascular fitness and the importance of regular aerobic exercise.

3. Obtain a copy of the video "The President's Council on Physical Fitness and Sports: On Your Mark," 1989, from Daniel J. Edelman, Inc., 1420 K. Street NW, 10th Floor, Washington, DC 20005, 1/2 inch VHS videocassette, 14 minutes. Write to publisher for price. This video will be a fun, motivational supplement to encourage physical fitness for third grade students.

Name _____ Date _____

## Activity 14-3. Exercise Message

| T | F | D | O | A | Y | M | E | N | G |
|---|---|---|---|---|---|---|---|---|---|

| U | L | K | S | I | C | R | H | V |
|---|---|---|---|---|---|---|---|---|

### Exercise keeps my body fit.

**Directions:** Decode the phrases below to find out how.

1. Makes my ___ ___ ___ ___ ___ ___ ___ strong!

2. Makes my ___ ___ ___ ___ ___ healthy!

3. Gives me ___ ___ ___ ___ ___ ___!

# Lesson 15. *Eating Lowfat Foods*

## Things to Know About Fat and Cholesterol

*Key Points:*

- We need fat in our diet.

- A high intake of total dietary fat is associated with an increased risk for obesity, heart disease, and some types of cancer.

- Choosing a diet low in fat can reduce our risk for certain diseases.

- The benefits and safety of lower fat diets for children are currently being debated.

- Whole milk is a major source of fat and saturated fat in children's diets.

- Children under two years of age should <u>not</u> have fat restricted in their diets.

*What's the difference between fat and cholesterol?*

Fat and cholesterol are similar substances, but they are not the same. Here are some of the ways in which they are different:

| | |
|---|---|
| Fat is a nutrient. We must have it in our diet. | Cholesterol is not a nutrient. We don't need it in the diet because we produce it in our bodies. |
| Fat provides energy or calories to the body. | Cholesterol does not provide energy/calories to the body. The only nutrients that provide energy are fat, protein, and carbohydrates. |
| Fat is found in foods from plants and animals. | Cholesterol is only found in foods from animals. For example, there is no cholesterol in potato chips, because they are made from potato and vegetable oil. These are both plant items. |

*What are the different kinds of fat?*

All fats were not created equal. Fats contain varying amounts of saturated fat, polyunsaturated fat, and monounsaturated fat. Foods that are high in saturated fat, like butter, tend to come from animal sources. Saturated fats tend to be solid at room temperature. Foods that are high in polyunsaturated fat, like vegetable oil, tend to come from plant sources. Polyunsaturated fats tend to be liquid at room temperature. Monounsaturated fats come from both plant and animal sources and are semi-solid at room temperature. All three kinds of fat contain nine Calories per gram.

*What are the different kinds of cholesterol?*

We get cholesterol from foods as well as make it in our bodies. Dietary cholesterol (the cholesterol in your food) contributes to raising the blood cholesterol in your body, but it is only one influencing factor. For example, a person could have a high blood cholesterol level even with a low dietary cholesterol intake because his/her body makes so much cholesterol.

Cholesterol does not mix with water. Since the blood is mostly water there must be a carrier to transport cholesterol and fat. These are lipoproteins. There are two kinds of lipoproteins that are used to evaluate one's risk for heart disease. They are Low Density Lipoprotein (LDL) and High Density Lipoprotein (HDL). They are made by our bodies. They are not found in foods.

A high level of LDL cholesterol in the blood tends to clog the arteries and leads to heart disease. Most people who have a high blood cholesterol level have a high LDL cholesterol level, too. A high level of HDL cholesterol is desirable, however, because it has a protective effect against heart disease.

*What is the connection between fat, cholesterol, and health?*

Most Americans consume too much fat and cholesterol. Too much fat, of any type, increases your risk for heart disease, obesity, some types of cancer, and possibly gall bladder disease. Too much saturated fat is a concern because it leads to elevated LDL cholesterol and thus promotes the development of heart disease. Too much dietary cholesterol may also lead to an elevated LDL cholesterol level, but the effect is not as great as that of saturated fat.

On the other hand, restricting fat and cholesterol during childhood may prevent proper growth. Although cholesterol is made in the body and is not a dietary essential, some fat is essential.

*How do arteries become clogged?*

Over a long period of time, a high blood cholesterol level can lead to clogged arteries. First, the artery must become injured. Small deposits of cholesterol and other substances collect at the injured site, the inside wall of the artery, and gradually grow larger. By the time an individual reaches middle age, these deposits (which are called "plaques") may become large enough to restrict the flow of blood. When blood flow to the heart is restricted, a heart attack occurs. When blood flow to the brain is restricted, a stroke occurs.

*What can be done during childhood to prevent heart disease?*

Heart disease begins in childhood and manifests later in life. The time to address fat is not after a heart attack but before. It makes sense to promote a heart-healthy (lowfat, low cholesterol) diet for children since it may help them prevent heart disease later in life. Also, it may help them to establish healthy eating practices while they are at an impressionable age. Nevertheless, it is critical that childrens' diets not be too restrictive in fat and cholesterol. Children need an adequate intake of fat and cholesterol for normal growth and development. There have been cases in which parents have gone overboard and have caused growth retardation in their children. Moderation is the key.

*What about the fat in milk?*

Milk is a major source of fat and saturated fat in children's diets. Most children over the age of two years would benefit from drinking lowfat milk (1% or 2%) instead of whole milk. The exceptions are children who are underweight and children who have been advised by their pediatrician to drink whole milk.

| Type of milk | Fat grams in 1 cup of milk | % of calories from fat |
| --- | --- | --- |
| Whole (3-4%) | 8 | 50 |
| 2% | 5 | 38 |
| 1% | 3 | 27 |
| Skim and Non-fat, dry | trace | less than 1 |

# Activity 15-1. Milk Carton Cutouts

## DIRECTIONS TO THE TEACHER

**Objectives**  (Cognitive Domain: Knowledge Level)

Students will recognize that different types of milk have different amounts of fat.

**Materials**

Student Activity Sheets (2)
Scissors
Paste

**Prerequisite Skills**

Cutting and pasting
Number order

**Procedure**

1. Discuss milk with students. Have students list different kinds of milk. Do students know differences between the types of milk? Some sample questions are:
    - Do you drink milk?
    - What kind of milk do you drink?
    - What kinds of milk are offered in the school cafeteria?
    - Have you ever tried a lowfat milk (2%, 1%, or skim)?
    - Do you like lowfat milk?

2. Explain to students how different kinds of milk vary in fat content. *(Refer to background information.)*

3. Distribute the activity sheets and explain the directions.

**Supplementary Activities**

1. Conduct a blind taste test of different kinds of milk. Ask students to rank their preferences. Discuss how fat influences the taste of milk.

2. Ask each child to record the amount of milk consumed in one day. Have students experiment with measuring cups, drinking glasses, and water to visualize the difference between four and eight ounce portions.

3. Obtain some nonhomogenized milk from a local farmer. Place milk in a glass container and demonstrate to students how cream (containing fat) rises to the top. Explain that lowfat and skim milk are made by "skimming" off the cream portion.

4. Collect milk carton samples from the school cafeteria. Read the labels to determine the fat content. Remember to check chocolate or other flavored milk cartons, if available.

Name _____ Date _____

## Activity 15-1. Milk Carton Cutouts

**Directions:** 1) Cut out the four milk cartons. 2) Place them in order from least fat to most fat. 3) Glue the milk cartons into the appropriate boxes on page 2.

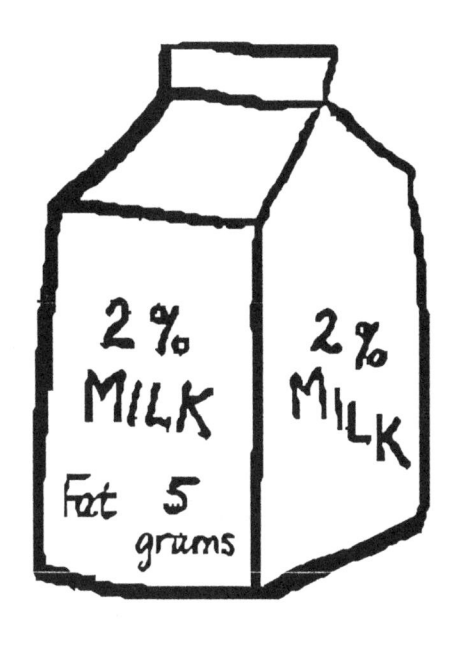

2% MILK — Fat 5 grams

SKIM MILK — Fat 0 grams

WHOLE MILK — Fat 8 grams

1% MILK — Fat 3 grams

Name _____ Date _____

## Activity 15-1. Milk Carton Cutouts, *page 2*

| | |
|---|---|
| **1**       *Least fat* | **2** |
| **3** | **4**       *Most fat* |

# Activity 15-2. Clogged Pipes

## DIRECTIONS TO THE TEACHER

**Objective** (Cognitive Domain: Comprehension Level)

Students will understand how too much fat in the diet can affect blood circulation.

## Materials

Student Activity Sheets (2)
Plastic straws (one per student)
Modeling clay
Eyedroppers (one per student)
Cups of water (one per student)
Red crayons (one per student)
Red food coloring (optional)

## Prerequisite Skills

Understanding of same / different

## Procedure

1. Catch your students' attention by introducing how blood travels around the body. Blood can make a round trip in less than a minute. It does this thousands of times a day.

2. Explain circulation to students.

   All parts of the body need nutrients and oxygen, which are carried in the blood.
   Blood travels to all parts of the body in the blood vessels.
   The heart pumps blood through the blood vessels.
   Sometimes the blood vessels become clogged with fat and fat-like substances.
   Eating too much fat, saturated fat, and cholesterol can cause clogs in the blood vessels.
   When blood vessels are clogged, the body doesn't get the nutrients and oxygen it needs.

3. Distribute straws, clay, eyedroppers and cups of water with red food coloring.
   Explain these analogies:

   - Straws are like blood vessels.
   - Clay is like fat.
   - Water is like blood (you may want to illustrate the water as red by adding food coloring).

4. Distribute the activity sheets and explain the directions.

## Supplementary Activities

1. Have students feel their hearts beating in their chests. They can feel blood flowing through their blood vessels by taking their pulse at their wrist or on the side of their neck. Have students take their pulse at rest and after twenty jumping jacks. Talk about why exercise causes an increase in the pulse rate. Discuss what is happening to their bodies. Are their hearts beating faster? Are they breathing faster? Do they feel warmer? Explain that their bodies use more energy when they exercise.

2. Obtain a copy of "The Heart Treasure Chest" from your local chapter of the American Heart Association. This kit includes numerous heart healthy activity ideas for young children.

3. Demonstrate the basic principle that oil does not dissolve in water. Most liquids will dissolve in water. The liquids that won't dissolve in water have something in common. What is it? To find out what that something is, perform an experiment using "test liquids" listed below.

   vinegar          baby oil
   grape juice      vegetable oil

   Conclude with the thought that the body is made of water. Blood is mostly water. Since fat won't dissolve in blood, it needs carriers to move fat through the blood. Protein helps carry fat.

4. February is American Heart Month. The American Heart Association makes a variety of educational programs available to teachers; contact your local chapter of the American Heart Association.

5. Share these fun facts with your students. Ask them to think of creative ways to illustrate the following:

   - The average child's heart beats about 90 times a minute or about 130,000 times a day. (Students can take their pulse rates to calculate how many times their own hearts beat per minute.)
   - A child's heart is the size of an orange.
   - An adult's heart is the size of a grapefruit.
   - The heart pumps nearly five quarts of blood every 60 seconds, or about 75 gallons per hour.
   - The heart pumps blood through more than 100,000 miles or veins and arteries to all parts of the body. Have students compare that figure to the distance they would travel if they crossed the United States 40 times or circled the earth 4 times.

Name _____ Date _____

## Activity 15-2. Clogged Pipes

**Directions:**

1) Hold a straw in one hand and place your other hand under the bottom of the straw. Gently blow through the straw. Can you feel the air moving easily through the straw?  Yes _____   No _____

2) Fill an eyedropper or baster with a small amount of water. Hold the straw and gently squeeze water into the top of the straw. Can you see the water flowing easily through the straw?  Yes _____   No _____

3) Push some modeling clay into the straw. Repeat steps 1 and 2. Can you feel the air moving through the straw?  Yes _____   No _____

   Can you see the water flowing through the straw?

   Yes _____   No _____

4) What happened when the straw became clogged?

   _____

5) What happens when your blood vessels become clogged? _____

6) How do you keep your blood vessels from becoming clogged? _____

© 1991 by The Center for Applied Research in Education

Name _____  Date _____

## Activity 15-2. Clogged Pipes, *page 2*

**Directions:** Find the body with the clogged blood vessel. Draw a circle around the clog.

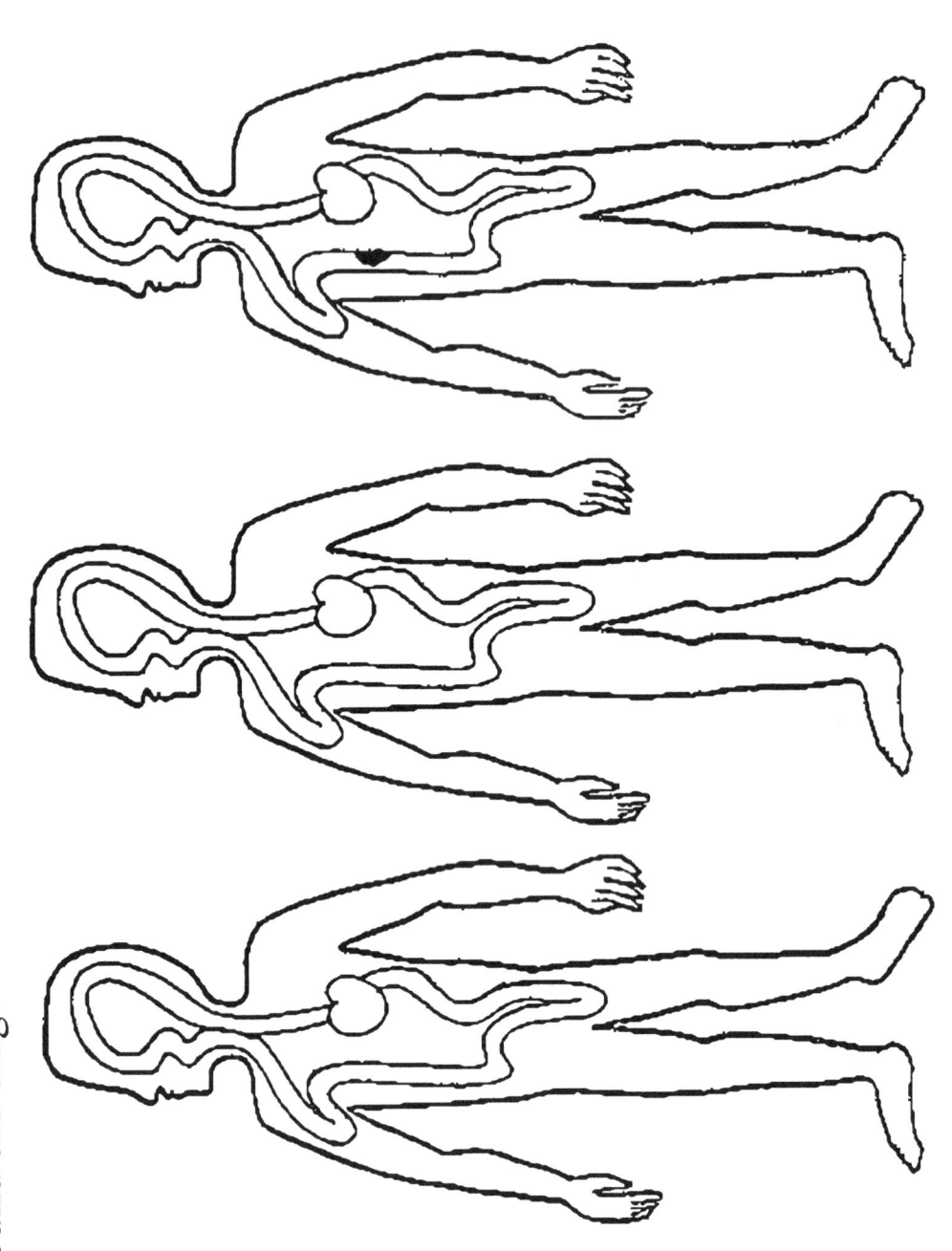

© 1991 by The Center for Applied Research in Education

# Activity 15-3. Fat Finder

## DIRECTIONS TO THE TEACHER

**Objective** (Cognitive Domain: Comprehension Level)

Students will distinguish between foods that have fat and foods that do not have fat.

## Materials

Student Activity Sheets (2)
Food samples (assortment of the following):

| peanuts | oil | apple |
| green pepper | potato chip | cheese (at room temperature) |
| raw potato | cracker | butter |
| bacon | mayonnaise | macaroni |

Brown paper towels or brown paper grocery bags

## Preparation

Place a small amount of each food to be used in a separate plastic bag or small jar.

## Prerequisite Skills

Experimental observation

## Procedure

1. Discuss sensory qualities of fat with students. Some sample questions are:
   How do you know if a food has fat? What does fat look like? What does fat feel like? What does fat taste like? What does fat smell like?

2. Explain how fat can be detected in foods: When you rub a food onto brown paper, fat will leave a wet spot on the paper. Water will also leave a wet spot, but a water spot will dry after a few minutes and will disappear. A fat spot doesn't dry. If you rub a food onto brown paper and it leaves a spot that doesn't dry, the food has some fat.

3. Distribute food samples, activity sheets, and explain the directions.

## Supplementary Activities

1. Another way to find the fat in foods is to read food labels. Ask students to go through their cabinets at home and to prepare a list of foods and their fat content.

2. Write a public service announcement that could be shared with other students in your school. Encourage students to increase their consumption of lowfat foods such as fruits, vegetables, and grains.

Name _____ Date _____

## Activity 15-3. Fat Finder

**Directions:** 1) Get a brown paper towel and a small sample of food. 2) Rub the food onto the paper towel. 3) Wait a few minutes. Does the food leave a spot that looks wet? If yes, place a check in the "Has fat" column. If no, place a check in the "Does not have fat" column. 4) Do the same thing for some other foods. 5) Answer the questions on page 2.

| Name of food | Has fat | Does not have fat |
|---|---|---|
|  |  |  |
|  |  |  |
|  |  |  |
|  |  |  |
|  |  |  |
|  |  |  |
|  |  |  |
|  |  |  |
|  |  |  |

© 1991 by The Center for Applied Research in Education

Name _____ Date _____

## Activity 15-3. Fat Finder, *page 2*

**Directions:** Answer the following questions based on what you observed.

1) Did the raw potato and potato chip give the same results? _____ If no, why were they different? _____

2) Do you think a French fry would test like a potato chip or the raw potato? _____

3) Did the macaroni have fat? _____

4) Since macaroni is made from grains, would you say that grains have fat? _____

5) How do you think a slice of plain bread would test? _____

6) Did the apple and green pepper give the same results? _____

7) Since apples are fruit and green peppers are vegetables, what can you say about the fat content of fruits and vegetables?

   _____

# Lesson 16. *Eating Plenty of Vegetables, Fruits, and Grains*

## Things to Know About Vegetables, Fruits, and Grain Products

*Key Points:*

- Foods high in starch and fiber are naturally low in fat and sodium, and high in vitamins and minerals.

*Why is there so much emphasis on vegetables, fruits and grain products?*

These foods are emphasized because of their carbohydrate content. By eating these foods you increase fiber and starch and decrease the fat in your diet. Foods from animals, such as meat, eggs, milk, and cheese, do not contain starch and fiber.

*What are carbohydrates in vegetables, fruits, and grain products?*

There are three types of carbohydrates -- sugar, starch, and fiber. Glucose is the predominant simple sugar. It is found with other simple sugars in fruit. Starch and fiber are types of complex carbohydrates found only in plants. They are called "complex" because chemically they are composed of chains of many glucose molecules. During digestion, starch is broken down into single sugar molecules to be used for energy. Fiber, however, cannot be digested by humans. Fiber passes down the intestinal tract undigested and forms bulk for the stool.

*What are the benefits of eating starchy foods?*

Starchy foods are plant foods. Most plant foods are naturally low in fat and sodium. They are high in fiber, vitamins, and minerals.

Starch provides energy. One to four hours after a meal, starch is digested, absorbed and is circulating to the cells for energy. When adequate complex carbohydrates are supplied to the body, proteins can be spared for use to promote growth and maintenance.

Complex carbohydrates take longer to digest than simple sugars. Therefore, they fill up children's stomachs for a longer period of time than simple carbohydrates. Thus, children do not get hungry as quickly.

*What are the benefits of fiber?*

Fiber helps remove waste from the body. Fiber acts like a sponge to hold water and thus increases the amount of water in the feces, making stools larger. Fiber helps prevent constipation and intestinal disorders.

High-fiber foods can help in weight control. A diet that is high in fiber is usually lower in fat and sugar. This can promote weight loss simply by decreasing calories, but fiber also has other advantages. High-fiber foods require more time to chew. It takes longer to eat a raw apple than to eat applesauce. If one takes longer to eat, one may be less likely to overeat. High-fiber foods also provide a feeling of fullness by adding bulk and filling up space in the stomach, thereby delaying hunger.

*Is all fiber the same?*

Not really. There are two types of dietary fiber: insoluble fiber found in wheat bran, vegetables and whole grain cereals; and soluble fiber, found in oat bran, barley, dried beans, fruit, and vegetables. Each plays an important but slightly different role in your body.

> Insoluble fiber: adds bulk to the diet, moving waste out of the body. It may also dilute some cancer-causing agents and decrease their period of contact with the intestinal wall. Thus a high-fiber diet many help reduce the risk of some types of colon cancer.

> Soluble fiber: may aid in the treatment of diabetes and high blood cholesterol. Soluble fiber may help diabetes by slowing absorption of sugar after a meal as well as by lowering fat levels in the blood. Soluble fiber helps people with high blood cholesterol by trapping bile salts, which contain cholesterol, and carrying them out of the body.

*Should children eat more fiber?*

Yes. Foods with fiber should be gradually added to a child's diet. However, too much fiber in a child's diet may fill the stomach and limit the total amount of food consumed. Children, as well as adults, should be encouraged to drink plenty of fluids when eating foods high in fiber. For example, children often snack on dry cereal without an adequate fluid intake. Since fiber absorbs water, constipation and hard, dry stools can result if adequate fluids are not provided.

*How can teachers encourage the consumption of vegetables, fruits, and grains?*

Teachers can arrange to have these foods as part of "classroom party treats." Use descriptors such as tasty, crunchy, refreshing, and delicious when mentioning these foods. Be sure to pack them in your lunch. Let your students know fruits, vegetables, and grains are important in your diet.

*How much starch and dietary fiber should children consume?*

This answer is controversial for adults and even more so for children. Most adults consume about 10 to 20 grams of dietary fiber per day. The recommendation for adults is to consume between 30 and 35 grams per day. However, it is unadvisable to add too much fiber too quickly. This can cause intestinal discomfort, such as bloating, diarrhea, and gas. Also, too much fiber can interfere with the absorption of other nutrients, such as iron, calcium, and magnesium.

Since recommendations are directed toward adults, the best advice for children may be to try for an average of about half whole grain and half enriched breads and cereals. This will provide the advantages without the shortcomings. Enriched products have iron, thiamin, riboflavin, and niacin. Whole grains have the benefit of vitamin E, trace minerals, and fiber.

# Activity 16-1. Starch and Fiber Chains

## DIRECTIONS TO THE TEACHER

**Objective** (Cognitive Domain: Comprehension Level)

Students will explain how starch and fiber differ by manipulating paper models.

## Materials

Student Activity Sheets (2)
Scissors
Stapler
Staple remover
Paste
Colored paper or paper to be recycled

## Prerequisite Skills

Reading skills
Cutting
Pasting

## Procedure

1. Discuss carbohydrates as the main source of energy for the body.

2. Introduce the term *complex carbohydrates*. Starch and fiber are called complex because they are made of many repeating units of sugar (the most basic carbohydrate). *(Refer to background information.)* For this activity starch and fiber will be thought of as chains with links that can either be broken or not broken.

3. Explain how long chains of starch and fiber are different because of the way the body can or cannot break the links of the chains. If the link can be broken then the carbohydrate can be used for energy.

4. Distribute the activity sheets. Read page 1 with the students, making sure they understand the difference between starch and fiber. Explain the directions. Instruct students to use the pattern to make more starch and fiber links. Be sure students label the cutouts as starch or fiber links. Label the staple remover "enzyme."

5. Hang the starch and fiber chains around the room.

## Supplementary Activities

1. Have students identify foods rich in starch and fiber on the school lunch menu.

2. Connect this activity with digestion. Starch enzymes are in saliva and the small intestine. From the small intestine the small units move through the blood to body cells. In body cells, the units are used for energy to keep the heart beating, muscles contracting, and for food waiting to be digested. All body activities, those we think about doing and do without thinking, require energy. Starch is an excellent source of energy.

Name _____ Date _____

# Activity 16-1. Starch and Fiber Chains

Starch and fiber are two kinds of carbohydrates. Starch links can be broken apart and used for energy. Fiber links cannot be broken apart. Fiber helps push waste out of the body.

**Directions:** 1) Cut out the link patterns on page 2. 2) Using the patterns, make and label ten fiber links. Paste one link together end to end. Loop the next link through the pasted one and repeat the pasting to form a fiber chain. 3) Make and label ten starch links. Staple the links to form a starch chain. 4) Use a staple remover (enzyme) to break the chain links. 5) Answer the following questions:

Which chain links could be broken apart with a staple remover (enzyme)?
       a. starch       b. fiber

Which could not be broken apart with a staple remover?
       a. starch       b. fiber

What "tool" in your digestive system works like a staple remover to break apart carbohydrate chains?
       a. enzymes       b. intestine

| Starch Foods | Fiber Foods |
|---|---|
| breads | whole grain bread |
| cereals | whole grain cereal |
| pasta (spaghetti, noodles) | vegetables |
| rice | fruits |
| beans and peas | nuts |
| potatoes | seeds |
| corn | beans |
| lima beans | peas |

What food groups have starch and fiber?

_____, _____, and _____.

# Activity 16-1. Starch and Fiber Chains, *page 2*

| Staple | Paste |
|---|---|
| Starch link | Fiber link |
| Staple | Paste |

cut along dotted lines

© 1991 by The Center for Applied Research in Education

# Activity 16-2. Fiber Foods

## DIRECTIONS TO THE TEACHER

**Objective** (Cognitive Domain: Application Level)

Given pictures of foods which contain fiber and those which do not, students will show which foods contain fiber by coloring appropriate choices.

## Materials

Student Activity Sheet (1)
Crayons

## Prerequisite Skills

Recognition of foods

## Procedure

1. Introduce the word "fiber." Fiber is the part of the plant that gives it structure. Only plant foods have fiber. Have students generate definitions of fiber, then look the word up in the dictionary. How close are the definitions?

2. Ask the students to name some plant foods. Ask them to identify to which food group each plant food belongs.

3. Distribute the activity sheet and explain the directions.

## Supplementary Activities

1. Children can see fiber in food. One way to make a lasting impression would be by drying celery. Place a piece of celery in a clear plastic bag. Leave it unsealed for a few months. The water will eventually evaporate and all that is left is the fiber. Let your students examine the remaining fiber.

2. Ask children to listen for the word <u>fiber</u> or look for it in advertising. What foods are usually advertised as high-fiber foods? Explain that cereals and breads are often associated with fiber because they are advertised most. But fruits, vegetables, nuts, and seeds are also excellent sources of fiber.

3. Invite a representative from your local Cancer Society to come to class and discuss the relationship between diet and cancer. The American Cancer Society has colorful posters for the classroom and brochures that can be sent home to parents. Investigate the options available in your area.

Name _____ Date _____

# Activity 16-2. Fiber Foods

Fiber is in <u>the whole grain breads, pasta, cereals, fruits, and vegetables</u> you eat, but fiber is <u>not</u> in meats and milk.

Fiber helps:
move waste out of the body
prevent cancer
prevent heart attacks

**Directions:** Put a circle around the foods that have fiber.

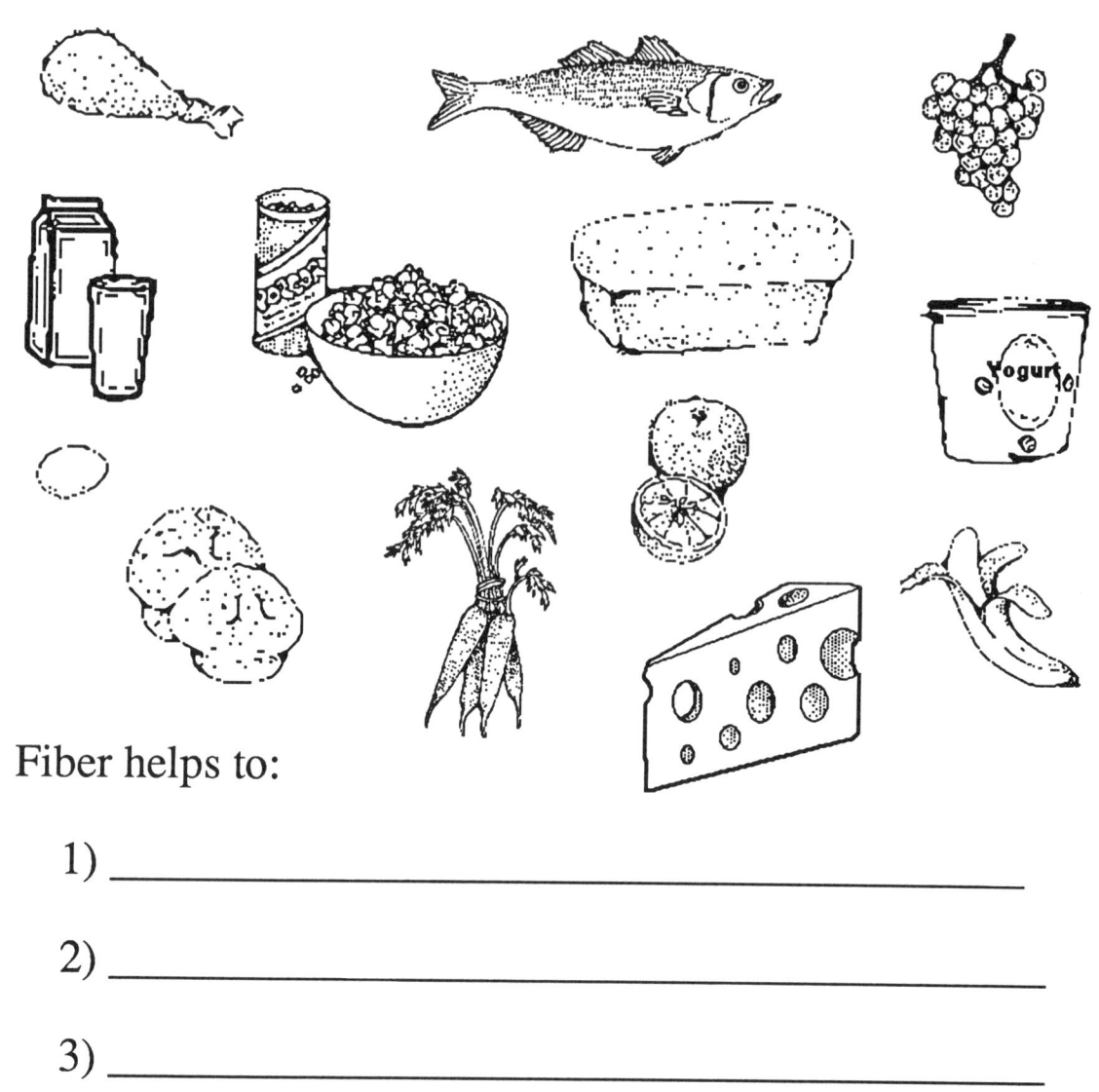

Fiber helps to:

1) _____

2) _____

3) _____

# Activity 16-3. Fiber Count

## DIRECTIONS TO THE TEACHER

**Objective** (Cognitive Domain: Knowledge Level)

Students will identify the fiber present in given foods by counting symbols.

## Materials

Student Activity Sheet (1)
Pencil

## Prerequisite Skills

Counting

## Procedure

1. Explain that fiber is found in fruits, vegetables, grains, nuts, seeds, and beans, but that different foods contain different amounts.

2. Introduce the concept of the symbol. In this activity the wheat symbol represents fiber. Fiber could be symbolized by other foods.

3. Distribute the activity sheet and explain the directions.

## Supplementary Activities

1. Have a "fiber" snack party. Provide raw vegetables, fresh fruits, and whole grain breads or cereals. Serve water or juice. Explain to the students that fiber takes up water and is necessary to move waste out of the body.

2. Demonstrate why you need to drink water when you eat fiber. Using a clear plastic tube about 3" in diameter, try to force a dry sponge through the tube. It won't slide. Now add water. The sponge, like fiber, takes up the water and slides through the tube.

Name _____ Date _____

## Activity 16-3. Fiber Count

**Directions:** Count the grains of wheat 🌾. Find out how much fiber is in each food.

## 1 🌾 = 1 gram fiber

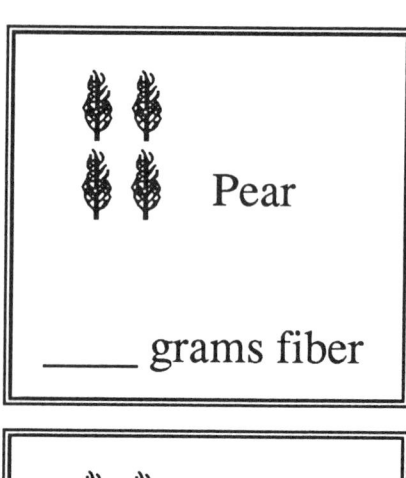

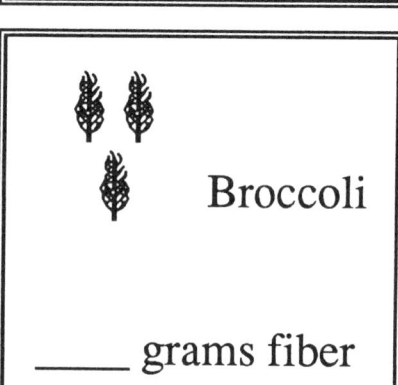

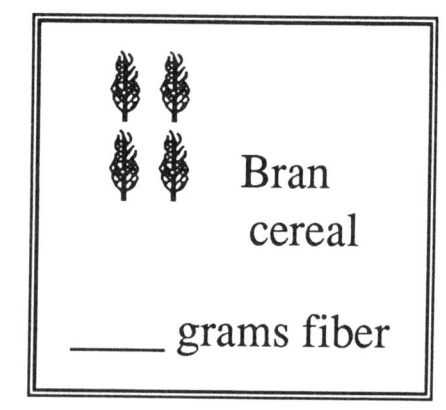

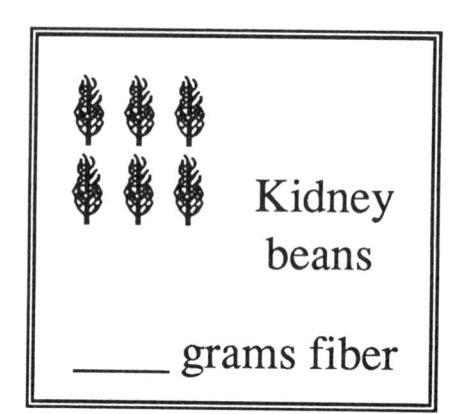

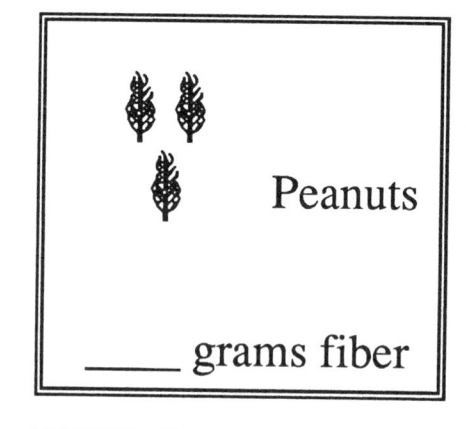

🌾 🌾
🌾 🌾   Pear

____ grams fiber

🌾 🌾 🌾
🌾 🌾 🌾   Kidney beans

____ grams fiber

🌾 🌾
🌾   Broccoli

____ grams fiber

🌾 🌾
🌾   Peanuts

____ grams fiber

🌾 🌾
🌾 🌾   Bran cereal

____ grams fiber

🌾 🌾
🌾   Wheat bread

____ grams fiber

## Try to eat at least 15 grams of fiber a day.

# Lesson 17. *Using Sugars in Moderation*

## Things to Know About Sugars

*Key Points:*

- Sugar and other carbohydrates that break down into sugar can cause tooth decay.

- Foods with sugars can be part of a healthful diet if used in moderation.

- Sugars are a source of energy (calories), but the foods that contain them are generally low in essential nutrients.

- Sugar has not been established as a risk factor for any chronic diseases.

*Is sugar really a health villain?*

The major health concern related to eating too much sugar is tooth decay. Tooth decay is a function of how much, how often, and what form of sugar is eaten. Sticky sweetened or starchy foods that stay on the teeth (like caramel, raisins, and soft bread) cause more decay than other foods. Sugary foods between meals are more likely to cause decay than those eaten with other foods at mealtime. The more frequently sugar is in contact with the tooth, the more likely decay will occur.

Hard candies are sucked on and kept in the mouth for a while, which means the teeth are bathed in sugar. Even bread and crackers can stick between the teeth and cause decay. On the other hand, presweetened juices and colas wash past the teeth, and therefore have limited contact with them. Cavity formation is also affected by how long the food stays in the mouth and whether you brush your teeth or rinse your mouth after eating. Foods such as fresh fruits, vegetables, and cheese help clean teeth and exercise gums. Still, it is wise to encourage students to brush and floss their teeth or rinse their mouths after eating. Children should be encouraged to visit the dentist at least once a year.

*Does sugar have any nutritive value?*

Sugar alone contributes calories but no vitamins or minerals. Sugar is considered a simple carbohydrate. It comes in various foods under many names, such as sucrose, lactose, fructose, and glucose. White and brown sugar, corn syrup, and honey do not contain any nutrients in significant amounts. Molasses, especially blackstrap molasses, does contain some B vitamins (thiamin and riboflavin) and minerals (calcium, iron, potassium), but in such small amounts as to be an insignificant nutrient value.

*Would the ideal diet for children be one void of all sugar?*

Not necessarily, since sugar in moderation is <u>not</u> bad. Over the past few years sugar has been given a bad name. Contrary to popular belief, sugar is not the cause of diabetes, obesity, heart disease, or criminal behavior. Studies in the past have also proven that sugar is not the cause of hyperactivity; however, one recent study has shown that children who were fed a sugar dose equivalent to two frosted cupcakes for breakfast had elevated levels of adrenaline leading to crankiness and anxiety. However, this study has not yet been replicated. No adverse effects were found for adults.

*Does this mean children can eat as much sugar as they want?*

Children should not be given an open invitation to consume unlimited sweetened foods. A major problem with diets high in sugar is that these foods may replace more nutritious ones. On the other hand, sugar can be valuable to some children who need to gain weight because it does provide a delicious, concentrated source of calories. Therefore it can be useful in a weight gain effort. But remember, many foods high in sugar are also high in fat.

The solution for children may not be to say "Don't eat sugar!" but to focus on the positive: "Eat Nutrition-Smart Sweet Foods." These foods taste good and provide many needed nutrients.

*How much sugar do American children eat, and what are the main sources of sugar?*

Americans eat about 125 pounds of sugar and sweeteners per person per year. Sugar is used in preparing foods at home, but more and more of the sugar in our diet comes from processed and convenience foods. Sugar and sweeteners, such as high fructose corn syrup, are added to many of our foods to make the flavor more appealing and to help preserve foods. Because sweeteners are added to so many foods, we may not realize how much we consume in a day.

*What can teachers do to encourage moderate use of foods containing sugar?*

First and foremost, teach children to read labels so they can find the sugar in foods in order to make informed decisions. Words that appear on a label and indicate sugar are:

- glucose (dextrose)
- sucrose (sugar)
- fructose (levulose)
- maltose (malt sugar)
- lactose (milk sugar)
- high fructose corn syrup
- corn syrup
- invert sugar
- molasses
- honey
- turbinado sugar

*How much sugar can children consume?*

There is no recommendation for children. It is recommended that healthy individuals over two years of age should eat only 10% of their daily calorie intake in the form of sugar. In a child's diet the total calorie range could be from 1300-3300 calories a day. This means a child could take in from 130-330 calories from sugar. This would be 33-82 grams of sugar a day. Studies show that children typically take in about 13-14% of their calories from sugar. Adults take in above 11%.

# Activity 17-1. Tooth Smart

### DIRECTIONS TO THE TEACHER

**Objective** (Cognitive Domain: Application Level)

By assembling a puzzle, students will discover which foods may lead to cavities and which foods decrease the risk of cavities.

### Materials

Student Activity Sheets (2)
Scissors
Paste

### Prerequisite Skills

Cutting and pasting
Shape matching (visual perceptual skills)

### Procedure

1. Explain that more people get tooth decay than any other disease.

2. Explain that after eating, tiny bits of food are left between the teeth. If you don't brush your teeth, bacteria can grow and eat away at the hard outside part of the tooth (the enamel). The result is a hole that is called a cavity.

3. Reinforce that some foods are more likely to cause cavities than others. These foods are usually sweet and sticky. However, they can also be bland and stick to the teeth, like bread or crackers.

4. Distribute the activity sheets and explain the directions.

5. Summarize by identifying foods that are wise snack choices for the teeth, such as fruits, vegetables, cheese, nuts, and beverages (especially water).

6. Point out other foods that should be used less frequently to reduce the risk of dental problems. Ask students to name foods that are sweet or that stick to their teeth.

7. Conclude with a reminder to brush and/or floss teeth after meals and snacks. You may want to mention toothpaste with fluoride helps fight tooth decay.

### Supplementary Activities

1. Invite a dentist or dental hygienist to your classroom. The specialist can promote good nutrition by discussing caries prevention and periodontal disease prevention. Ask the guest to demonstrate proper brushing and flossing. Periodontal disease prevention includes calcium/phosphorous balance by increasing lowfat dairy products; providing vitamins C and B which may help maintain periodontal health, and eating firm, fibrous foods which stimulate tissues, bone, and salivary glands.

2. Children's Dental Health Month is February and is sponsored by the American Dental Association. To send for a catalog that features classroom aids, write to the American Dental Association, Order Department, 211 East Chicago Ave., Chicago, IL 60622; (800) 621-8099, ext. 2639. Be sure to contact your local dental association for more information on National Children's Dental Health Month events.

3. For younger children, you want to explain that we have two sets of teeth -- "baby" and permanent -- and that we lose all our baby teeth, one at a time, from about the age of six.

4. Have a tooth counting contest. As a homework assignment, have each child count the exact number of teeth in his or her mouth, then print the tally on a small sheet of paper. The next day, collect the tallies and add them up, keeping the total a secret. Then ask the children to guess the total number of teeth for the entire class. Give a new toothbrush and packet of dental floss to the student who comes closest to guessing the total.

5. Set up a dental health learning center using publications from government and professional organizations. Write to: National Institute of Dental Health, 9000 Rockville Pike, Building 31, Rm. 2C36, Bethesda, MD 20892 for more information. Refer to the address of the American Dental Association in Supplementary Activity #2.

Name _____ Date _____

## Activity 17-1. Tooth Smart

**Directions:** Cut out the shapes below. Find the tooth on page 2. Some shapes fit onto the tooth, some do not. Paste those that fit onto the tooth in the right places. Those that don't fit should be pasted at the bottom.

- water
- peanut butter & jelly
- crackers
- candy
- vegetables
- cheese
- gumdrops
- raisins
- bread & honey

© 1991 by The Center for Applied Research in Education

Name _____ Date _____

## Activity 17-1. Tooth Smart, *page 2*

Foods that stick to teeth may cause cavities.

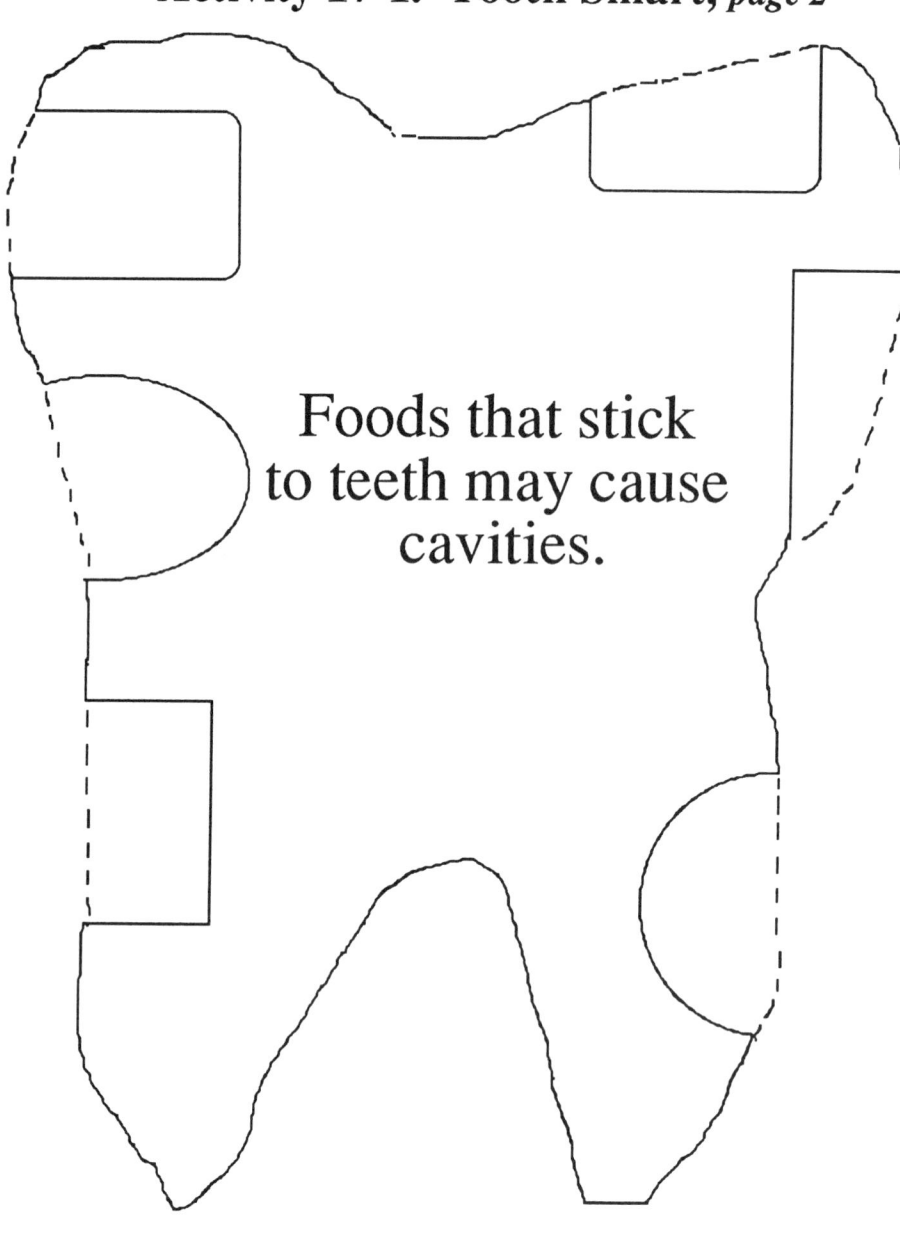

Foods that do not stick to teeth are less likely to cause cavities.

© 1991 by The Center for Applied Research in Education

# Activity 17-2. Ingredient Smart

## DIRECTIONS TO THE TEACHER

### Objective (Cognitive Domain: Application Level)

Students will discover that sugar has many names by locating a pseudonym for sugar on food labels.

### Materials

Student Activity Sheets (2)
Pencil

### Prerequisite Skills

Reading

### Procedure

1. Discuss the meaning of ingredients -- the parts that make up a whole. Many foods are mixtures of ingredients. For example, a peanut butter and jelly sandwich is made of two slices of bread, two tablespoons of peanut butter, and two teaspoons of jelly. Of course, there are also ingredients that make up the bread, such as flour, eggs, salt, and so on.

2. Introduce sugar as a common ingredient added to food. Sugar as a sweetener is added to enhance flavor, but it is also used as a preservative. Nutritionally, sugar provides only calories (energy) to a food.

3. Ingredients on a food label are listed in descending order. The ingredient in the greatest amount is listed first and so on. Many products have sugar listed as the first ingredient.

4. Distribute the activity sheets and explain the directions.

### Supplementary Activities

1. Ask students to bring in food product boxes. Take time in class to read the lists of ingredients, counting the number of sugars in foods. Remind students that sugar is not bad but it offers no nutritional benefit other than calories (energy). Generally speaking, when sugar is added to a food the nutrient density goes down.

2. Have a cookie-tasting party. Ask a parent volunteer to make a batch of cookies. Divide the batch in half. Make half the cookies with the amount of sugar called for in the original recipe and the other half with half the sugar. Don't tell your students which is which and let them taste the two and compare. Which do they like better? If the students like the cookies with less sugar, have them write a letter that can be taken home asking if they can help make cookies with less sugar than the original recipe.

Name _____  Date _____

## Activity 17-2.  Ingredient Smart

**Directions**: A food label lists the ingredients in a food. Use your dictionary to find the meaning of the word <u>ingredient</u>. Write the definition.

_____

_____

Sugar is an ingredient in many foods. Sugar is not bad, but be aware of where it is hidden in foods. There are many ingredient words on food labels that mean sugar. Below is a list of sugar names.

| <u>Sugar Names</u> ||
|---|---|
| brown sugar | malt flavoring |
| corn syrup | malt syrup |
| corn sweetener | maltose |
| dextrose | molasses |
| fructose | raw sugar |
| glucose | sorbitol |
| high fructose corn syrup | sugar |
| honey | turbinado sugar |
| invert sugar | |

© 1991 by The Center for Applied Research in Education

Name _____ Date _____

## Activity 17-2. Ingredient Smart, *page 2*

**Directions:** Look at the list of sugar names on page 1. Circle all the sugar names in each of the food ingredient lists below.

### Cereal

**Ingredients:** rice, sugar, brown sugar, salt, honey, malt syrup

### Cookie

**Ingredients:** bleached flour, sugar, molasses, partially hydrogenated vegetable shortening, brown sugar, cocoa, water, modified food starch, baking soda

### Cake Mix

**Ingredients:** sugar, enriched flour, vegetable oil, cornstarch, cocoa, flavor, salt, dextrose

### Candy

**Ingredients:** peanuts, corn syrup, sugar, milk, butter, salt, flour, egg whites, flavors

### Cake Frosting

**Ingredients:** sugar, margarine, water, corn syrup, cocoa, starch, butter, salt, flavor, dextrose

### Soda

**Ingredients:** Carbonated water, sugar, caramel color, phosphoric acid, flavors, caffeine

**The ingredient listed first is the one in the greatest amount by weight.**

© 1991 by The Center for Applied Research in Education

# Activity 17-3. Sugar Decoder

## DIRECTIONS TO THE TEACHER

**Objective** (Cognitive Domain: Knowledge Level)

Given an assortment of foods, students will identify high-sugar and low-sugar foods.

**Materials**

Student Activity Sheets (2)
Pencil
Visual aid of one teaspoon of sugar in a baby food jar, plastic bag, or a packet of sugar

**Preparation**

Measure and display a teaspoon of sugar
Glass of water

**Prerequisite Skills**

Vowel recognition

**Procedure**

1. Introduce the concept of "hidden sugar." Sugar dissolves in water and cannot be seen in most foods.

2. Dissolve a teaspoon of sugar in a glass of water. Can it be seen? Can it be tasted?

3. Distribute the activity sheets and explain the directions.

4. Conclude that it is okay to eat foods with sugar, but they should be eaten in moderation and only occasionally.

5. Clarify that the number of vowels in a food name does not determine the sugar content. To avoid misconception tell the children that this activity was designed to name foods so the number of vowels would correspond with the number of teaspoons of sugar.

**Supplementary Activities**

1. Set up a learning station or bulletin board with a visual display of sugars in foods. Display either a box or model of the food, or the name of the food with a plastic bag or jar containing the number of teaspoons of sugar present in the food. On the following page is a possible list of foods and their sugar content.

|  | **Food** | **Teaspoons of sugar** |
|---|---|---|
| Desserts | Apple Pie - 1 slice | 4 |
|  | Cheesecake - 1 slice | 6 |
|  | Chocolate Chip Cookies - 2 small | 1 |
|  | Chocolate Pudding Pop - 1 pop | 2 1/2 |
|  | Instant Chocolate Pudding - 1/2 cup | 6 |
|  | Jell-o - 1/2 cup | 4 |
|  | Pecan Pie - 1 slice | 7 |
|  | Snack Cupcake | 3 |
| Candies | Chocolate Bar with Almonds - 1.45 ounce | 5 1/2 |
|  | Chocolate Covered Granola Bar - 1 bar | 5 1/2 |
|  | Jelly Beans - 10 per ounce | 4 |
|  | Peanut Butter Cups - 2 cups | 6 |
| Drinks | Apple Juice - 6 ounces | 5 |
|  | Cola - 12 ounces | 9 1/2 |
|  | Fruit Flavored Drink from powder - 1 cup | 5 1/2 |
|  | Orange Juice from Concentrate - 6 ounces | 5 1/2 |
| Cereal and | Frosted Mini-Wheats - 4 lg. biscuits | 1 1/2 |
| Bakery | Glazed Yeast Doughnut - 1 doughnut | 2 |
| Products | Homemade Bran Muffin - 1 small | 3 |
|  | Honey Smacks - 3/4 cup | 4 |
|  | Maple flavored Oatmeal - 1 packet | 3 |
|  | Raisin Bagel - 1 bagel | 2 |
|  | Toaster Pastry | 4 |
|  | Waffle with 2 Tbsp. syrup | 7 |

2. Determine the number of teaspoons of sugar in a breakfast cereal. The breakfast cereal must provide additional carbohydrate information at the bottom of the panel listing nutrition information. Collect empty cereal boxes. Only use the boxes with "Carbohydrate Information." Lead the students to find the nutrition information panel on the side of the box which contains the words: "Carbohydrate Information." Look below this heading for the line stating: "sucrose (or fructose) and other sugars." Here's an example:

| **CARBOHYDRATE INFORMATION** | (per serving) |
|---|---|
| Starch and related carbohydrates | 12 g (grams) |
| *Sucrose and other sugars* | 12 g |
| Dietary fiber | 3 g |
| Total carbohydrates | 27 g |

One serving of this cereal has 12 grams of sugar. How many <u>teaspoons</u> of sugar does this equal? Four grams of sugar equals one teaspoon. Therefore, if 12 grams of sugar is present in one serving of cereal, then this would be equal to 3 teaspoons of sugar. Keep in mind that most of us eat two or three "servings" of cereal in our bowl. Therefore, the amount of sugar may be doubled or tripled. Many nutritionists and dentists recommend choosing cereals that contain 6 grams or less of sugar per serving. An exception to this rule is cereals that contain dried fruit or raisins. These cereals may contain up to 12 grams of sucrose and other sugars and still be acceptable. The dried fruit contributes about 4-7 grams of naturally occurring sugar and also provides several vitamins, minerals, and fiber.

For homework, ask students to calculate the number of teaspoons of sugar in their family's favorite cereals. Ask your students to generate a list of breakfast cereals with less than 6 grams of sugar per serving.

Name _____ Date _____

## Activity 17-3. Sugar Decoder

**Directions:**

1. Underline the vowels in each food on page 2. Vowels are the letters a, e, i, o, u, and y.
2. Count the number of vowels. Write the total number in the box.
3. Draw as many teaspoons of sugar in the blank that matches the number of teaspoons in the food.

Here is an example for you.

```
                                              teaspoons sugar

   a p p l e   p i e   =  | 4 |   ♉ ♉ ♉ ♉
   ‾         ‾     ‾ ‾
```

This means that one piece of apple pie has 4 teaspoons of sugar in it.

Now complete the problems on the next page.

© 1991 by The Center for Applied Research in Education

Name _____ Date _____

## Activity 17-3. Sugar Decoder, *page 2*

Remember the vowels are a, e, i, o, u, and y.

Sweet Snacks                                          teaspoons sugar

jelly beans (10)          = ☐      _____

one can ice cold soda pop = ☐      _____

pudding pop               = ☐      _____

a chocolate bar           = ☐      _____

cupcake                   = ☐      _____

Which snack has the most sugar?

_____

Which snacks have less than 5 teaspoons of sugar?

_____

_____

_____

# Lesson 18. *Using Salt and Sodium in Moderation*

## Things to Know About Salt and Sodium

*Key Points:*

- Sodium is an essential nutrient.
- Sodium and salt should be used in moderation.
- The sodium content of food appears on some food labels.

*What is sodium?*

Sodium is a mineral that occurs naturally in almost all foods, with additional amounts found in many foods and beverages. Often when we think of sodium we think of SALT. The chemical name for salt is sodium chloride. Salt contains sodium and chloride.

*Why is sodium important?*

Sodium is important because it attracts water into the blood vessels and helps maintain normal blood volume and blood pressure. Sodium is also needed for proper functioning of nerves and muscles.

*How much sodium do we need?*

We only need about 500 milligrams of sodium per day. However, it would be very difficult and not very appetizing to eat this small amount. Thus, it is important to choose a level where one can comply. For example, a low sodium diet in a hospital is 2000 milligrams. Most Americans take in 4000-6000 milligrams per day. A safe and adequate intake of sodium is set at 1300-3300 milligrams a day.

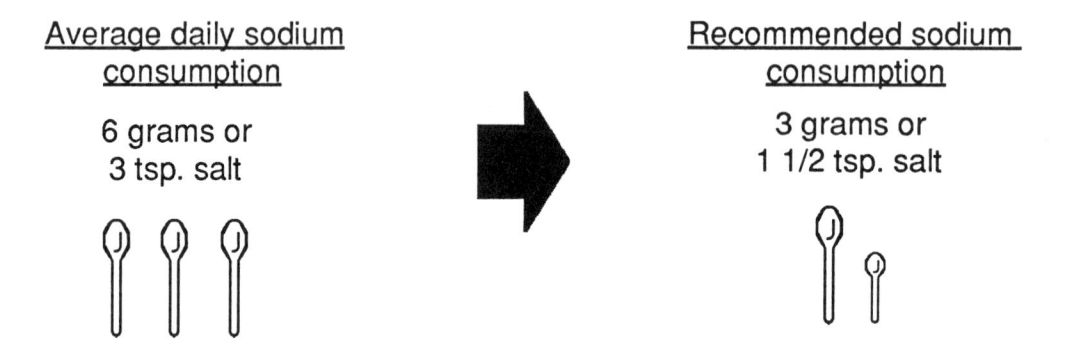

| Average daily sodium consumption | Recommended sodium consumption |
|---|---|
| 6 grams or 3 tsp. salt | 3 grams or 1 1/2 tsp. salt |

*How does the body handle excess sodium?*

Each kidney filters and regulates the blood sodium level by keeping the amount of sodium needed and removing any excess. You know how thirsty you get after you eat salty food? The excess sodium in the blood triggers the thirst center in the brain, and tells you that you need to drink. Drinking liquids provides fluid to help excrete the excess sodium into your urine.

*What is the connection between sodium and high blood pressure?*

High intakes of sodium are known to raise blood pressure in some sodium-sensitive individuals. Not everyone is equally susceptible to high blood pressure. There are a few risk factors that make some individuals more likely candidates for the disease. Risk factors include a family history of the disease among certain groups, such as blacks, obesity, and a high sodium intake. We cannot predict who will develop high blood pressure, but we know that American children eat much more sodium than they actually need.

*Where is sodium found in your diet?*

Sodium is in most of the foods we eat. Some of it may occur naturally in our food, such as the sodium in a carrot or in milk. Other sodium comes from the salt we add during cooking or at the table. Most sodium added during processing comes from salt, but other ingredients and additives used by manufacturers contain sodium as well.

Foods that provide significant amounts of sodium in the diets of Americans (excluding sodium added during cooking or at the table) include bread and bakery products, cured and processed meats, canned and some frozen vegetables, and milk products, especially many cheeses. Salt or sodium in other forms is also used in many sauces, soups, salad dressings, and in many breakfast cereals.

Children are not born with a preference for salt. If processed foods high in sodium and salted foods are limited in childhood, children may be less likely to acquire a preference for salt. This is particularly beneficial for children of families who have a genetic tendency toward hypertension.

*How can children cut down on their sodium intake?*

Since children may already have developed a preference for salt, they may need to change their preference by gradually lowering the amount of salt in their diet. Studies show that children who gradually reduce the amount of salt they eat lose their desire for the salty taste. Starting with the diet they presently consume, and making gradual changes, is the key to lowering salt consumption. For example, if children are used to salting their food before they taste it, they can be encouraged to taste it first. If after tasting the food they must add salt, try shaking salt in the palm of their hands and gradually adding less and less. A second tip would be to moderate choices by choosing a tuna sandwich a few times a week instead of a bologna sandwich. The changes will become more desirable as children lose the desire for the salty taste.

*How do we identify sodium on food labels?*

Understanding what the food labels mean can help you know how much sodium is in the food. You may see these claims used on food labels:
        "sodium free"         less than   5 milligrams of sodium in 1 serving
        "very low sodium"    less than  35 milligrams of sodium in 1 serving
        "low sodium"         less than 140 milligrams of sodium in 1 serving

A sodium health claim can not be used if the sodium is more than 140 milligrams.

Students must be taught to be aware of serving sizes. If they eat three servings of a food and one serving contains 140 milligrams of sodium, in actuality they have eaten 420 milligrams of sodium. This is no longer a low sodium food.

# Activity 18-1. Sodium Smart

### DIRECTIONS TO THE TEACHER

**Objective** (Cognitive Domain: Comprehensive Level)

Students will predict which of two foods contains more sodium.

### Materials

Student Activity Sheet (1)
Student Answer Sheet (1)

### Prerequisite Skills

Understanding of sodium
Less than, greater than

### Procedure

1. Define sodium as an essential nutrient.

2. The sodium content of foods is listed on food labels. However, the amount of salt in foods is not listed.

3. Distribute the activity sheet and explain the directions.

4. Distribute the answer sheet and discuss results.

### Supplementary Activities

1. Discuss why sodium-containing ingredients are added to foods. They function as leavening agents, flavor enhancers, preservatives, thickeners, binders, emulsifiers, and mold inhibitors. Conduct a cooking lesson. Have your students bake yeast bread without salt, baking powder, or baking soda. What happens?

2. Discuss how sodium functions in the body. It attracts water into the blood and helps maintain blood volume and blood pressure. If we eat too much sodium it continues to draw more water into the blood and the blood volume increases and blood pressure goes up.

Name _____ Date _____

## Activity 18-1. Sodium Smart

**Directions:** In each question below, circle the food that you think has more sodium.

1. 5 saltines           or 1 slice of American cheese           ?

2.  Milkshake or  French fries?

3.  Old-fashioned oats or  1 packet of instant oatmeal?

4. One 10 oz.  soup or 1/2  teaspoon of table salt?

5. Fast food fries  or 1 fast food apple pie           ?

6. 1 oz. corn chips           or one medium 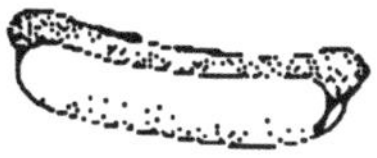 hot dog?

7. 4 oz.  hamburger meat or  2 slices of bologna?

8. 1/2 cup fresh or frozen cooked green beans           or 1/2 cup           ?

9. 1/2 cup canned corn           or 1/2 cup frozen corn 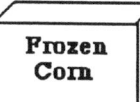          ?

© 1991 by The Center for Applied Research in Education

# Activity 18-1. Sodium Smart (answer sheet)

| Right answers | Wrong answers |
|---|---|
| 1. 1 slice of American cheese (450 mg) |  1. 5 saltine crackers (165 mg) 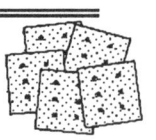 |
| 2. "Fast food" milkshake (300 mg) |  2. Regular size "fast food" French fries (109 mg)  |
| 3. 1 packet of instant oatmeal (300 mg) |  3. Old-fashioned oats (less than 5 mg)  |
| 4. 10 oz. can of soup (1500 mg) |  4. 1/2 teaspoons of table salt (1050 mg)  |
| 5. 1 "fast food" apple pie (427 mg) |  5. Regular size "fast food" French fries (201 mg)  |
| 6. 1 medium hot dog (450 mg) |  6. 1 oz. corn chips (245 mg)  |
| 7. 2 slices of bologna (400 mg) |  7. 4 oz. hamburger meat (70 mg)  |
| 8. 1/2 cup canned green beans (350 mg) |  8. 1/2 cup fresh or frozen cooked (less than 10 mg)  |
| 9. 1/2 cup canned corn (350 mg) |  9. 1/2 cup frozen cooked corn (less than 10 mg) 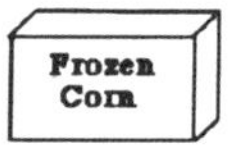 |

© 1991 by The Center for Applied Research in Education

# Activity 18-2. Sodium Inspector

## DIRECTIONS TO THE TEACHER

**Objective** (Cognitive Domain: Analysis Level)

Students will differentiate between sodium free, very low sodium, and low sodium products by utilizing given criteria and nutrition information on a food label.

## Materials

Student Activity Sheets (2)
Pencil

## Prerequisite Skills

Understands "greater than, less than" signs (>,<)

## Procedure

1. Discuss sodium content with students. Some sample questions are:

    • Why is sodium added to foods?
    • Can you tell if a food has a lot of sodium in it? How?
    • Why might people want to eat foods with only a little sodium in them?

2. Distribute the activity sheets and explain the directions.

## Supplementary Activities

1. Order the Sodium Display Kit from Penn State Nutrition Center, 417 E. Calder Way, Penn State University, University Park, PA 16801-5663. Set up the display as a learning station or bulletin board. The kit teaches the difference between sodium and salt, compares the amount of sodium the average American consumes to the amount recommended, and compares the sodium content of different foods. Call 814-865-6323 for ordering information.

2. Mrs. Dash is a sodium substitute herb flavoring used to enhance the taste of food. The company provides a hot line and will answer any questions concerning sodium in foods. The Hot Line number is 800-622-DASH. Explain and discuss why food companies provide services such as these to its customers.

Name _____ Date _____

# Activity 18-2. Sodium Inspector

<u>Sodium</u> is a nutrient that is found in many foods. We can read a food label and find out how much sodium is in a food. Sometimes a food label also makes a statement about the sodium content.

| What label says | What it means |
|---|---|
| "sodium-free" | < 5 milligrams of sodium in 1 serving |
| "very low sodium" | < 35 milligrams of sodium in 1 serving |
| "low sodium" | < 140 milligrams of sodium in 1 serving |
| (< means less than) | > 140 no statement allowed |

**Directions:** 1) Read the food labels. 2) Circle the word "sodium." 3) Find out how much sodium is in a serving. Decide which statement can be used. 4) Write it at the bottom of the label. The first one is done for you.

Rye Wafers
Nutrition Information Per Serving
Serving size: 8 crackers
Servings per container: 9
Calories................................ 90
Protein............................ 2 grams
Carbohydrate................ 18 grams
Fat..................................... 1 gram
Sodium..................... 0 milligrams

sodium free

(The wafers have 0 milligrams of sodium in 1 serving. Since 0 milligrams < 5 milligrams, we can use the words "sodium free.")

© 1991 by The Center for Applied Research in Education

Name _____ Date _____

## Activity 18-2. Sodium Inspector, *page 2*

### Wheat Snacks

Nutrition Information (per serving)
Serving Size .............. 12 crackers
Servings per container ............ 15
Calories ................................. 70
Protein ........................... 1 gram
Carbohydrate ................... 9 grams
Fat ................................. 3 grams
Sodium ................. 70 milligrams

_____

### Pretzels

Nutrition Information
per serving
Serving size ........... 1 oz.
Servings per package ... 8
Calories ..................... 110
Protein ............... 3 grams
Carbohydrate ... 23 grams
Fat ....................... 1 gram
Sodium .... 20 milligrams

_____

### Microwave Popping Corn
### Natural Flavor

Nutritition Information Per Serving
Serving size: 4 cups popped
Servings per bag: 2

Calories ............................... 200
Protein ........................... 4 grams
Carbohydrate ............... 22 grams
Fat .............................. 11 grams
Sodium .................200 milligrams

_____

### Snack Mix

Nutrition Information
Per Serving

Serving size          2/3 cup
Servings per carton      6
Calories               120
Protein             3 grams
Carbohydrate       19 grams
Fat                 5 grams
Sodium         3 milligrams

_____

Remember: If you want to find out about nutrition, read the label.

# Activity 18-3. Sodium Vending

## DIRECTIONS TO THE TEACHER

**Objective** (Cognitive Domain: Analysis Level)

Students will identify some foods that don't taste salty yet may contain sodium.

**Materials**

Student Activity Sheet (1)
Pencil

**Prerequisite Skills**

Seriation of numbers
Reading and writing

**Procedure**

1. Introduce sodium as a necessary nutrient needed by our hearts, muscles, and nerves to function properly and to maintain fluid balance.

2. Explain that our food supply has so much sodium that we often get more than we need. Convenience foods or processed foods contribute more sodium to the American diet than sodium from the salt shaker.

3. Explain sodium is in salt. Salt is a taste recognized by our taste buds. Some foods taste salty, so we know they have sodium. Many other foods have sodium yet we can't taste it.

4. Distribute the activity sheet and explain the directions.

**Supplementary Activities**

1. Discuss the senses. Taste is a sense that relates to nutrition because taste can make eating pleasurable. The tongue has 12,000 taste buds located all over the tongue. Each area of the tongue has a different set of taste buds. The four tastes are bitter, sour, salty and sweet. Discuss how salty foods taste. Make a collage of salty tasting food.

2. Ask your students how they feel after eating a salty food. They'll probably say thirsty. Salt pulls water. You can demonstrate this by putting lettuce, which is 97% water, in a bag, adding salt, and letting it sit overnight. The salt will pull the water out of the lettuce, and it will wilt. Explain that this demonstrates the same concept as when they get thirsty. As a result of consuming salt, the body triggers the brain to drink water.

3. Make cookies or cake (from scratch). Use half the batter with salt, the other half without. What happens? Can the students taste the difference?

Name _____ Date _____

# Activity 18-3. Sodium Vending

Sodium is a nutrient found in many foods. Salt has sodium.

**Directions:** Look at the foods in the vending machine on the left. The number of milligrams (mg) of sodium in each food is listed. In the blank vending machine on the right, rank the foods by the number of milligrams, from the least to the most sodium. The first and last ones are done for you.

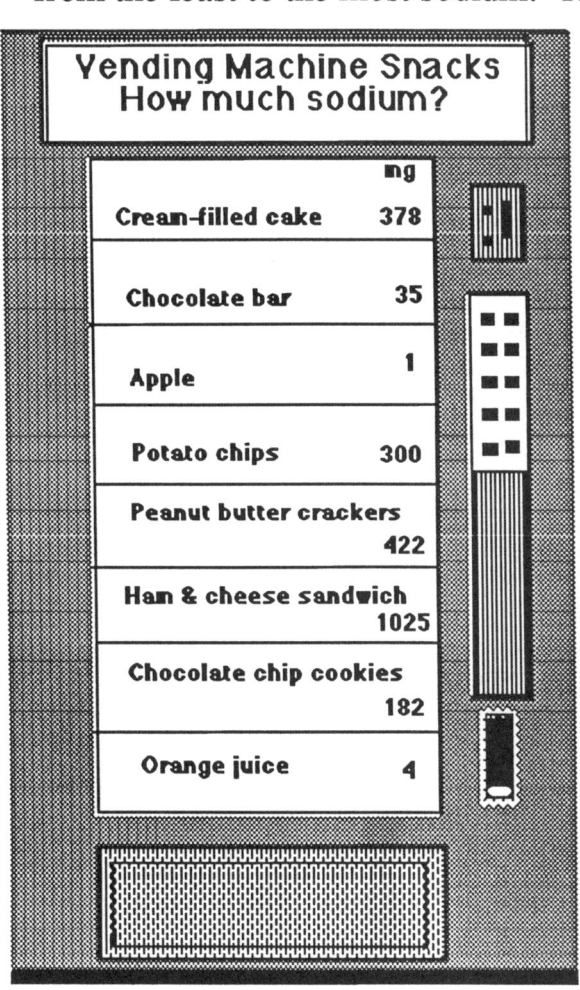

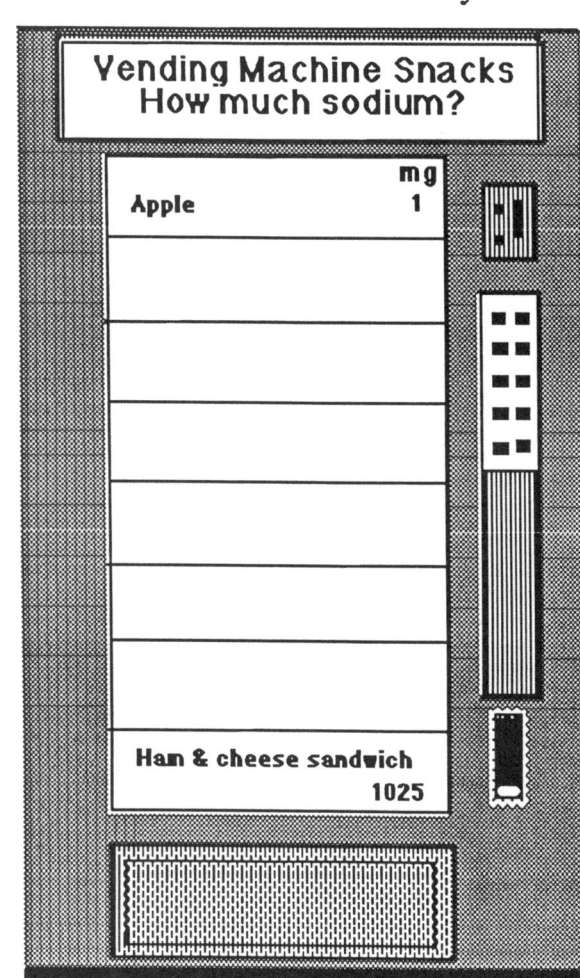

**Vending Machine Snacks — How much sodium?**

| Food | mg |
|---|---|
| Cream-filled cake | 378 |
| Chocolate bar | 35 |
| Apple | 1 |
| Potato chips | 300 |
| Peanut butter crackers | 422 |
| Ham & cheese sandwich | 1025 |
| Chocolate chip cookies | 182 |
| Orange juice | 4 |

**Vending Machine Snacks — How much sodium?**

| Food | mg |
|---|---|
| Apple | 1 |
|  |  |
|  |  |
|  |  |
|  |  |
|  |  |
|  |  |
| Ham & cheese sandwich | 1025 |

**Some foods taste salty, some don't.**

1. Potato chips taste salty. But they are not the highest in sodium content. Which three snacks are higher?

   _____

   _____

   _____

2. A food may not taste s ___ ___ ___ ___ but still have s ___ ___ ___ ___ ___ .

# Unit 4. EATING THROUGHOUT THE DAY

Lesson 19 <u>Breakfast</u>
    19-1. Mystery Message
    19-2. Time to Eat
    19-3. Breakfast on the Run

Lesson 20 <u>Lunch</u>
    20-1. Bag Lunches
    20-2. Menu of Color
    20-3. Fill in the Menu

Lesson 21 <u>Supper</u>
    21-1. Families
    21-2. Supper Steps
    21-3. Microwaving

Lesson 22 <u>Snacks</u>
    22-1. Choosing Snacks
    22-2. Snack Track
    22-3. Popcorn Percents

Lesson 23 <u>Convenience Foods and Vending Machines</u>
    23-1. Fat Pats
    23-2. Shopping
    23-3. Snack Cents

Lesson 24 <u>Advertising</u>
    24-1. Commercials
    24-2. Slogan Power
    24-3. Ads, Ads, Ads

Lesson 25 <u>Cultural Foods</u>
    25-1. Favorite Food Flags
    25-2. Cultural Foods
    25-3. Cultural Foods Search

# Lesson 19. *Breakfast*

## Things to Know About Breakfast

*Key Points:*

- Children who eat breakfast are better able to pay attention in school.

- A variety of foods, both traditional and nontraditional, are good breakfast choices.

- Foods high in complex carbohydrates and low in simple carbohydrates (sugars) -- such as bread -- are most desirable.

*Why should children eat breakfast?*

Over twenty-five years ago, the Iowa Breakfast Studies concluded that children who eat breakfast perform better in school. This wasn't news to the many teachers who had observed behavioral differences between children who eat the morning meal and children who skip it. However, the Iowa Breakfast Studies and several more recent studies provide support for teachers, parents, and health professionals who promote breakfast.

Breakfast can be literally translated as "breaking the fast." A child who eats a bedtime snack at 9 p.m. and gets up at 7 a.m. has been without food for ten hours. Since children have small stomachs and relatively high energy needs, they need to replenish their energy supply in the morning.

When a child skips breakfast, energy must come from blood glucose that has been stored in the body. (Glucose is also called blood sugar.) Without breakfast, there is an inadequate supply of glucose to get the child through to lunch. Thus, a child who skips breakfast will typically experience a "mid-morning slump." About three hours after getting up, the child will feel tired and weak and may be unable to concentrate on his or her school work. Eating breakfast will not make children smarter, but it will increase their attention span, making it possible for more learning to take place.

Breakfast eaters have also been shown to consume more essential nutrients like calcium, fiber, vitamins C, thiamin, and riboflavin, than do breakfast skippers.

*What should a child eat for breakfast?*

Essentially, any nutritious food can be included in the morning meal. If a child doesn't like traditional breakfast foods like cereal and toast, he or she should be encouraged to make alternative selections. Some ideas include: leftovers from the evening meal, macaroni and cheese, pizza, yogurt, graham crackers and peanut butter. Of course, a breakfast will provide more nutritional benefits if it includes foods from several food groups.

*What's wrong with doughnuts and coffee cakes?*

Aside from being very high in fat, these foods tend to be high in simple carbohydrates (sugar) and low in complex carbohydrates (starch and fiber).

Ideally, breakfast meals should be high in complex carbohydrates and low in simple carbohydrates. A breakfast high in simple carbohydrates, such as two doughnuts and 1/2 cup of orange juice, will raise the blood glucose level very quickly, but then it will drop. About two hours after the meal, the blood glucose level will actually be lower than it was before the meal. This drop in blood glucose is referred to as the "mid-morning slump." The tiredness and weakness experienced during the slump is the same as skipping breakfast. Thus, eating a breakfast high in simple sugars will have the same effect as eating no breakfast at all. Both will result in a mid-morning slump.

A meal high in complex carbohydrates, such as whole wheat toast with peanut butter, yogurt and fruit, will enable the blood glucose level to remain above the fasting level for about four hours.

*Which cereal is best?*

Although few cereals are poor nutritional choices, the best choices meet the following criteria:

> Sugar - less than 6 grams per serving
>        - may have up to 12 grams per serving if the cereal has dried fruit or raisins
> Fiber - at least 3 grams per serving
> Iron - at least 25% of the U.S.RDA

Cereals that provide 100% of the U.S. RDA for vitamins and minerals are not necessary.

*How can you tell how much sugar and fiber is in a serving of cereal?*

"Carbohydrate Information" on the side of the cereal box lists three forms of carbohydrates (sucrose and other sugars, starch and related carbohydrates, and dietary fiber) with the grams provided per serving. Since your students probably think of sugar in teaspoons more than grams, you can teach them to convert grams to teaspoons. Since there are four grams of sugar per teaspoon, the number of teaspoons of sugar in one serving can be found by dividing the number of grams by four. To determine fiber, simply use the chart. A cereal with three or more grams of fiber per serving meets the guidelines.

When selecting cereals, many times tradeoffs must be made. Some cereals may be low in sugar but also low in fiber. One cereal may not meet both guidelines. Rotating cereals from day to day or mixing cereals together can help achieve the guidelines. Also, fresh fruit could be added to the breakfast to increase fiber.

# Activity 19-1. Mystery Message

## DIRECTIONS TO THE TEACHER

**Objective** (Cognitive Domain: Comprehension Level)

Students will summarize the importance of eating breakfast by writing one reason why breakfast is important.

**Materials**

Student Activity Sheet (1)
Pencil

**Prerequisite Skills**

Letter and number recognition

**Procedure**

1. Discuss breakfast with students. Some sample questions are:

    - Do you eat breakfast?
    - Why do you/don't you eat breakfast?
    - What are your favorite foods to eat for breakfast?
    - Have you ever skipped breakfast?
    - How do you feel when you skip breakfast?

2. Explain the importance of breakfast. (*Refer to Background Information*).

3. Distribute the activity sheet and explain the directions.

**Supplementary Activities**

1. Plan to eat a breakfast in the classroom. Give students suggestions for packing a bag breakfast. For example, yogurt, cheese, bagels, muffins, fruit, juice, and peanut butter sandwiches. If your school has a breakfast program, you might also plan to have the class meet for breakfast in the cafeteria.

2. Ask students to write a "Morning Story" describing the morning activities of a child who eats breakfast and how the child feels after eating breakfast.

3. September is American Breakfast Month. Don't let the school year get started without teaching your students the importance of good nutrition with a variety of lessons on breakfast. Go around the room and ask students what they ate for breakfast that morning and tally the responses for each food group. Continue tallying breakfast choices for the entire month, then have the students graph the results. Students can specify which foods are nutrition smart, such as lowfat cereal, fresh fruit, lowfat milk; and which foods aren't so smart, like doughnuts, candy, soda, and so on. By the end of the month, children will have a better understanding of what a good breakfast should include.

Name _____ Date _____

## Activity 19-1. Mystery Message

**Directions:**
1) Each letter of the alphabet has been given a number.
2) Solve the Mystery Message by writing the letter on the line above each number. Here is an example.

| A | B | C | D | E | F | G | H | I | J | K | L | M |
|---|---|---|---|---|---|---|---|---|---|---|---|---|
| 1 | 2 | 3 | 4 | 5 | 6 | 7 | 8 | 9 | 10 | 11 | 12 | 13 |

| N | O | P | Q | R | S | T | U | V | W | X | Y | Z |
|---|---|---|---|---|---|---|---|---|---|---|---|---|
| 14 | 15 | 16 | 17 | 18 | 19 | 20 | 21 | 22 | 23 | 24 | 25 | 26 |

$\underline{H}\ \underline{A}\ \underline{V}\ \underline{E}\quad \underline{F}\ \underline{U}\ \underline{N}$
 8   1   22   5      6   21   14

___  ___  ___  ___  ___  ___  ___  ___  ___
 2   18   5   1   11   6   1   19   20

___  ___  ___  ___   ___  ___
 7   5   20   19    13   5

___  ___  ___  ___  ___
 7   15   9   14   7

Is this message true?   Yes _____   No _____
Write one reason why breakfast is important.

Breakfast is important because _____
_____

# Activity 19-2. Time to Eat

## DIRECTIONS TO THE TEACHER

**Objective** (Cognitive Domain: Application Level)

Students will discover why breakfast is important by comparing the number of hours between supper and breakfast and the number of hours between breakfast, lunch, and other snacks throughout the day.

## Materials

Student Activity Sheet (1)
Pencil

## Prerequisite Skills

Understanding of basic time concepts
Ability to utilize information presented on a chart

## Procedure

1. Discuss telling time to the nearest hour and how to calculate the passage of time in hours.

2. Discuss the need to eat food for energy. Reinforce that a constant supply of food helps the body run efficiently. Some sample questions are:

    - What time do you eat breakfast?
    - How long do you go from your last meal of the day to your first meal of the next day?
    - How can skipping breakfast affect your ability to learn during the morning hours of school?
    - Do you notice that we usually eat more often later in the day than in the morning, yet we must perform at our peak early in the day and early in the afternoon?

3. Distribute the activity sheet and explain the directions.

## Supplementary Activities

1. Have the children keep their own record of the times they eat meals and snacks. Ask them to count the time that lapses between feedings. Ask each child to compare his or her pattern to Ben's.

2. Have students keep a one week record of the actual time they eat breakfast. Does the time differ on the weekend?

Name _____  Date _____

## Activity 19-2. Time to Eat

Just as a car's engine needs fuel to run, your body needs food to help you go. A regular supply of food keeps your engine running smoothly. Without food you'll slow down and lose steam. Without energy, you may not feel like keeping up with your classmates.

**Directions:** Look at when Ben eats from Monday morning to Tuesday morning. Answer the questions.

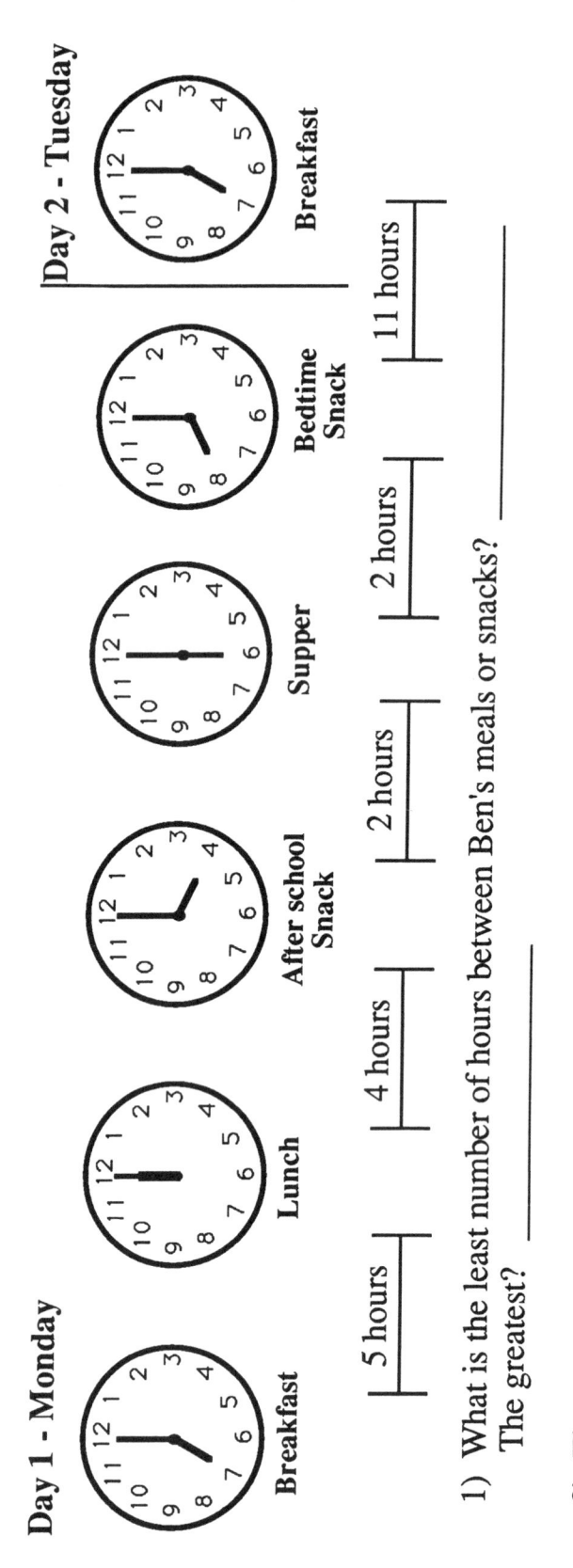

Day 1 - Monday

Breakfast — Lunch — After school Snack — Supper — Bedtime Snack

|— 5 hours —|— 4 hours —|— 2 hours —|— 2 hours —|

Day 2 - Tuesday

Breakfast

|— 11 hours —|

1) What is the least number of hours between Ben's meals or snacks? _____ The greatest? _____

2) The greatest number of hours is between _____ and _____.

3) Circle the nutrition-smart reason for eating breakfast.
   a. I get to pick what I eat and I can make it myself.
   b. I have used up most of my energy supply and need a refill.
   c. I get a new toy in my cereal box.

© 1991 by The Center for Applied Research in Education

# Activity 19-3. Breakfast on the Run

## DIRECTIONS TO THE TEACHER

**Objective** (Cognitive Domain: Knowledge Level)

Students will identify nutritious fast-to-prepare foods for breakfast.

**Materials**

Student Activity Sheet (1)
Pencil

**Prerequisite Skills**

Ability to form a circle, an "X," and to draw lines

**Procedure**

1. Discuss a family's busy schedule. Tell students that sometimes meals are skipped while the family is busy at other activities. Mention that breakfast is the most frequently skipped meal, yet breakfast is considered to be the most important meal of the day.

2. Reinforce these ideas

    - If you don't eat for 10-12 hours your body will be "running on empty."
    - People who eat breakfast may accomplish more work and are physically and mentally more alert.
    - Breakfast provides nutrients your body needs to function and feel alert.

3. Reinforce that skipping breakfast is not a good idea, but that children do not need to sit down to a traditional breakfast like eggs and bacon or pancakes. Instead, they can eat fast, nutrition-smart meals in a short time.

4. Introduce these times to the students. Did you know it takes:

    - 19 seconds to pour milk or juice into a glass to drink?
    - 54 seconds to cut an English muffin in half and place 1/2 of a cheese slice on each muffin and place it in a broiler or microwave?
    - 35 seconds to toast bread, and while the bread is toasting slice a banana and then spread peanut butter and the banana over the toast?
    - 31 seconds to pour cereal, banana slices, and milk into a bowl?
    - 41 seconds to slice a bagel and add sliced turkey breast on top?

    Now have them offer some suggestions for other fast nutrition-smart breakfasts.

5. Distribute the activity sheet and explain the directions. This is especially important for beginning readers.

Supplementary Activities

1. Have students time their breakfast from preparation to clean-up. Ask them to compare which takes longer, a breakfast prepared on a school day or a breakfast prepared on the weekend.

2. As children grow older and begin to make their own decisions, they sometimes choose to sleep rather than take the time to eat breakfast. The nutritional needs for breakfast are as great during adolescence as they are when they are younger. Discuss with the children some fast, easy breakfasts they can prepare in less than five minutes. Examples are peanut butter and jelly sandwich, grilled cheese sandwich, yogurt and fruit, cereal and fruit, milk and toast, and warmed leftovers from last night's supper.

3. Bring in some foods that can be eaten at breakfast or that simulate breakfast foods, such as materials like confetti in a cereal box, sponge for toast with liquid soap to spread, and so on, and then time the children as they prepare a fast meal. You'll need a stop watch or a clock with a second hand. Time and record the activity from preparation to clean-up.

4. Show "What's for Breakfast?" from The Most Important Person film set, available from Encyclopedia Britannica, 310 S. Michigan Ave., Chicago, IL 60604. Avg. 5 minutes. Other topics include: "Tasting Party," "Have a Snack and Foods Around Us." $450.00 films, $300.00 videotape and $155.00 filmstrips. Phone is 312-347-7900.

5. Show the film or video The New Eating on the Run (2nd edition, 1986), available from Alfred Higgins Productions, Inc., 6350 Laurel Canyon Blvd. #305, North Hollywood, CA 91606. (800) 766-5353. For 16 mm film, $415; for video $375. The grade level is 4-6 and adult, but many primary classes may find the presentation appropriate.

Name _____ Date _____

## Activity 19-3. Breakfast on the Run

Ben gets up late and his mom yells, "School starts in twenty minutes, don't forget breakfast." Ben goes into the kitchen and here is what he sees.

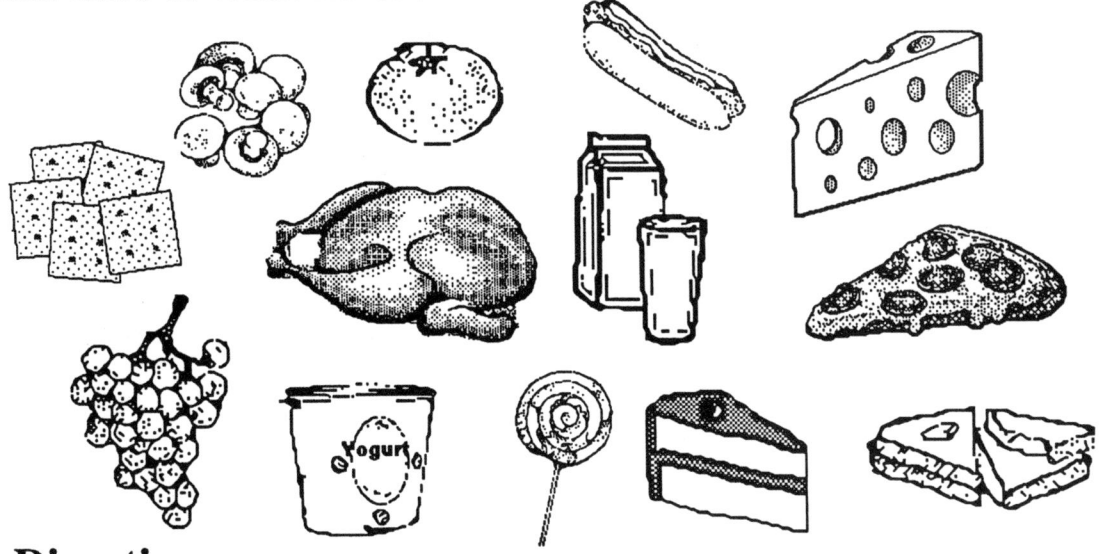

**Directions:**
1) Circle the foods above that would be ready to eat fast.
2) Put an X on those fast foods that are nutrition-smart.
3) Look at all the fast nutrition-smart foods Ben could eat. Draw a line from the foods to Ben to show what you would choose for his breakfast.
4) Make a picture of a fast breakfast you eat.

# Lesson 20. *Lunch*

## Things to Know About Lunch

*Key Points:*

- School lunches are provided so that children meet at least one third their RDA. Brown bag lunches from home should meet the same goal.

- Teachers, parents, and the school food service can work together to support nutrition education in the classroom and cafeteria.

*Why should children eat lunch?*

Eating lunch promotes a good afternoon at school. Learning is more difficult when children are hungry. The School Lunch Program offers nutritious meals to students by providing at least one third of the nutrient needs included in the RDA. School lunch helps promote the health and well-being of children while setting an example that a balanced meal contains milk, meat or alternatives, grains, fruits, and vegetables.

Federal guidelines require that lunches served to children in grades K-3 provide the following foods:

| Food Groups | Serving Size |
|---|---|
| Milk | 8 oz. (1 cup) |
| Meat or meat alternate | 1 1/2 oz. |
| Vegetable or fruit | 2 or more servings both total 1/2 cup |
| Bread or bread alternate | 8 servings a week |

*Are school lunches supporting the Dietary Guidelines?*

Recently the school lunch program has come under attack for failing to provide children with lunches that meet recommendations for fat, sodium, sugar, and fiber. Some parents and teachers assume that the foods served do not support the nutrition education that is being conducted in the classroom.

Nevertheless, many school food service programs have been successful in serving well-accepted healthy meals. For example, skim milk and lowfat milk are offered along with whole milk. Many of the luncheon meats that are used in sandwiches and on salad bars are 95% fat free and lower in sodium. Many foods that were once fried, like chicken and potatoes, are being baked. When foods are fried, vegetable shortening is replacing animal fat. Finally, salad bars are regular features in some schools and fresh fruit is served as dessert.

Most schools offer both lowfat chocolate and white milk. Some offer lowfat chocolate milk once a week while others offer it every day. If a child does not drink white milk, chocolate milk is an acceptable alternative. Chocolate milk consumed by a child provides more calcium, protein, vitamins A and D and riboflavin than white milk left in the carton!

If your school is currently taking steps or has already taken steps to reduce the fat, sugar, and sodium, and increase complex carbohydrates in the lunches, then the teachers and food service personnel should tell the parents of these changes. Newsletters or labeling items on the lunch menu will draw attention to the positive steps your school is making to promote wellness within your community.

*What about brown bag lunches?*

Preparing a bag lunch gives parents an opportunity to share information about food and nutrition with their children. Children are more likely to eat and enjoy a lunch that they've helped prepare themselves. When choosing items for a bag lunch, it is a good idea to follow *A Pattern for Daily Food Choices* (see Unit 2) and the Dietary Guidelines. This doesn't mean that children need to eliminate all of their favorite foods, but it does mean balancing the foods that are higher in fat, sugar, or sodium with other foods that contain less of these components.

- Use a variety of foods from the major food groups. *(See Unit 2, lessons 6 through 11 for suggestions of variety within food groups.)*

- Keep nutrients in mind. Foods high in fats and sugars can add pleasure, but without the necessary nutrients. Lunch time beverages, desserts, and chips are all possible sources of extra sugars and fats.

- Go lightly on bread spreads high in fat, such as butter, margarine, and mayonnaise. Better choices are mustard, ketchup, or barbecue sauce.

- Include foods with dietary fiber, such as fruits with the peel, vegetables, and whole grain bread products.

- Choose naturally low-sodium foods, such as fresh fruits and raw vegetables, lean meats and poultry.

- Use the 80/20 rule of thumb: 80% of the bag lunch should be nutrient-dense foods from the major food groups. Only 20% should be from the fats and sweets group. This means only one small "extra" from the fats and sweets group.

- Use lower fat luncheon meats (95% fat free) and lowfat cheeses and lower sodium meats and cheeses.

# Activity 20-1. Bag Lunches

## DIRECTIONS TO THE TEACHER

**Objective** (Cognitive Domain: Analysis Level)

Students will identify nutrition-smart foods by choosing nutritious foods to fill a lunch bag.

## Materials

Student Activity Sheets (2)
Pencil
Crayons
Scissors
Glue

## Prerequisite Skills

Ability to classify foods by groups

## Procedure

1. Discuss with the students the fact that the School Lunch Program sets regulations for the kinds and minimum amounts of foods to be served. Despite these regulations, many children choose to bring a lunch from home and obviously these are not regulated. Nevertheless, the same principle should apply.

2. Distribute the activity sheets and explain the directions.

## Supplementary Activities

1. Food availability changes with the seasons of the year. Discuss with your class how lunch bag items change from fall, winter, spring, and summer. Most obvious will be changes in fruits and vegetables, but don't forget hot and cold. A thermos of soup or chili taste good on a cold day, but not nearly as inviting in the heat of early fall or late spring. To follow up the discussion, have four examples of bag lunches representing the foods available at different seasons. Ask the children to match the bag lunch to the correct season.

2. Pack a mystery lunch box. Blindfold one student. Ask him or her to reach into the box and try to name the foods by touch. Another similar activity would be for the blindfolded child to describe what he or she feels and have the class try to name the foods based on his or her description.

3. Refer to the book <u>Lunch Box Treats</u>, by Nancy Skodack, M.S., R.D., Texas Monthly Press, P.O. Box 1569, Austin, TX 78767, 1989. The cost is $8.95. The book offers 120 recipes for healthy, fun lunches. You may want to inform your students' parents about this resource in a newsletter or gift suggestion list at the holidays.

4. Older students should be able to look at the items in a school lunch bag and name the major nutrients provided in the foods. For example, a sandwich with turkey provides complex carbohydrate, protein, fat, and iron but is missing vitamins A and C and calcium. Ask the students what other foods they could pack in the lunch bag to supply the missing nutrients.

5. Discuss with your students how they can pack an environmentally sound lunch. A lunch box is recycled day after day but bags can also be recycled. If the children draw designs on their bags they may be more apt to recycle them. Instead of packing food in plastic bags use containers that can be reused.

    Environmentally speaking, a reusable container with a lid is the best way to pack your lunch. This is because over its lifetime it is going to displace a lot of disposable products. Aseptic juice containers (juice box) are popular for lunch. Discuss with your class the more environmentally aware option of putting juice in a thermos. Some schools have recycling programs in which aluminum cans can be recycled.

    Learn what is being recycled in your municipality. There is generally a hotline number. If not, call your town clerk, state recycling coordinator, or the Environmental Defense Fund at 1-800-235-5333. You can also look under recycling in the yellow pages.

Name _____ Date _____

## Activity 20-1. Bag Lunches

**Directions:** 1) Put an X on the food that doesn't belong in each food group. 2) Of the two foods left, color the one you like best. 3) Cut out the foods you colored. 4) Go to the next page.

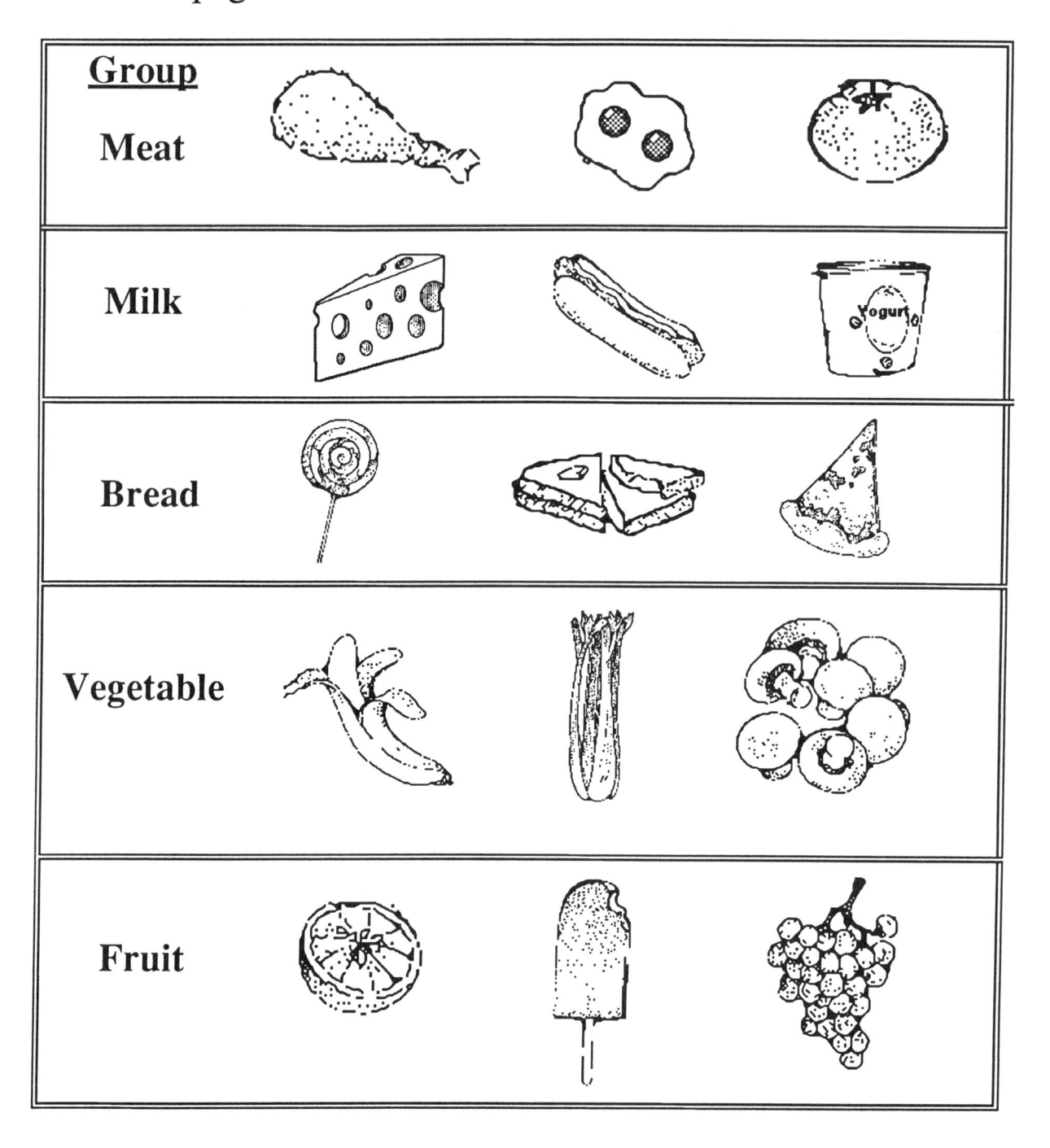

| Group | | | |
|---|---|---|---|
| **Meat** | chicken leg | fried eggs | tomato |
| **Milk** | cheese | hot dog | yogurt |
| **Bread** | lollipop | sandwich | pizza slice |
| **Vegetable** | banana | celery | mushrooms |
| **Fruit** | orange slice | popsicle | grapes |

© 1991 by The Center for Applied Research in Education

Name _____ Date _____

## Activity 20-1. Bag Lunches, *page 2*

**Directions:** Place the foods you colored on the correct food groups. Paste them on the lunch bag.

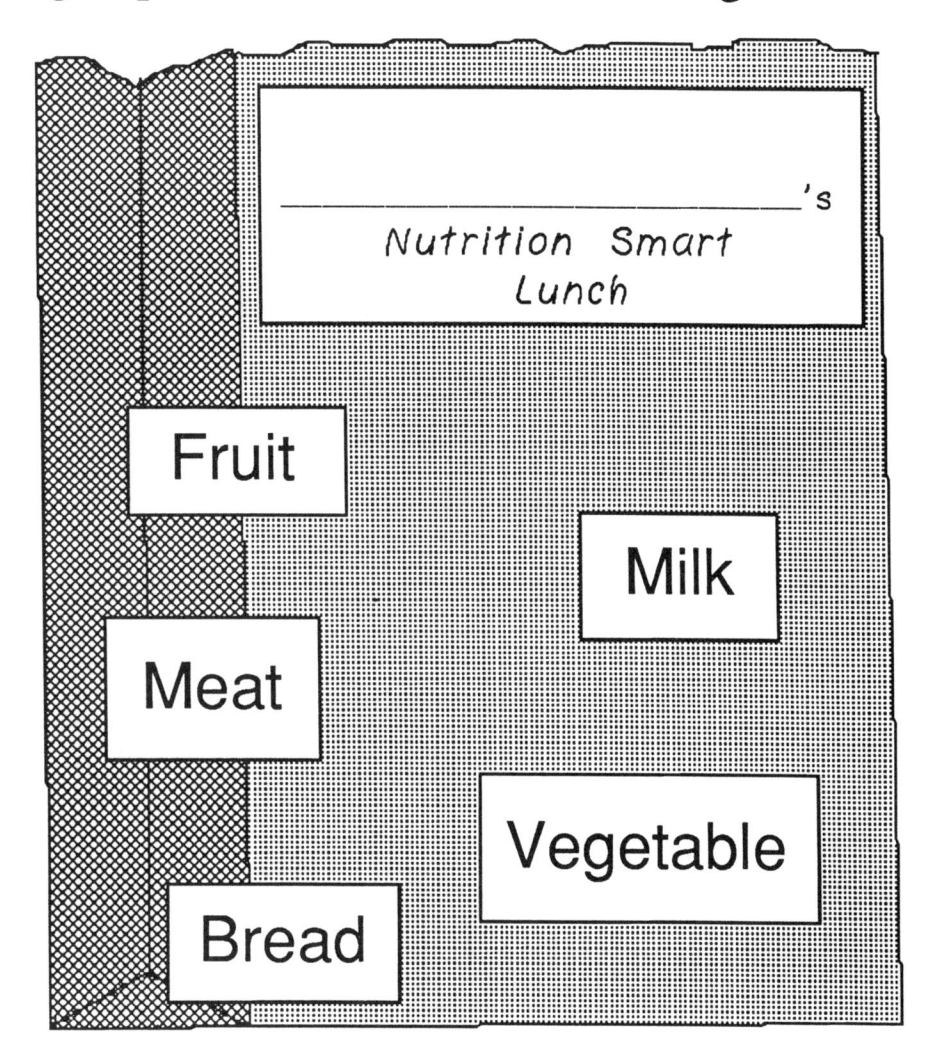

_____'s
Nutrition Smart
Lunch

Fruit

Milk

Meat

Vegetable

Bread

Now your lunch bag is full of foods from all the food groups.
Super!
You packed a nutrition-smart lunch.

# Activity 20-2. Menu of Color

## DIRECTIONS TO THE TEACHER

**Objective** (Cognitive Domain: Comprehension Level)

After coloring a menu, students will infer that the school lunch menu offers a variety of foods from all the food groups.

**Materials**

Student Activity Sheet (1)
Crayons

**Prerequisite Skills**

Identification of colors

**Procedure**

1. Discuss the many ways we can categorize food, such as by color, texture, taste, temperature, nutritional value, and so on.

2. Review with students the idea that food groups are based on nutrient value. Foods in the same food group are strong in the same nutrients. Remind students that no one food group offers all the nutrients we need to grow and stay healthy.

3. Discuss the role of the School Lunch Program and how it was developed to offer children the essential nutrients. Tell the students that regulations are set so that food services must offer a specific amount of foods from each food group for each lunch.

4. We eat with our eyes before we eat with our mouths. The way a food looks can make a difference in how appealing a meal looks to us. Remind students that the more colors they see on a plate the more appealing that meal can be.

5. Distribute the activity sheet and explain the directions.

**Supplementary Activities**

1. Using your own school lunch menu and the color code for food groups used in this activity, ask the children to color over the entree on the menu with the appropriate color. Do they see a variety of colors? They should.

2. Have each child think about his or her favorite foods in each food group served in the school cafeteria. Have each child write a thank you letter to the food service personnel. Letters may include naming the foods that are favorites.

3. Have students imagine that mashed potatoes were purple or milk was green. Would it taste different? Experiment with food coloring. Have a taste test, then try a blind test. Can students tell the difference blindfolded?

Name _____     Date _____

## Activity 20-2. Menu of Color

**Directions:** Color each box of the menu the color of the food group. Some boxes can have more than one color. Notice the colorful menu.

| Meat = red | Vegetables = green | Bread = brown |
| Milk = blue | Fruit = purple | Fats and Sugars = yellow |

### School Lunch Menu

| Monday | Tuesday | Wednesday | Thursday | Friday |
|---|---|---|---|---|
| Tuna Salad | Hot Dog on a roll | Meat Loaf and Gravy | Lasagna | Taco |
| Bun | Green beans | Mashed Potatoes | Bread | Corn |
| Carrots | Orange Slices | Whole wheat Roll | Tossed Salad | Pear |
| Red Grapes | Cookie | Baked Apple | Pineapple | Yogurt |
| Milk | Milk | Milk | Milk | Milk |

© 1991 by The Center for Applied Research in Education

# Activity 20-3. Fill in the Menu

## DIRECTIONS TO THE TEACHER

**Objective** (Cognitive Domain: Application Level)

When given an incomplete school lunch menu, students will discover the missing food group and change the menu by adding a specific food from the missing group.

## Materials

Student Activity Sheet (1)
Pencils

## Prerequisite Skills

Charting information

## Procedure

1. Discuss the components of a school lunch.

2. Remind the students that each food group is offered at lunch in order to provide them with the nutrients needed for growth. If any one of the food groups is missing, the nutrients needed for growth will also be missing. Although we can occasionally skip some food groups, if we did this with any regularity we might miss major nutrients needed for growth.

3. Distribute the activity sheet and explain the directions.

## Supplementary Activities

1. Make a transparency master of your school lunch menu. Ask the children to write down the foods that they choose not to eat. Then ask them to write down beside that food what nutrients the food has to offer. Finally, ask them to think if there are other foods they eat at breakfast or supper that will provide these nutrients. For example, if a student never eats carrots she/he would write down carrot. Beside carrot she/he would record vitamin A. Other foods that she/he may eat with vitamin A are milk, ice cream, ready-to-eat cereals, sweet potatoes, apricots, cantaloupe, peaches, broccoli, kale, collard greens, V-8 juice, canned vegetable soup, spinach, or watermelon. The children will see there are other options, but they should think about the foods they eat throughout the day to get all the nutrients needed for growth.

2. Arrange a tour of your school's lunch facilities or invite the food service director to visit your class. Discuss the components of a nutritious school lunch. Review the weekly school lunch menu to identify the food groups. Ask the director to talk about how meals are planned and prepared.

Name _____ Date _____

## Activity 20-3. Fill in the Menu

This is what must be included in the school lunch menu each day.

### Food Groups

1 serving Milk (milk, cheese, or yogurt)
1 serving Meat ( meats, fish, chicken, beans, or eggs)
2 or more servings of Vegetable or Fruit
1 to 2 servings Bread (breads, pasta, and rice)

**Directions:** Look at the menu below. A food is missing in each lunch. Write the missing food group on the bottom line. Fill in the empty box with a food from the missing group. The first one is done for you.

| School Lunch Menu | | | | |
|---|---|---|---|---|
| Monday | Tuesday | Wednesday | Thursday | Friday |
| Whole Wheat Roll | | | Potato Wedges | |
| Cabbage Salad | Milk | Carrots & Celery Sticks | | Spaghetti & Meatballs |
| Oven Baked Cod | Orange | Turkey & Cheese | Milk | Garlic Bread |
| Milk | Green Beans | Sliced Peaches | Apple | Tossed Salad |
| *Kiwi* | Cornbread | Milk | Chicken Nuggets | Banana |

*Fruit* _____  _____  _____  _____

# Lesson 21. *Supper*

## Things to Know About Supper

*Key Points:*

- Children are often involved in family meal preparation either out of necessity or a desire to participate.

- Convenience foods are becoming common suppertime entrees.

- Understanding a child's suppertime environemnt can help a teacher understand the family's dynamics.

*What has happened to the traditional supper?*

Over the years, there have been trends away from the traditional supper. Economic and social forces have dramatically changed American lifestyles. These changes create significant differences in the way we allocate time, energy, and money to food. Children are affected by all of these trends in the ways in which their family makes food choices.

Families are spending less time preparing supper, sharing more responsibility for food preparation, and opting to pay extra for convenience food items. Mothers still tend to make the food purchasing decisions, but they are cooking less and men are cooking more. Children and teens are participating in food shopping and meal preparation.

With more mothers working outside the home there is an increase in "latch-key children." The six million latchkey children between the ages of 6 and 11 not only influence the way families eat, but also the way food is marketed. According to J. Stanton, Ph.D., Professor of Food Marketing, St. Joseph University, Philadelphia, PA, 13 percent of latch-key children make their own dinner; 8 percent make the family dinner. We are now seeing changes in the way food is marketed in order to accommodate this trend.

*How does a change in supper traditions affect children?*

As more children eat alone, there is less family influence on children's eating habits. Children now make daily decisions about their diets. They have fewer opportunities to observe their parent's food choices. The outcome of this phenomena will be increased use of convenience foods, as well as food prepared away from home.

Even with these changing trends, children are still depending on parents for nutrition information. According to the Kellogg Children's Nutrition Survey, the schoolchildren surveyed said they depend on their families for nutrition information more than any other source (35 percent), with school second (29 percent), and physicians third (16 percent). These findings imply that educating family members is the key to helping children make healthful food choices.

Teachers can help educate family members through nutrition newsletters. Teachers can remind parents that if they don't want their children eating pop, chips, and high-fat, low-nutrition foods, they shouldn't buy them. Likewise, when children do the shopping, parents should set guidelines for what is purchased and make sure the children follow the guidelines.

*What does suppertime mean to children?*

Supper is more than just a time to eat. The dynamics of the family during meal preparation, meal time, and cleanup are significant in how the child perceives the meal and eating experiences. The environment at the table can have a negative or positive influence on nutrient intake. If eating is to be successful, it must occur in a setting that is pleasant and free from stress and unreasonable parental demands. Although suppertime is out of the hands of the teacher, recognizing a child's perception of suppertime can better help the teacher understand the whole child.

*How can teachers help promote family suppertime?*

Encouraging pleasurable eating at suppertime can be accomplished in many ways. Teachers can encourage children to become involved in meal planning, shopping and preparation. This process will not only start good habits early, but can make suppertime more fun. Children can help in a variety of ways, such as setting the table, tearing lettuce leaves for salad, pouring milk or juice, and eventually, with supervision, preparing or cooking some foods. This involvement can help the family decrease the time it takes for meal planning and preparation. The process can also encourage parents and children to interact with one another.

Suppers need to be viewed as a time to share the day's activities with family members. Teachers can reassure children that it is okay if their family is not the stereotypical family consisting of mother, father, brother, and sister. Their family is made up of any members that we come in contact with in our household. Family may be grandparents, aunts, uncles, step-family members, a foster family, even housemates.

# Activity 21-1. Families

## DIRECTIONS TO THE TEACHER

**Objective** (Affective Domain: Knowledge Level)

Students will identify the person(s) he/she eats with during suppertime.

**Materials**

Student Activity Sheet (1)
Crayons

**Prerequisite Skills**

Coloring

**Procedure**

1. Define suppertime as the time of day when the evening meal is prepared, eaten and cleared away. Suppertime is also called dinnertime by some people. It is usually the main meal of the day.

2. Discuss suppertime with children. Some questions you might ask are:

    •With whom do you eat at suppertime?
    •What do you like to talk about during suppertime?
    •What do you like to have going on around you while eating?

2. Distribute the activity sheet and explain the directions.

**Supplementary Activities**

1. Have each student make a collage of pictures and words that tells something about him- or herself (things he/she likes to eat, do, family, etc.)

2. Have each student write a thank you letter to the person that prepares most of his or her suppers. The letter should include a list of favorite foods.

Name _____ Date _____

## Activity 21-1. Families

**Directions:** Suppertime can be a fun time to share with those you care about. Sharing about your day can help you learn more about one another. Draw a picture of the people you eat supper with.

No matter if your family is big or small,
wide or tall,
your own family is the best of all.

# Activity 21-2. Supper Steps

## DIRECTIONS TO THE TEACHER

**Objective** (Cognitive Domain: Comprehension Level)

Given ten steps for preparing a meal, students will predict the appropriate order of events by sequencing them correctly.

## Materials

Student Activity Sheets (2)
Scissors
Glue
Pencil or markers

## Prerequisite Skills

Sequencing skills
Cutting and pasting

## Procedure

1. Ask your students who in their families help in mealtime preparation. Generate ways children can help. *(Refer to Things to Know About Supper.)*

2. Distribute the activity sheets and explain the directions.

3. Conclude by having the children verbalize the steps they can do by themselves to help their families prepare for dinner.

## Supplementary Activities

1. Plan a meal for the class to celebrate a holiday or special event. Divide the children into groups: those who will plan the meal, those who will prepare, those who will set up the eating area and serve, and those who will clear the area and clean up.

2. Meal planning is a good time to reinforce measuring skills. Ask questions such as: Would you eat a teaspoon or a cup of mashed potatoes? Would you put a teaspoon or a half-cup of margarine on bread?

3. When preparing meals, children can never be reminded enough to wash their hands. Discuss with your students how germs are spread by dirty hands.

Name _____ Date _____

## Activity 21-2.  Supper Steps

**Directions:**

1) Cut out the Steps to Prepare Supper and put them in order.  The steps are followed before, during, and after suppertime.
2) After you finish cutting, follow the directions on the next page.

## Steps to Prepare Supper

| Clear the table | Eat supper |

| Serve the food | Set the table |

| Wash hands | Package leftovers |

| Do the Shopping | Do the dishes |

| Plan a meal | Make the food |

© 1991 by The Center for Applied Research in Education

Name _____  Date _____

## Activity 21-2. Supper Steps, *page 2*

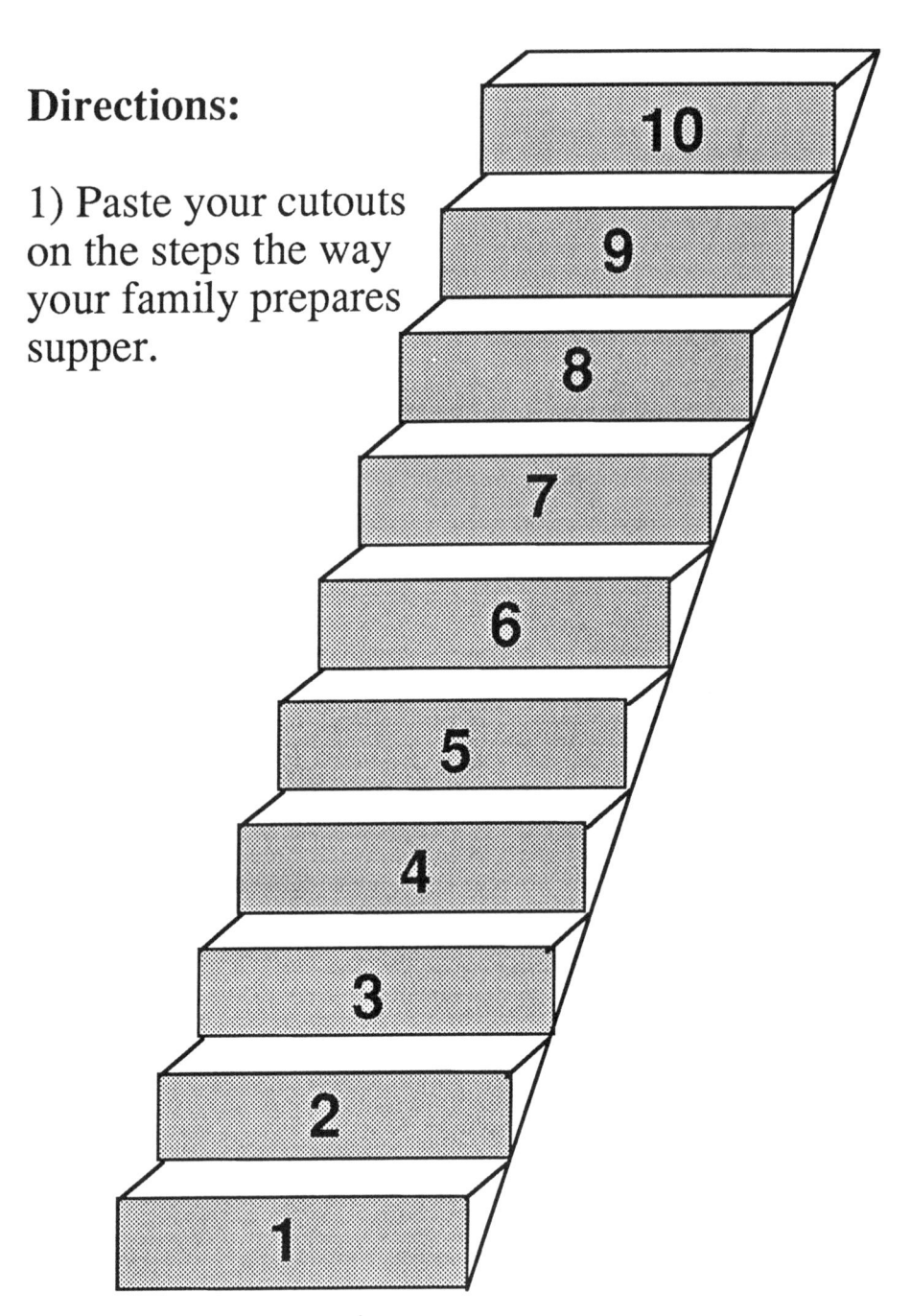

**Directions:**

1) Paste your cutouts on the steps the way your family prepares supper.

2) Mark a check √ next to the steps you can do with help.

3) Put 2 checks √ √ next to the steps you can do by yourself.

# Activity 21-3. Microwaving

## DIRECTIONS TO THE TEACHER

**Objective** (Cognitive Domain: Comprehension Level)

Students will distinguish between appropriate and inappropriate uses of the microwave oven.

**Materials**

Student Activity Sheet (1)
Pencil

**Prerequisite Skills**

Reading   (children who cannot read should not be operating a microwave oven)

**Procedure**

1. You should conduct a needs assessment before doing this activity. About 70% of your students should answer *yes* to the questions for this activity to be relevant. Ask the following questions:

    • Do they push buttons?
    • Do they read the timer?
    • Do they put food in?
    • Do they take food out?

    Inform your students that a recent <u>Good Housekeeping</u> Survey found 65% of children between the ages of 4 and 12 use a microwave oven at home.

2. Ask your students if there are rules for safe microwaving that they follow.

3. Distribute the activity sheet and explain the directions.

**Supplementary Activities**

1. Invite a home economist to your classroom to talk about microwave cooking. Some points she might want to introduce are:

    - Microwave ovens are cool inside, but dishes can get very hot from the heat of the food.
    - Some microwave food packages are designed to heat and crisp food (like pizza, French fries, and popcorn). These may contain heat susceptors that get extremely hot.
    - Steam should be allowed to escape during cooking. Leave a vent when covering food.
    - Always uncover dishes away from the face.
    - Sugar molecules attract microwaves, so fillings such as jelly in doughnuts or fruit in pastries can get scalding hot in just a few seconds. This is true even when the pastry feels cool on the outside.

- Foods do not cook evenly in a microwave oven. Therefore, stirring, rearranging and rotating food helps the cooking process.
- Never cook an egg in its shell. Steam and pressure can build and cause the egg to burst.
- Never heat baby bottles in a microwave.

2. Set up a nook in your classroom with the right equipment for the microwave. Talk with your students about the right and wrong equipment to use in a microwave oven. For example, only paper towels designed for the microwave are safe. Dyes, colors, and tints in regular paper towels are not compatible with food, and some may contain ingredients that are not approved by the FDA for food contact. Paper towels are used for two functions: to keep food dry or moist.

   Strong, high-quality plastic wrap labeled microwave safe won't melt during cooking and can withstand the steam. When food is covered with plastic wrap it is important to vent the wrap to allow air to escape.

   Wax paper can be used to help prevent splattering.

   Do not reuse trays and containers provided with microwave convenience foods. They have been designed for one-time use with that specific food.

   Margarine, yogurt tubs, and reusable containers are often used to store leftovers and warm the food in them. Such containers are not meant to be heated. The heat can make the container too hot to handle, or even melt the plastic and start a fire. Furthermore, they may contain chemicals that can leach into the hot food.

   Metal pans are not safe in the microwave oven.

   Glass containers not designed for the microwave may explode on removal. Show your students where to find the words "microwave safe" on dishes.

   Tell children to never run a microwave oven when it is empty.

   Remind children to always use a hot pad when they remove dishes from the oven.

3. Help your students understand the mystery of microwaving. "Heat-susceptor" packaging is a microwaving concept that could arouse the curiosity in your students. Heat susceptors are thin, gray strips or disks of metallized plastic that absorb microwaves. They act like a drying pan in the oven, becoming very hot in a short amount of time. Bring in some examples for your students to examine. The heat susceptor is the large silver surface on which pizza cooks. In microwave popcorn, you can hold the bag up to the light and see the strip.

4. Discuss the environmental issues surrounding the packaging of microwave foods. Many foods come in boxes with trays and plates, or with bowls with lids that are not recyclable. Discuss with students the idea that special trays, dishes, and bags for microwaving are often marketing gimmicks.

Name _____ Date _____

## Activity 21-3. Microwaving

**Directions:** Read the "Rules for Safe Microwaving."

**Rules for Safe Microwaving**
1. Only use the microwave oven to heat food or drinks.
2. Read the food package directions before cooking.
3. Use a hot pad when taking food out of the oven.
3. Be careful opening heated packages; steam can burn your face and fingers.
4. Stir food before eating. Hot spots can burn your mouth and throat.

Read the sentences below. Is Ben following the rules while using the microwave? Draw a ☺ by the **right** use. Draw a ☹ by the **wrong** use.

1. ____ Ben tries to use the microwave to dry out his wet mittens.
2. ____ Ben reads the package directions before cooking his dinner meal.
3. ____ Ben places the heated package on the counter top and slowly opens the package away from his face.
4. ____ Ben stirs his food before he eats it.
5. ____ Ben gives his 3-year-old brother a package of food to microwave.
6. ____ Ben uses a hot pad to protect his fingers when he removes the food from the oven.

© 1991 by The Center for Applied Research in Education

# Lesson 22. *Snacks*

## Things to Know About Snacks

*Key Points:*

- Snacks help children meet their nutritional needs.

- The most nutrition-smart snacks are foods found in the basic food groups.

- Foods that are categorized into the fat and sweet group should be chosen as only occasional snacks.

- Lean meats, lowfat milks, crackers, bread, fruits, and vegetables are anytime snacks.

*What is a snack?*

A snack is a small amount of food eaten between meals. Snacks traditionally are thought of as something you can hold in your hand, such as an apple or vending machine goodie. But, any food, ranging from celery with peanut butter to a small bowl of cereal, can be a snack. Fruit makes a fabulous snack because it comes in its own package and is a juicy, tasty treat. Too often people reach for chips, cookies, candy bars, crackers, and ice cream before considering other snack options.

*Should we promote snacks?*

Snacks are a part of almost everyone's lifestyle. Just the thought of snacks may trigger ideas of fun and socializing. Children typically enjoy the taste of snack foods and the atmosphere in which they are served. But too often children hear their parents say "Don't eat that snack, it will spoil your dinner." As a result, children are made to feel guilty about snacking. If timed right snacks can be part of a healthy diet. Snacks actually help children meet their nutritional recommendations. Studies show that children who eat snacks have diets that are more adequate in nutrition than those who don't eat snacks. So, we should think of snacks as "small planned meals," not as extra food between meals. There is no reason to feel guilty about eating them if they are planned to complement regular meals, and do not cause the child to exceed caloric needs.

*How should children choose snacks?*

Considering food preferences, children can be taught to choose snacks based on nutrition benefits and how the food complements the total diet. For example, if a child chooses yogurt as a snack, that is a good nutrient choice. But if the child had milk at all three meals and cheese at lunch, but no fruits or vegetables all day, yogurt is not the best snack choice.

Moderation must be applied when choosing snacks high in fat, sugar, and sodium, such as chips, cookies, and candy. If a food is nutrient dense, if offers a high proportion of nutrients in relation to calories per serving. Children who choose nutrient-dense snacks are helping to meet their energy and nutrient needs.

*What are some nutrient-dense snacks?*

A quick look at the snack food ranking chart on the next page supports the idea that foods closer to their natural state are more nutrient dense, and foods that have been processed have more fall into the meat, milk, grain, vegetable and fruit groups are nutrient dense. Foods that fall into the fats and sweets group are low in nutrient density.

When looking for nutrient-dense snacks, don't be misled by the term "natural." A snack that carries the words "natural" on a label is not guaranteed to be low in fat, sugar, or sodium. Marketers use it to get consumers to buy their products. Similarly the term "light" or "lite" is often misleading.

*Are there "bad" snacks?*

Foods, including snack foods, are not "good" or "bad" by themselves. No single food offers all of the essential nutrients in the amounts needed by the body. If a cookie after school is offered with a glass of milk, and if the milk would not be chosen without the accompanying cookie, then the nutritional benefits speak for themselves.

There may, however, be "bad snacking habits." Snacks may be eaten not only out of hunger but also out of boredom or habit. Too often, eating takes place without thinking about what's being eaten, how much, or why. This can lead to overeating or turning to food to cope. Children should learn to be aware of their snacking so that healthier snacking patterns can be carried over into adulthood.

## Snack Food Rankings

### Food Class

Raw vegetables
Fruit or vegetable juice
Cereal
Milk
Fresh fruit
Pumpkin or sunflower seeds
Yogurt, flavored
Cheese
Milkshake
Peanuts
Rolls, bread, bagels
Pudding
Peanut butter
Graham crackers
Ice cream
Dried fruit
Crackers or pretzels
Cookies or cake
Canned fruit
Granola bars
Potato chips
Pies, pastry, doughnuts
Popcorn
Jello
Candy
Soft drinks

**High Nutrient Density** (top)

**Low Nutrient Density** (bottom)

Data from Gillespie, A. 1983. Assessing snacking behavior of children. *Ecology of Food and Nutrition* 13: 167-172.

# Activity 22-1. Choosing Snacks

## DIRECTIONS TO THE TEACHER

**Objective** (Cognitive Domain: Knowledge Level)

Given a list of fifteen snack choices, students will identify nutrition-smart snack food choices.

## Materials

Student Activity Sheet (1)
Pencil

## Prerequisite Skills

Letter finding skills

## Procedure

1. Define a nutrition-smart snack as one that provides nutrients that help you grow. Foods in the meat, milk, vegetable, fruit, and grain group are nutrition smart.

2. Distribute the activity sheet and explain the directions.

3. Wrap up with a discussion of why the five foods that are not in the search are not considered nutrition smart. These foods offer very few nutrients in comparison to the number of calories from fat or simple sugars.

## Supplementary Activities

1. Ask the students to name their favorite snacks. How many of their favorite snacks appear in the list of healthy snacks?

2. Ask the students to name more healthy snack food choices and create their own word search. Have the students exchange word searches.

3. Browse through the snack foods section of a store or look through the choices in a vending machine. Have students identify which food choices are nutrition smart.

Name_____ Date_____

## Activity 22-1. Choosing Snacks

**Directions:** Ten of the fifteen snacks listed are healthy snack choices. Only the healthy choices can be found in the word search below. Answers are found going down, across, and diagonally.

Snacks
Juice
Soda
Milk
Nuts
Apple
Lollipops
Popcorn
Raisins
Potato chips
Yogurt
Pork rinds
Crackers
Sandwich
Marshmallows
Pretzels

| S | E | Y | O | G | U | R | T | A |
|---|---|---|---|---|---|---|---|---|
| A | P | P | L | E | N | S | I | C |
| N | I | R | Q | M | O | J | A | R |
| D | B | A | E | H | P | U | F | A |
| W | H | I | G | T | Z | I | V | C |
| I | D | S | L | E | Z | C | M | K |
| C | R | I | C | S | T | E | I | E |
| H | W | N | U | T | S | X | L | R |
| J | K | S | N | I | Y | M | K | S |
| U | P | O | P | C | O | R | N | O |

Which is your favorite
*NUTRITION SMART*
snack?
_____

# Activity 22-2. Snack Track

## DIRECTIONS TO THE TEACHER

**Objective** (Cognitive Domain: Comprehension Level)

After recording snacking habits for several days, students will summarize habits to identify possible patterns.

## Materials

Student Activity Sheet (1)
Pencil

## Prerequisite Skills

Basic knowledge of time
Reading/writing
Chart reading

## Procedure

1. Discuss patterns with students. Some sample questions are:

    - What are things that you do every day at the same time of day?
    - Do you always have an after-school or bedtime snack?
    - Is the snack always the same?

2. Discuss the usefulness of keeping food records. Some sample questions are:

    - Do any of you keep a diary? If so, why?
    - Keeping food records is something like a diary. Have any of your family or friends kept food records?
    - Food records can help you understand what foods you eat and why. We often eat snacks without giving the foods much thought. Would you like to keep a record of your snacks for several days so that you can learn more about your snacking patterns?

3. Distribute the activity sheet and explain the directions. Review with students how to use the big and small hands properly on the clock.

## Supplementary Activities

1. Discuss the nutrient value of different snack foods. Ask students to bring in the label of their favorite snack food. What nutrients are present, which ones are lacking? If this was the only snack you ever ate how would you get a variety of nutrients?

2. Ask students to draw a floor plan of their home, labeling the rooms. Instruct them to write the word "FOOD" in each room food is stored in their home. Then write "SNACK" in all the rooms where they have a snack. Discuss snacking behaviors with the students. The emphasis of this lesson is on awareness. Avoid passing judgment on students' behavior. Instead, lead the students to draw their own conclusions.

Name _____ Date _____

## Activity 22-2. Snack Track

**Directions:** Using the chart below, keep track of your snacking habits for three days. Follow the example on the first line of the chart.

| Day I snacked | What I ate | Time I snacked | Who I snacked with | How I felt | What I was doing |
|---|---|---|---|---|---|
| example Wednesday | graham crackers and peanut butter | (clock showing ~8:00) | me (sister) Dad friend brother Mom babysitter other | (happy) sad (hungry) bored excited | Doing homework. |
|  |  | (clock) | me sister Dad friend brother Mom babysitter other | happy sad hungry bored excited |  |
|  |  | (clock) | me sister Dad friend brother Mom babysitter other | happy sad hungry bored excited |  |
|  |  | (clock) | me sister Dad friend brother Mom babysitter other | happy sad hungry bored excited |  |

My favorite snack is _____. When I snack, I like to _____.

© 1991 by The Center for Applied Research in Education

# Activity 22-3. Popcorn Percents

## DIRECTIONS TO THE TEACHER

**Objective** (Cognitive Domain: Comprehension Level)

Students will distinguish between three different snacks by answering questions utilizing information provided in a pie graph.

## Materials

Student Activity Sheet (1)
Pencil

## Prerequisite Skills

Reading a pie graph

## Procedure

1. Remind students that popcorn in its natural state is a great low-calorie, high-fiber snack. But as oil, butter, or margarine and salt are added, the nutritional quality of popcorn changes.

2. Discuss with students the increasing popularity of microwave popcorn as a snack food. Ask students for some reasons they think microwave popcorn is so popular. Some answers may be: it's easy, fast, needs no appliances other than the microwave, nothing to wash afterwards, parents let children make it "by themselves."

3. Discuss with the students that along with the convenience may come some nutritional disadvantages, such as more fat, sodium, artificial colors, and artificial flavors.

4. Discuss reading a pie graph.

5. Distribute the activity sheet and explain the directions.

6. Conclude that the popcorn that remains fat free and sodium free is hot-air popped. Unfortunately, some children may find it lacking in flavor. Therefore, if microwave popcorn is the popcorn of choice, children should learn to read labels and be aware of comparing brands for the best choice.

## Supplementary Activities

1. Bring to class the labels from ready-to-eat popcorn and microwave popcorn. Compare the information on the label, such as: 1) the serving size (make sure when making comparisons that they are not comparing a 4 cup serving to a 3 cup serving), 2) calories per serving, 3) grams of fat per serving, and 4) milligrams of sodium.

2. Discuss with children variations in food products. One brand of popcorn may have bigger kernels than another brand. This means a cup of one brand of popcorn may contain fewer actual pieces. Bring in several brands of popcorn and have the students make comparisons by measuring the popped corn into cup containers.

3. Have a popcorn party. Serve hot-air, ready-made, and microwave popcorn. Can the students taste a difference? Ask for their comments. Try some of these toppings to enhance the flavor of hot-air popcorn: parmesan cheese or chili powder, or try:

   <u>Cajun Corn</u>: for 2 1/2 quarts popped corn

         1 tablespoon melted margarine
         1 teaspoon paprika
         1/2 teaspoon onion powder
         1/2 teaspoon garlic powder
         1/4 teaspoon cayenne pepper
         1 teaspoon lemon pepper

   (you need the margarine to help the herbs stick to the popcorn)

4. Conduct a blind taste test. Students can "taste" for fat, flavor, or salt. Provide at least three types of popcorn (for example hot-air, stove-top popped in oil, ready-made, or microwaved.) Have the students rank them on flavor. Be sure to serve water to drink in between bites.

5. The best way for students to recognize fat in popcorn is to observe the stain it leaves on a paper towel. After the students have tried ranking the popcorn according to flavor, ask them to observe the grease spots left on the paper towel. Now ask the students to rank them by grease stains from none to highest by each kind of popcorn. Explain that fat is a nutrient that adds flavor to foods. Many processed foods add fat. The grease spots they see are actually fat that was absorbed by the paper. The children may also find grease (or fat) on their fingers.

6. Think about other foods that are generally thought to be nutritious. The way these foods are prepared or served can alter the nutritional value. Compare foods such as raisins to chocolate covered raisins, and plain yogurt to a yogurt sundae. Ask your students to generate similar examples.

Name _____ Date _____

## Activity 22-3. Popcorn Percents

Directions: Use the pie graphs to answer the following questions.

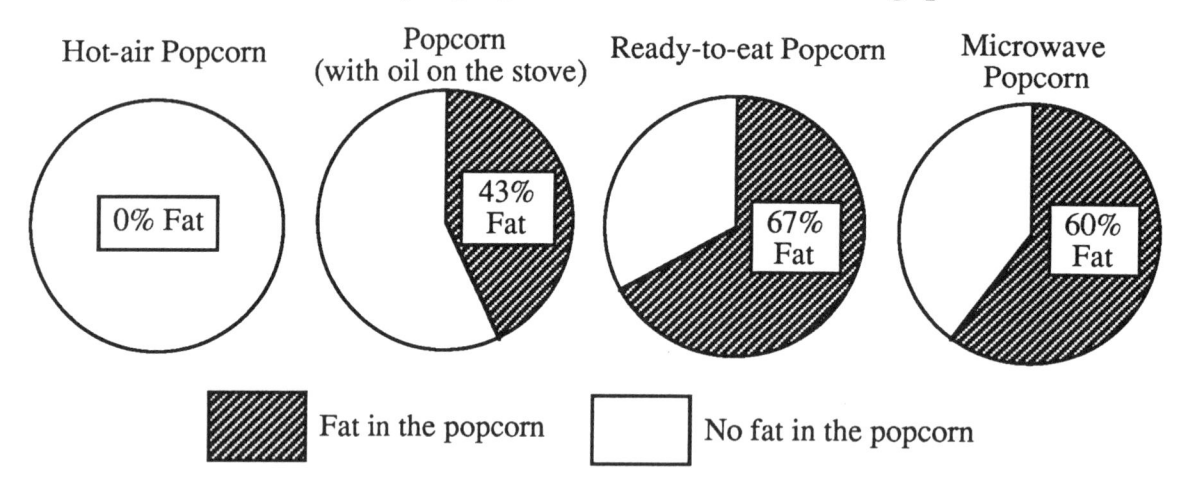

Hot-air Popcorn — 0% Fat

Popcorn (with oil on the stove) — 43% Fat

Ready-to-eat Popcorn — 67% Fat

Microwave Popcorn — 60% Fat

▨ Fat in the popcorn  ☐ No fat in the popcorn

1. Which popcorn has the least amount of fat? _____

2. Which popcorn has the greatest amount of fat? _____

3. Which has more fat, stove-popped or hot air-popcorn? _____

4. Why do you think hot-air popcorn has no fat but stove-popped popcorn has fat? _____

5. What kind of popcorn do you make at home?

_____

**Depending on how it is popped, popcorn can be a nutrition smart snack.**

© 1991 by The Center for Applied Research in Education

# Lesson 23. *Convenience Foods and Vending Machines*

## Things to Know About Convenience Foods and Vending Machines

*Key Points:*
- Some nutrition-smart foods can be found in convenience stores and in vending machines.

*Are convenience foods part of our children's lives?*

Convenience plays a dominant role in the lifestyles of children. As more mothers work, there are more latchkey children. The millions of latchkey children between the ages of 6 and 11 not only influence the way families eat and the way food is marketed -- many of these children make their own dinner and some even make the family dinner. As a result, food is being marketed to children, with packaging designed especially for children, such as smaller containers and shatterproof materials. Convenience foods are even labeled especially for children by stating the intended age of the consumer, such as 3 to 10, 2 to 8, or 4 to 10.

Convenience stores are also becoming a common alternative to the grocery store. Families are more often stopping at convenience stores to make quick food purchases rather than waiting in line at the supermarkets. During these stops, parents may give children the opportunity to purchase snacks. The convenience store has also become an after-school hangout in which children spend their own money on food without the guidance of an adult.

Vending machines are popping up everywhere, even in some schools. Some vending machines may offer only candy and soda, but some provide pizza, French fries or popcorn with a microwave oven for speedy preparation. In any case there are always foods available that catch the eye of children.

*Is "convenience" synonymous with "bad"?*

No. Although many convenience foods are high in fat and sodium, many are not. The major issue is the frequency at which convenience foods are being eaten. When discussing convenience foods with your students, try to avoid the words "good" and "bad." A more appealing way to discuss these choices might be <u>anytime</u> foods or <u>sometime</u> foods. Examples of anytime foods might be an apple or orange juice. Examples of sometime foods might be potato chips, cola, or a candy bar. This way children will not think of any food as bad, but will recognize that all choices should be made wisely.

The foods offered in vending machines often reflect the consumption trends of our society. Today many vending items have reformulated products with a reduced fat content and the elimination of cholesterol or cholesterol-raising tropical oils (coconut and palm oil.) Sometimes, turkey and vegetable sandwiches and pasta salads with low-calorie dressing can be obtained in a vending machine. Some vendors have even gone so far as to provide nutrition fact sheets at the machine. Experiments in schools have shown that children choose more nutritious snacks if they are offered side by side with sugary foods. For example, if apples are made available in vending machines, children choose candy less often. When milk is made available, soft drink sales drop.

*How can teachers help children make wise choices?*

Teachers can help children learn to choose convenience foods wisely. The variety of snack foods available at convenience stores and vending machines is often limited. The key is learning to choose the most nutrients for the dollar. Convenience stores and vending machines may be one of the first places children learn to spend their own money on food. Because everyone wants a bargain, why not teach children to shop for the most nutrients for the dollar? Children should recognize they are spending money to purchase foods to make their body strong in order to be the best they can be.

Children are not born with the ability to choose a nutritious diet. Their food habits, like those of adults, are learned through experience. One part teachers can play in this whole process is to provide experiences of choice in the classroom. Opportunities to compare labels and taste a new lowfat or low-sodium food can be provided in school. Children can also learn from field trips to supermarkets, convenience stores, and fast food places where they can actually discuss food choices together. A teacher's influence can help moderate children's intake of less nutritious foods while teaching them about foods that will help them grow and be strong.

*What if a child chooses "sometime" choices all the time?*

When suggesting a change in habits, children (and adults) can't make too many changes at once. It is advisable to focus on one change at a time. For example, often children pick potato chips and a cola beverage when at a convenience store or vending machine. The cola beverage has no nutrients, only calories. Instead of criticizing or even mentioning the potato chips, it makes sense to concentrate on the one change that would make the most nutritional difference first. Suggest that the children replace the cola beverage with a more nutrient dense carton of milk or fruit juice. Giving students alternatives or having them help you list alternatives can be beneficial. Many children may not yet be aware of the fruit juice and single serving of milk available in convenience stores and vending machines. Bringing this to their attention may be all the encouragement they need.

# Activity 23-1.  Fat Pats

## DIRECTIONS TO THE TEACHER

**Objective** (Cognitive Domain: Comprehension Level)

Students will convert the grams of fat in convenience foods to pats of butter.

## Materials

Student Activity Sheets (4) (two sets to choose from depending on the appropriateness for your class)
Yellow crayon or marker

## Prerequisite Skills

Activity 23-1A: Graphing skills
Activity 23-1B: Constructing a bar graph
Division by four

## Procedure

1. Discuss why it is important to know how much fat is in the foods we eat. Discuss the link between fat and heart disease.

2. Discuss how we can't see fat in food, but we can see butter or margarine, and they are mostly fat (and water).

3. Choose the appropriate worksheet depending on the level of your class. One worksheet requires the student be capable of dividing by 4; the other doesn't.

4. Distribute the activity sheets and explain the directions.

## Supplementary Activities

1. Fat display kits are available from the PENN STATE NUTRITION CENTER, 417 E. Calder Way, Penn State University, University Park, PA 16801-5663. Telephone: 814-865-6323. The display can be used in a learning center or as a bulletin board. Call or write for ordering information.

2. Bring some snack food and convenience food labels into class. Ask the students to look for the grams of fat, and convert the grams to pats of butter.

Name _____ Date _____

## Activity 23-1A. Fat Pats

**Directions:**

Below is a list of foods and the grams of fat in each food.

Use this list to fill in the bar graph on page 2.

| | |
|---|---|
| Fish sandwich | 20 grams |
| 6 chicken nuggets | 16 grams |
| Chocolate chip cookie | 16 grams |
| Apple pie | 12 grams |
| French fries | 12 grams |
| Hot fudge sundae | 12 grams |
| Plain hamburger | 12 grams |
| Whole milk | 8 grams |
| Skim milk | 0 grams |

© 1991 by The Center for Applied Research in Education

Name _____ Date _____

## Activity 23-1A. Fat Pats, *page 2*

**Directions:** Using a yellow crayon, color each column to show the number of grams of fat in that food. Answer the questions.

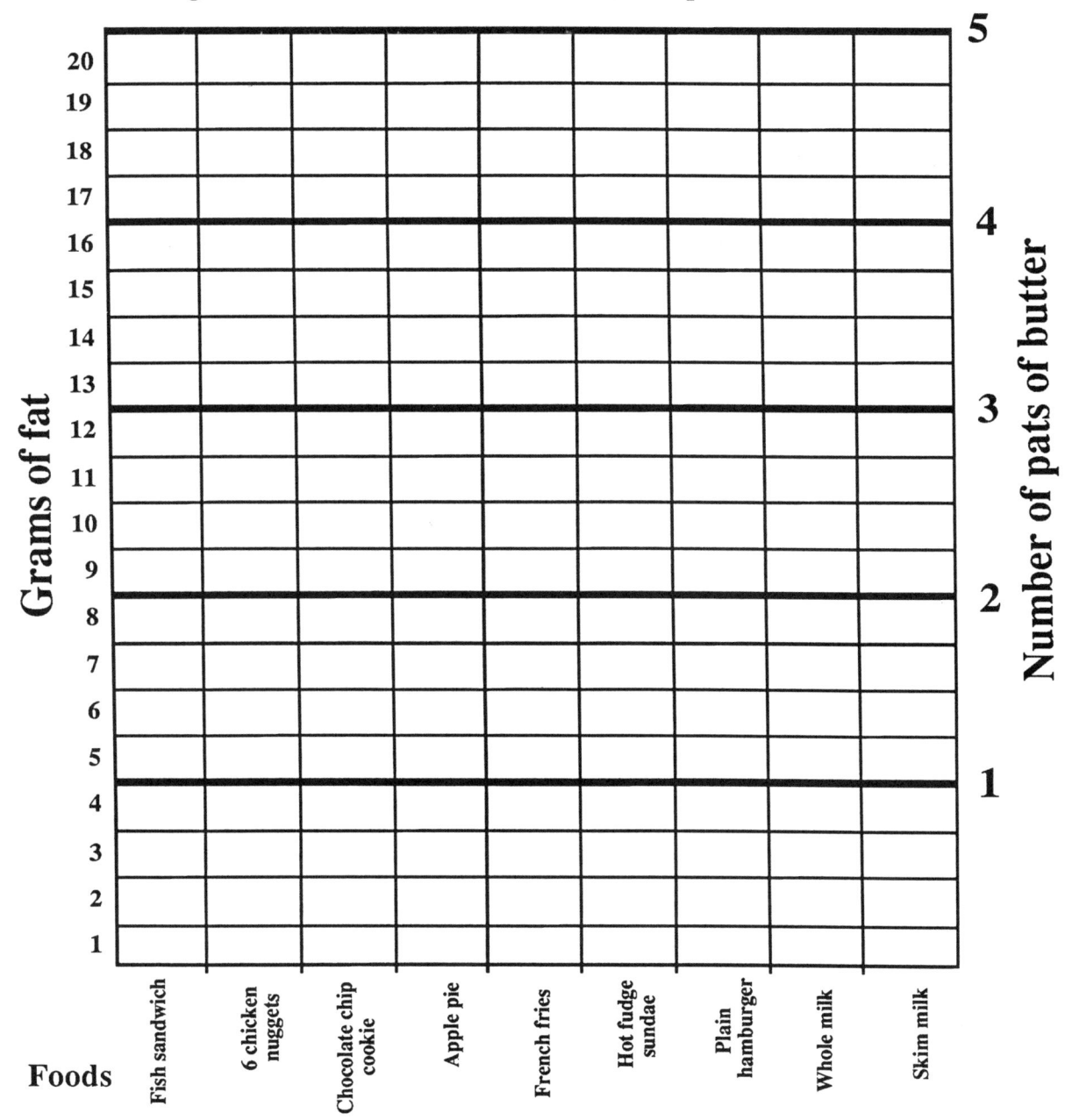

**Grams of fat** (y-axis: 1–20)

**Number of pats of butter** (right y-axis: 1–5, with 4 grams = 1 pat)

**Foods** (x-axis): Fish sandwich, 6 chicken nuggets, Chocolate chip cookie, Apple pie, French fries, Hot fudge sundae, Plain hamburger, Whole milk, Skim milk

1) As your graph shows, four grams of fat equals 1 pat of butter. Which food has the amount of fat found in 5 pats of butter? _____

2) Which food has no fat? _____

Name _____ Date _____

## Activity 23-1B.  Fat Pats

Fat is in many foods, but we don't always see the fat. Grams are the unit used to measure fat in foods. Below is a list of foods and the grams of fat. In order to help you "see" the fat, you can change grams of fat to pats of butter, all you need to do is divide by 4.

**Directions:** Divide the grams of fat by 4 to find how many pats of butter are in each food.

Ex:      20  grams  ÷  4  =  5  pats of butter

| | | |
|---|---|---|
| Whole milk | 8 grams ÷ 4 | = __2__ pats of butter |
| Skim milk | 0 grams ÷ 4 | = _____ pats of butter |
| Fast food big burger | 36 grams ÷ 4 | = _____ pats of butter |
| 6 chicken nuggets | 16 grams ÷ 4 | = _____ pats of butter |
| 1 slice cheese pizza | 4 grams ÷ 4 | = _____ pats of butter |
| Baked potato/cheese | 32 grams ÷ 4 | = _____ pats of butter |
| Plain hamburger | 12 grams ÷ 4 | = _____ pats of butter |
| French fries | 12 grams ÷ 4 | = _____ pats of butter |
| Chocolate chip cookie | 16 grams ÷ 4 | = _____ pats of butter |
| Apple pie | 12 grams ÷ 4 | = _____ pats of butter |
| Hot fudge sundae | 12 grams ÷ 4 | = _____ pats of butter |

Now go to page 2 and follow the directions.

© 1991 by The Center for Applied Research in Education

Name _____ Date _____

## Activity 23-1B. Fat Pats, *page 2*

**Directions:** Using the information from page 1, color the bar graph to show the number of fat pats in convenience foods. Use a yellow crayon to color in your graph. Answer the questions below.

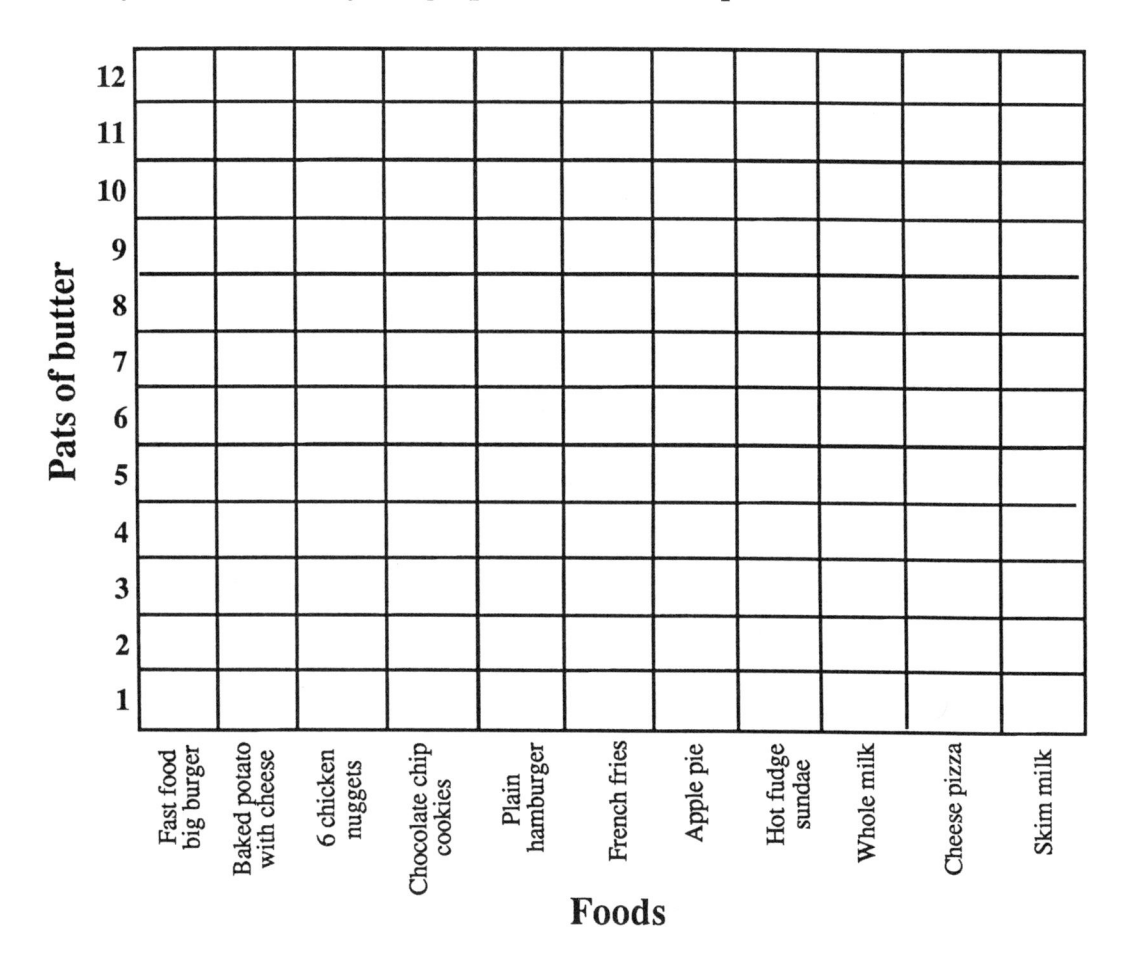

**Pats of butter**

12
11
10
9
8
7
6
5
4
3
2
1

Fast food big burger | Baked potato with cheese | 6 chicken nuggets | Chocolate chip cookies | Plain hamburger | French fries | Apple pie | Hot fudge sundae | Whole milk | Cheese pizza | Skim milk

**Foods**

1) Which food has the most fat pats? _____

2) What is the difference between whole milk and skim milk in grams of fat? _____ (Hint: ____ - ____ = ____)

3) If you ate a plain hamburger, French fries, and a hot fudge sundae, how many grams of fat would you eat? _____
(Multiply the pats of butter by 4)

© 1991 by The Center for Applied Research in Education

# Activity 23-2. Shopping

## DIRECTIONS TO THE TEACHER

**Objective** (Cognitive Domain: Analysis Level)

Students will identify nutrition-smart snacks in a list of convenience foods.

## Materials

Student Activity Sheet (1)
Pencil

## Prerequisite Skills

Addition/Subtraction facts
2-digit plus or minus a 1-digit number -- no regrouping

## Procedure

1. Ask students to name places in the community that have vending machines. Discuss what people are usually doing in those places. Vending machines are provided for convenience for people to have snacks while working, playing, traveling, and so on. They usually are not intended for providing a complete meal. Discuss why it is important for people who frequently shop at vending machines to stop and think about the nutritional quality of the food choices offered.

2. Distribute the activity sheet and explain the directions.

3. Follow-up discussion could include questions such as

    • What are the three nutrition-smart choices? (pretzels, juice, milk)
    • Why are pretzels nutrition smart? (They are made from bread with no fat.)
    • Why is juice nutrition smart? (It is made from fruit and provides vitamin C.)
    • Why is milk nutrition smart? (It provides protein, calcium, and other vitamins and minerals the body needs to grow.)

## Supplementary Activities

1. Discuss with your students the environmental issues that surround vending foods. Proper disposal of waste materials is just one issue, packaging is another. You might start the discussion by asking your students what types of waste they often see in city parks or streets. Many times it is soda cans, bottles, or bags and containers from convenience food items. Discuss the environmental impact, what they can do as consumers, and what issues must be taken care of by industry and the government. You may want to mention that several food companies are sponsoring programs aimed at controlling packaging waste. Del Monte Foods based in San Francisco, Pepperidge Farms in Norwalk, Connecticut, Quaker Oats in Chicago, Illinois, and McDonalds in Oakbrook, Illinois, are just four of the major food companies. Have your students write for consumer information.

2. Follow the same procedures, as discussed above, with fast food restaurants.

Name _____ Date _____

## Activity 23-2. Shopping

**Directions:** Find the snacks you can choose from a vending machine. Add or subtract the numbers below each line. Then go to the vending machine to find the matching letter. Be sure to answer question 7.

**Vending Machine**

| 1 j | 2 u | 3 g | 4 a | 5 p | 6 r |
| 7 m | 8 i | 9 l | 10 k | 11 e | 12 z |
| 13 o | 14 c | 15 h | 16 i | 17 t | 18 s |

Here's one done for you.

a   p   p   l   e
(2+2) (10-5) (2+3) (11-2) (5+6)

1. ___  ___  ___  ___  ___  ___  ___  ___
   (1+4) (10-4) (5+6) (15+2) (6+6) (7+4) (5+4) (17+1)

2. ___  ___  ___  ___  ___
   (11-10) (0+2) (3+5) (12+2) (15-4)

3. ___  ___  ___  ___
   (4+3) (15-7) (2+7) (16-6)

4. ___  ___  ___
   (8-5) (0+2) (13-6)

5. ___  ___  ___  ___  ___
   (8+6) (8+7) (9+7) (5+0) (9+9)

6. ___  ___  ___  ___  ___  ___
   (7+7) (12+1) (6+7) (5+5) (6+2) (9+2)

7. Three of the six vending machine choices are nutrition smart. (Circle) them.

# Activity 23-3. Snack Cents

## DIRECTIONS TO THE TEACHER

**Objective** (Cognitive Domain: Application Level)

Given a price list, students will use this information to answer a variety of questions that focus on nutritional aspects of snacks.

## Materials

Student Activity Sheets (2)
Pencil

## Prerequisite Skills

Basic knowledge of monetary concepts
Reading/writing
Understanding of less than and greater than

## Procedure

1. Begin with a discussion of convenience foods. Some questions are:

    • Do you stop at a convenience store for snacks?
    • Do you think about the foods in convenience stores in terms of food groups?
    • Visualize the layout of the store. Where are foods in the food groups found?

2. Distribute the activity sheets and explain the directions.

## Supplemental Activities

1. Using page 1 of this activity, ask the students to add the costs for foods in each food group. Convert cents to dollars and cents.

2. Set up a convenience food corner in your classroom. Provide students with the nutrition information on the products, and ask them to select the snacks that provide the most nutrients for the dollar. Place six boxes or bags in the convenience food corner. Label them meat, milk, fruit, vegetable, grains, fats, and sweets. Ask the students to categorize the snack foods into the appropriate box or bag. Somewhere in the corner write out the message: "Nutrition smart snacks are lean meats, lowfat milks, fruits, vegetables, or grains."

Name_____Date_____

# Activity 23-3. Snack Cents

**Directions:** Below is a list of snacks you can buy at the convenience stores and their prices. The snacks appear again in their food groups. Place the price next to the snack foods. The first box has been done for you. Answer the questions on the next page.

## Snack Prices

| Candy bar.....45¢ | Pretzels.........69¢ | Chips......69¢ |
|---|---|---|
| Milk.........70¢ | Yogurt..........89¢ | Apple......35¢ |
| Pie..........65¢ | Raisins..........50¢ | Peanuts....49¢ |
| Fruit juice.....79¢ | Soda...........69¢ | Brownie...65¢ |
| String cheese..69¢ | Cupcakes........65¢ | Cookie.....59¢ |
| Doughnut.....49¢ | Animal crackers...79¢ | Beef jerky..99¢ |

## 4 Food Groups

**Fruits & Vegetables**

Apple    **35¢**    _____
Raisins  **50¢**    _____
Fruit juice  **79¢**  _____

**Milk & Milk Products**

Milk          _____
String cheese _____
Yogurt        _____

## Other Group

**Fats & Sweets**

Candy bar  _____
Chips      _____
Pie        _____
Soda       _____
Brownie    _____
Cupcakes   _____
Cookie     _____
Doughnut   _____
Beef jerky _____

**Meats**

Peanuts   _____

**Breads & Cereals**

Pretzels  _____
Animal crackers  _____

© 1991 by The Center for Applied Research in Education

Name_____Date_____

# Activity 23-3. Snack Cents, *page 2*

When answering the questions below remember this general rule:
**Choosing snacks from the major food groups helps you make nutrition-smart snack choices. The snacks found in these groups are usually packed with more nutrients, which makes them the nutrition-smart way to shop.**

Questions

1) If you were thirsty and had 75¢ to spend, which drink would be the

   nutrition-smart choice? _____

2) Give one reason why you think an apple is 35¢ while a slice of apple pie cost 65¢. _____

   _____

3) There are three foods you can you buy in the milk group. List them from least expensive to most expensive:

   least  _____

   _____

   most  _____

4) Animal crackers and cookies are both enjoyable snacks.

   Which one is more nutrition smart? _____

   Why? _____

5) There are four things you could buy with 50¢. List them.
   Put a check √ next to the items you might choose. If they are nutrition-smart choices, add an extra check √√.

   _____     _____

   _____     _____

# Lesson 24. *Advertising*

## Things to Know About Advertising

*Key Points:*

- Not all nutrition-smart foods are advertised.

- Advertisers use tactics geared toward children to lure them into buying a food product. Children need to recognize these tactics.

- Foods which are advertised are often those that are processed and contain high amounts of salt, fat, and sugar.

*How are children affected by advertising?*

Children can get hooked on a food before even tasting it. How? Through advertising. From the commercials they see on television to the advertisements on billboards and in magazines, advertisements are everywhere! The affect of these advertisements is sometimes not realized until a child begins begging for the newest cereal just seen on television.

According to research conducted at Cornell University's Human Development and Television Research Lab, it is not until children are eight years old or so that they begin to realize that the intent of advertising is to get them to do something.

Foods that get advertised are often those that are processed and contain increased amounts of salt, fat, and sugar. The purpose of an advertisement is to get people to buy the food. Because foods are advertised on television or other media does not mean they are nutrient dense. There are many delicious and nutritious foods that are not often advertised; these include strawberries, cabbage, kidney beans, and barley.

Children are also affected by peer pressure. Advertisers have clever ways of playing on a child's need to be accepted by his peers. Many children choose products because "everyone is getting it" or "it's the cool cereal to choose."

All these clever advertisements help influence childrens' ideas of what they want to eat. If children gain guidance from teachers and parents, they can learn to be aware of how advertisements influence their food choices.

*How can children understand the effect of advertising?*

Children must learn how to identify the tactics that advertisers use to influence children's purchasing habits. These tactics may be emotional appeal, attention getters, or sales pitches with promises and incomplete truths. A teacher can help by pointing out these strategies. This will help children make choices that are based on sound information, not just sales pitches and empty promises. An excellent resource to help children make informed choices is *Penny Power* magazine, a Consumer Reports publication for young people.

Often, prizes in food packages are included to persuade children to buy the food product. However, children need to realize that prizes do not make the food better for their bodies.

*Some facts about television and advertising:*

- The average American child watches almost 28 hours of television a week. In a year he or she will see between 30,000 and 40,000 commercials. More than half the commercials are for foods, and most of the foods are highly sugared cereals and snacks.

- By the time the average American child has reached the teen years, he or she has spent more time watching television than being in school.

- For each hour of television watched, the likelihood of a child becoming obese is increased by 2% per year (Pediatrics, Volume 75, Number 5, May, 1985).

- Children aged 7 to 11 spend about $5 billion a year and influence an additional $50 billion in family spending (Consumers Union Report).

- An analysis of television advertising in 1977 indicated that only 25% of food advertising time was devoted to food in the Basic Four Food Groups; another study found 64% of food commercials directed at children were for sugared foods. Think what those figures must be like today!

# Activity 24-1. Commercials

## DIRECTIONS TO THE TEACHER

### Objective (Cognitive Domain: Analysis Level)

Given a list of television commercials, students will separate advertised foods into the appropriate food group.

### Materials

Student Activity Sheet (1)
Pencil

### Prerequisite Skills

Reading
Food group knowledge

### Procedure

1. Introduce commercials. Commercials can be divided into two categories. One type of commercial attempts to sell a product or service. Another type is a public service message. Define these types and have students generate examples of each.

2. Discuss with your students the number of commercials aired on Saturday morning.

3. Have students guess at the intended audience. Remind the students that these are developed for children.

4. Distribute the activity sheet and explain the directions.

### Supplementary Activities

1. Tape Saturday morning television. Plan to watch a half hour or fifteen minutes of the tape. Ask your students to raise their hands when a commercial begins and the cartoon ends. After each commercial, stop the tape. Discuss with your students the difference between the cartoon and the ad. Point out that the intent of advertising is to get you to buy. Ask the students what catches their attention. What makes them want to buy the product? If it is a food product, what food group does the product go into?

    Conclude that not all foods needed to help them grow are advertised. Although advertised food has a place in the diet, there are many other tasty foods to choose from.

2. Ask children to watch television on Saturday or after school (a time geared towards children) and to keep a record of the number of food commercials. Ask them to place the advertised foods into food groups. What foods are advertised most often?

Name _____ Date _____

## Activity 24-1. Commercials

Ben watched TV for a half hour on Saturday morning. Here is a list of the commercials he watched.

**Happy Morning Cereal**
**Milk for My Body**
**Freddie's Fast Food**
**Star Toys**
**Crunchy, Munchy Cereal**
**Brite Tooth Toothpaste**

**Gooey, Chewy Cookies**
**Drug-free Schools**
**Ready, Set, Go Cereal**
**Jumping Jack Tennis Shoes**
**Gummy, fresh Raisins**
**Kool-Man Drinks**

**Directions:** In the above list, (circle) all the foods that were advertised. Write those foods under the matching food group.

| Fruit | Vegetable | Meat |
|---|---|---|
|  |  |  |
| Milk | Bread | Fats and Sweets |
|  |  |  |

1) Which food group was advertised most?

   _____

2) If you bought only foods advertised, would you get all the food needed to grow and be healthy?
   YES     or     NO

© 1991 by The Center for Applied Research in Education

# Activity 24-2. Slogan Power

## DIRECTIONS TO THE TEACHER

**Objective** (Cognitive Domain: Synthesis Level)

Students will generate a slogan for a given food. Each slogan must be written utilizing a specified tactic.

## Materials

Student Activity Sheet (2)
Pencil

## Prerequisite Skills

Reading
Writing

## Procedure

1. Ask your students to name foods commonly advertised.

2. Ask them to name some foods not advertised.

3. Discuss the concept that advertisers pay for commercial spots or ad layouts in magazines. Some food producers can afford advertising; some can't.

4. Distribute the activity sheets and explain the directions.

5. Explain that this activity sheet offers advertising slogans for foods not commonly advertised.

6. Discuss how the slogans are used to sell the food. Advertisers may use an emotional appeal, a famous person, testimonials, or a bandwagon approach to help sell a food. Possible questions for discussion:

    • What are the tactics used to get consumers to buy the product?
    • What do advertisers want their customer to know about the food being advertised?
    • Do students think that advertising a food would encourage more people to buy it?

## Supplementary Activities

1. In small groups have your students plan and conduct an advertising campaign to promote a food not commonly advertised. Each group will select one food to be promoted. Make sure the food is a nutrition-smart food that falls into one of the basic food groups. Encourage your students to be creative, designing posters, pamphlets, buttons, or coupons to promote the food.

2. Allow your students to apply the advertising tactics used in food commercials to a food that is not commonly advertised. Divide the class into groups. Ask each group to select a food and write a commercial for the product they selected in using some tactics such as promises, movie stars or athletes, catchy songs, dancing, and so on. Ask the groups to plan props and costumes to use in the commercial. Have the groups perform the commercials for the class. You may select a group or two to perform the commercials in the cafeteria during lunch.

3. Ask your students to bring in advertisements from magazines. Categorize the ads based on the advertisers' selling techniques.

4. Show the film, "Seeing Through Commercials," Barr Films, PO Box 7878, Irwindale, CA 91106-7878. 1977. $340.00. Phone 818-338-7878. This film can be borrowed from the Food, Nutrition and Information Center (FNIC), National Agriculture Library, Rm. 304, Beltsville, MD 20705, (301) 344-3719.

Name _____ Date _____

# Activity 24-2. Slogan Power

Below is 1) a food not usually advertised, 2) an advertising tactic, and 3) a slogan using the tactic. The tactic in the slogan is underlined.

**Directions:** Using the underlined tactic, write your own slogan under each picture.

1) **Animal Crackers**

2) **Advertising Tactic Used:**

   Bandwagon--
   Everybody's Doing It

3) **Our slogan:** Big or small, short or tall, everyone loves animal crackers.

4) **Your slogan:** _____

---

1) **Kidney Beans**

2) **Advertising Tactic Used:**

   Emotional appeal for good health

3) **Our slogan:** Kidney beans help the heart.

4) **Your slogan:** _____

---

1) **Cornbread**

2) **Advertising Tactic Used:**

   Famous person

3) **Our slogan:** Rocky Star eats cornbread.

4) **Your slogan:** _____

Name _____  Date _____

## Activity 24-2. Slogan Power, *page 2*

1) **Lowfat Cottage Cheese**

2) **Advertising Tactic Used:**

   Famous sports hero

3) **Our slogan:** Lowfat cottage cheese helps Mac Runner win every time.

4) **Your slogan:** _____

===

1) **Blueberries**

2) **Advertising Tactic Used:**

   Testimonial

3) **Our slogan:** Blueberries make me a blue ribbon winner.

4) **Your slogan:** _____

===

1) **Lettuce**

2) **Advertising Tactic Used:**

   Emotional appeal for good health.

3) **Our slogan:** Salads -- fresh and healthy.

4) **Your slogan:** _____

# Activity 24-3. Ads, Ads, Ads

## DIRECTIONS TO THE TEACHER

**Objective** (Knowledge Domain: Analysis Level)

Given a food advertisement and descriptions of advertising techniques, students will identify the technique employed in the ad.

## Materials

Student Activity Sheets (2)
Crayons or markers
Pencil

## Prerequisite Skills

Reading/writing
Coloring

## Procedure

1. Select a food product advertisement aimed at children in a well-known magazine.

2. Open a discussion about the advertisement. Some questions are:

   • What in this ad gets your attention?
   • How does the ad make you feel?
   • Would you try this product?

3. Explain that advertisers use certain tactics in order to sell a product. *(Refer to Things to Know About Advertising.)* Discuss what tactic was used in the advertisement you selected.

4. Distribute the activity sheet and explain the directions.

## Supplementary Activities

1. Set up a learning station with food advertisements from magazines. On the back of each advertisement place a label that designates the tactic used. Instructions will direct the child to look at the ad and decide what tactic is used. Then place the ad in a box or an envelope labeled Testimonial, Bandwagon, Famous Person, or Emotional Appeal for Health. Have the child check his or her answer by looking at the back side of the ad. It may be helpful to have a sample ad on the outside of each box or bag to guide your students as they categorize the ads.

2. Conduct a survey of food advertisements. Ask students to go through a magazine, counting the food ads and categorizing each ad by food groups. Ask the student to graph the results. Picture graphs may be a fun way to display the results. Draw a conclusion about food advertising and nutrition-smart foods based on what food groups are advertised most.

Name _____ Date _____

## Activity 24-3. Ads, Ads, Ads

### Directions:

1) Look at the advertisement on the next page.

2) How does the advertisement make you feel?
   a. thirsty
   b. sad
   c. happy

3) Think about how the ad gets your attention. Is it the words, the girl, or the cool drink? Which of these got your attention?

   _____

   _____

4) Think about the message used to make you want to buy the drink. Which of the following was used? Circle your answer.
   a. testimonial -- ordinary person explains how the product helped him
   b. bandwagon -- everyone's doing it; you should too
   c. famous person -- star sells the product
   d. emotional appeal for health -- it's good for you

5) Would you buy this drink?   yes _____   no _____

6) Color the ad so that it would get your attention.

Name _____ Date _____

# Activity 24-3. Ads, Ads, Ads, *page 2*

**NEW!**

**Light Natural Flavor**

*Enriched with Vitamin C*

LEMONADE

"So rich in Vitamin C it makes you smile both inside and out."

© 1991 by The Center for Applied Research in Education

# Lesson 25. *Cultural Foods*

## Things to Know About Cultural Foods

*Key Points:*

- All cultures have basic food groups.

- Studying cultural foods can help children accept new foods and cultural diversity.

- People throughout the world have the same nutritional requirements, but they meet those needs through different combinations of foods.

*What are some similarities and differences among diverse cultures?*

People all over the world need nutrients that are found in foods from the milk, meat, grain, fruit, and vegetable groups. But not all cultures use foods from all the food groups. For example, a culture may not consume milk or milk products but choose alternate foods as sources of calcium. The foods may differ in how they are prepared, what ingredients are added, and the way the foods are served. Families in different cultures have different traditions surrounding food and mealtimes. Religious beliefs may also influence food choices.

*How do teachers address cultural differences?*

The "melting pot" theory has traditionally been the way of discussing cultural differences in America. However, this approach has become replaced by the "salad bowl" theory as a new way of approaching cultural diversity. We need to learn that different cultures should be appreciated rather than hidden or melted together. We wouldn't enjoy a salad if it had just one vegetable in it. Each culture offers its unique flavors to enhance the overall flavor of the salad. Rather than melting in and losing some of its flavor or culture, the "salad bowl" lets each culture retain its identity.

*How are food preferences formed?*

Food preferences are shaped by ethnic heritage and the family food style to which we are accustomed. When you ask students what foods they think of when you mention each of the food groups, they may have entirely different answers. One student may like rice, another potatoes. Fish to one child could mean red snapper, to another, trout from an icy cold stream, or tuna right from the can. Likes and dislikes can come from exposure to foods or the lack of exposure. Just talking about food differences can accustom children to different foods and in turn broaden their food preferences. Examining a child's origin can be an excellent way to explore the ways in which his/her ethnic heritage influences food preferences. Introducing children to the customs of their classmates can make them aware of the variety and uniqueness of different cultures.

*What are foods from other countries that Americans eat?*

Many restaurant and fast food establishments feature foods that originated in other countries. Tacos, pizza, egg rolls, and gyro sandwiches are now as American as apple pie. This is one way to teach children what others in different countries may eat. By exposing children to different cultural foods at an early age, you are opening their minds to new horizons and taste buds to new flavors.

# Activity 25-1. Favorite Food Flags

## DIRECTIONS TO THE TEACHER

### Objective (Cognitive Domain: Application Level)

Students will prepare a national flag that includes a reproduction of the flag, the name of the country, and a food associated with the country.

## Materials

Student Activity Sheet (1)
Crayons or markers
Magazine pictures
Chart of national flags (in encyclopedia)
Tape
Pencils
Paste
3 x 5 inch cards

## Prerequisite Skills

Copying geometric shapes

## Procedure

1. Discuss the "salad bowl" theory of a nation. Encourage students to share some nationalities represented in their family's heritage.

2. Have students pick one nationality of their ethnic heritage or a country of their choice.

3. Explain that there are foods associated with various countries. These food associations are often influenced by available crops, climate, and traditional preparation methods.

4. Distribute the student activity sheet and explain the directions. Allow students to work independently or in small groups to complete the activity sheet.

## Supplementary Activities

1. Have students attach their flags to the respective countries on a map. This could be used as a bulletin board or as a lesson in geography/mapping skills.

2. Have students research main crops produced in a given country. Discuss possible relationships between crops and associated national foods.

3. Have students identify food groups for foods pictured on flags. Have students generate a menu for an ethnic meal that includes all food groups.

4. Invite students to bring in an ethnic dish to share at an ethnic feast. Award prizes for students who taste all foods contributed.

5. As a gift idea, students could collect recipes for favorite ethnic dishes and organize them into a recipe book.

Name _____ Date _____

## Activity 25-1. Favorite Food Flags

**Directions:**
1) Choose a country. Find the flag of that country.
2) Draw the flag on a piece of 3 x 5 inch paper.
3) Color the flag.
4) On the back of your flag write the name of the country.
5) Cut out a picture of a food from this country. Paste the picture under the name of the country.
6) Write the name of the food under the picture.
7) Tape your flag to your pencil.
8) Follow the sample below.

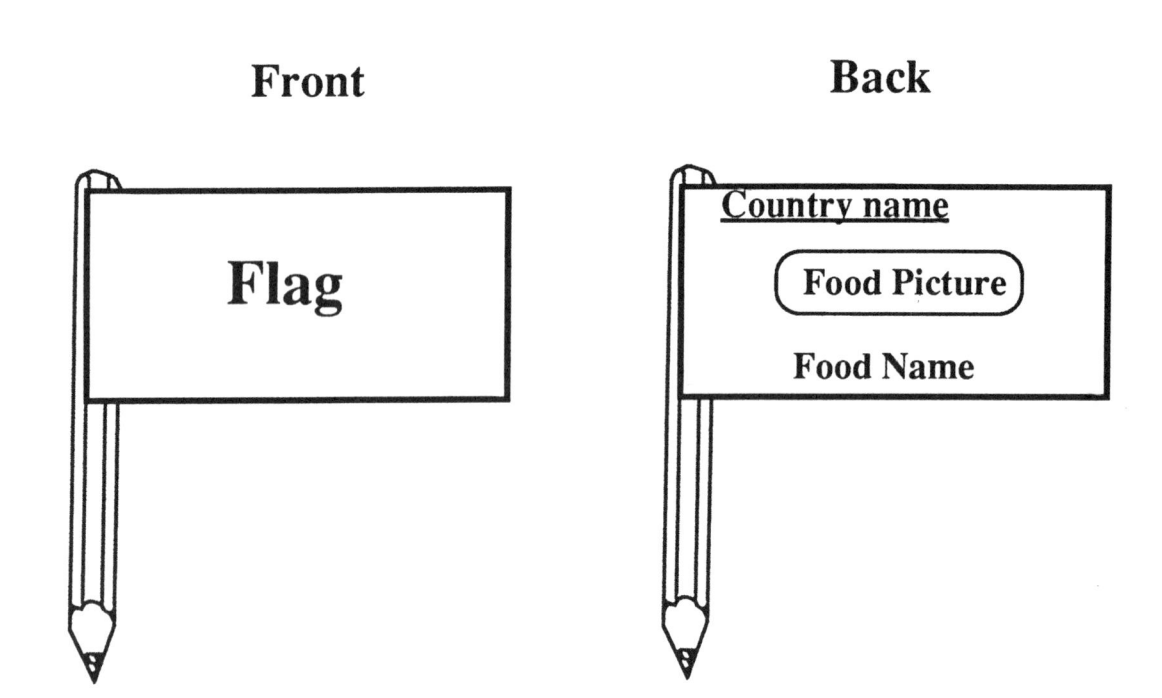

**Front**  **Back**

**Flag**

Country name
Food Picture
Food Name

**Remember:**
Many foods make an exciting diet.

# Activity 25-2. Cultural Foods

## DIRECTIONS TO THE TEACHER

**Objective** (Cognitive Domain: Knowledge Level)

Students will match traditional foods to the appropriate country.

## Materials

Student Activity Sheets (2)
Pencil

## Prerequisite Skills

Reading/writing
Completing a chart

## Procedure

1. Introduce the idea of cultural foods. Explain that many cultures start with the same basic foods, but the spices and methods of preparation may differ. Ask the students how they might find out what ingredients, spices and methods of preparation are used for a particular food. The responses should move toward a recipe (or a list of ingredients).

2. Distribute the activity sheets and explain the directions.

## Supplementary Activities

1. Look for cultural foods on your school lunch menu. Discuss the origin of these foods.

2. Plan a trip to a local ethnic grocery store or invite the store manager to your class. Discuss likenesses and differences in cultures. If you visit the store be sure to call ahead and ask for permission to visit.

3. Encourage your students to look beyond themselves and reach out to others. The Tapori Children's movement is an international organization whose 300 full-time volunteers work with needy children and families in 19 countries around the world. The organization encourages children from every nation to share their diverse experience and ideas with one another by submitting articles to the monthly newsletter. The Tapori newsletter is a forum for children to express their thoughts and feelings, and learn about one another's cultures. For more information about Tapori or to subscribe to their monthly newsletters ($7.00), contact Tapori, 172 First Ave., New York, NY 10009, (212) 228-1339.

4. Order your free cultural calendar. This calendar, issued in two-year cycles and published by the National Conference of Christians and Jews (NCCJ), highlights the major festivals of nine ethnic cultures and is well suited for discussing cultural diversity. Order from NCCJ, 71 Fifth Ave., Suite 1100, Dept. 1M, New York, NY 10003.

Name _____ Date _____

# Activity 25-2. Cultural Foods

**Directions:** Look at each recipe ingredient list below. Answer the questions on the next page.

### Cheeseburgers

1 pound ground beef
6 slices American cheese
6 sliced rolls
lettuce, tomato, pickle, etc.

### Spanish Rice

2 sweet bell peppers, chopped
1 medium onion, chopped
1 lb. ground beef
1-16 oz. can tomato puree
3 cups white rice

### Chili Con Carne

1 pound ground beef
1 tbsp. chili powder
1 medium onion
1/2/ tsp. salt
1/4 tsp. ground hot pepper
2-15 oz. cans tomato sauce
1-15 oz. can tomato puree

1-16 oz. can pinto beans
1 tbsp. flour
1/2 tsp. paprika
1-6 oz. can green chilies

Top with cheddar cheese

### Italian Lasagna

2 lbs. lasagna noodles
1-8 oz. can tomato puree
1-8 oz. can tomato paste
1-8 oz. can crushed tomatoes
1/2 lb. ground beef
1/2 tsp. each of basil, thyme, oregano,
marjoram, parsley
1/4 tsp. pepper
1 bay leaf
1 lb. ricotta cheese
1 lb. mozzarella cheese
1 tbsp. parmesan cheese

© 1991 by The Center for Applied Research in Education

Name _____ Date _____

# Activity 25-2. Cultural Foods, *page 2*

1) Look and see if all food groups can be found in each recipe. Write an ingredient in each space. The first column has been done for you.

|  | Cheeseburger | Chili | Lasagna | Rice |
|---|---|---|---|---|
| **Meat** | beef |  |  |  |
| **Fruit/Vegetable** | tomato, lettuce, pickle |  |  |  |
| **Breads/Cereals** | roll |  |  |  |
| **Milk** | American cheese |  |  |  |

2) In order to have all food groups at a meal, what could you serve with chili? _____ with rice? _____

3) Look at the chart to find out what ingredients can be found in all four recipes? _____ and _____

4) Draw a line to match the four recipes with the country.

United States — Lasagna
Spain ⟶ Cheeseburger
Mexico      Rice
Italy         Chili

Although foods may be prepared differently in different countries, ingredients can be mixed to make nutritious meals.

# Activity 25-3. Cultural Foods Search

## DIRECTIONS TO THE TEACHER

**Objective** (Cognitive Domain: Knowledge Level)

Given a list of cultural foods, students will list each as a lowfat or high-fat food.

## Materials

Student Activity Sheets (2)
Pencil

## Prerequisite Skills

Letter finding skills

## Procedure

1. Review the dietary guideline relevant to fat consumption. Explain that lowfat foods do have fat, but not as much as high-fat foods. Remind students that some fat is needed in the diet, and that some foods do not contain any fat.

2. Distribute the activity sheets and explain the directions.

## Supplementary Activities

1. Introduce a world map. Mark Italy, Mexico, and China. Discuss how you can get from your hometown to one of these countries. Children may suggest a car, train, or plane ride to get to Mexico; a plane or boat to get to Italy or China.

2. Invite a travel agent to your classroom to discuss travel, food, and cultural differences among these three countries.

3. Make fortune cookies. Share the cookies with another classroom. CAUTION: Teacher may need to do the frying to prevent injury from burning or splattering.

*FORTUNE COOKIES     (30 servings)

| Ingredients | Materials Needed | One-by-one Recipe |
|---|---|---|
| 5 cups flour | pastry brush | 2 tablespoons flour |
| 3 cups brown sugar | electric frying pan | 1 tablespoon brown sugar |
| 3/4 cup cornstarch | pancake turners | 2 teaspoons cornstarch |
| 2 cups oil | small bowls | 1 teaspoon oil |
| 5 cups cold water | measuring spoons | 3 tablespoons cold water |
| oil for frying pan | | |

DIRECTIONS: Stir the first three ingredients together. Stir in oil and add water. Beat hard, batter should be thin. Pour circular shapes into lightly oiled electric frying pan set at 350°. Fry five minutes. Turn and fry five minutes more. Remove. Insert fortune. Fold in quarters. Set on paper towels to cool until hard.

Name _____ Date _____

## Activity 25-3. Cultural Foods Search

**Directions:** Use the word list to find the words in the word search below and on page 2. The words across ( → ) indicate foods or cooking methods high in fat. The words down ( ↓ ) indicate foods that are low in fat.

```
d e e p f r i e d c v i
a q j r b i d p d p j l
c h i p s c y e c u b o
b c y i t e c j e n e m
c h i m i c h a n g a s
k i s a o z s e f l n y
t l h r u h l g f o s p
v i s k q e m t g x n z
```

**Mexican**

beans
chili
chimichangas
chips
deep fried
rice

**Rewrite words high in fat ( → ).**

_____

_____

_____

**Rewrite words low in fat ( ↓ ).**

_____

_____

_____

# Activity 25-3. Cultural Foods Search, *page 2*

## Chinese

battered
chop suey
crispy
deep fried
lomein
rice

**Rewrite words high in fat ( → ).**
_____
_____
_____

**Rewrite words low in fat ( ↓ ).**
_____
_____
_____

| r | m | l | l | k | c | f | l | m | d | d |
|---|---|---|---|---|---|---|---|---|---|---|
| e | s | z | o | y | h | a | c | o | v | u |
| t | s | i | m | z | o | b | p | r | q | t |
| v | h | d | e | e | p | f | r | i | e | d |
| u | c | r | i | j | s | g | x | c | i | w |
| g | d | h | n | y | u | k | p | e | o | b |
| i | b | a | t | t | e | r | e | d | f | x |
| c | r | i | s | p | y | w | a | j | e | n |

| o | r | d | n | m | p | a | r |
|---|---|---|---|---|---|---|---|
| s | a | u | s | a | g | e | t |
| b | a | l | f | r | e | d | o |
| d | s | c | o | i | f | u | m |
| z | x | e | q | n | r | g | a |
| d | c | r | e | a | m | i | t |
| w | l | m | v | r | i | h | o |
| k | n | t | y | a | i | j | p |

## Italian

alfredo
cream
marinara
sausage
tomato

**Rewrite words high in fat ( → ).**
_____
_____
_____

**Rewrite words low in fat ( ↓ ).**
_____
_____
_____

© 1991 by The Center for Applied Research in Education

# ANSWER KEY

## Unit 1: Eating to Grow

**1. Growing Up**

1-1. Things That Grow
 6 of these things grow
 4 of these things do not grow

1-2. Growing Bigger
 egg - 1, tadpole - 2, frog - 3
 seed - 1, sprout - 2, plant - 3

1-3. How Big Am I?
 Answers will vary

**2. Nutrients to Grow On**

2-1. Riddle
 water

2-2. Food Energy
 1. cheddar cheese
 2. green pepper
 3. apple
 4. chicken leg
 5. cheddar cheese
 6. apple and green pepper

2-3. Nutrient Words

```
c a r b o h y d r a t e x
w o x g k m v i t a m i n
a i l e m i s g l e p m h
t a n d w n d i l i r s n
e d j x g e o t y e o f y
r h u l r r y a e s t d w
a p q i j a e u o r e y z
p y r m w l r g e o i a z
s o t f a t o i r y n l o
```

 P
 caRbohydrate
 O
 faT
 watEr
 vItamin
 miNeral

**3. What's Inside Me?**

3-1. Bone Smart
 Not applicable

3-2. Muscle Smart
 Students should circle
  bicycling
  cheering and jumping
  playing basketball
  skating
  playing football

3-3. Body Smart
 1. Y (false)
 2. D (false)
 3. K (false)
 4. N (true)
 5. T (false)
 6. S (true)

 My Body Works On Nutrients

**4. After I Swallow, What Happens?**

4-1. Fun Facts
 Answers will vary

4-2. Where the Food Goes
 Not applicable

4-3. Digestion Action
 mouth - hammer - mash
 esophagus - slide - slide
 stomach - hand mixer - mix
 intestines - scissors - breaks apart
 intestines - pipe - moves out or leaks

# UNIT 2: Eating All Kinds of Food

## 5. Introducing A Pattern for Daily Food Choices

**5-1. Beary-Good Eating**
orange - fruit - yellow
chicken leg - meat - red
carrots - vegetable - green
yogurt - milk - blue
cheese - milk - blue
banana - fruit - yellow
fish - meat - red
muffins - bread - orange
steak - meat - red
loaf of bread - bread - orange

**5-2. Eating Advice**

| E | S | C | T | B |
|---|---|---|---|---|
| O | P | B | M | C |
| C | L | A | L | N |
| D | M | E | B | T |
| B | H | C | I | N |
| E | L | K | M | E |

STOP AND THINK

**5-3. Serving Numbers**
bread - 6    fruit - 2
milk - 2     vegetables - 3
meat - 2

## 6. The Meat Group

**6-1. Meat and Legume Scramble**
chicken
turkey
lean beef
lean pork
lentils
navy beans
lima beans
kidney beans
black-eyed peas

Protein plus exercise builds strong muscles

## The Meat Group (continued)

**6-2. Protein Smart**
steak - A
chicken leg - A
nuts - P
fish - A
beans - P
egg - A
turkey - A
rice - P
Plants and animals

**6-3. Green Eggs and Ham**
1. have protein
2. have iron
3. are in the meat group
4. are animal products
5. can be eaten in many ways

## 7. Breads, Grains, and Cereals

**7-1. Grain Word Search**

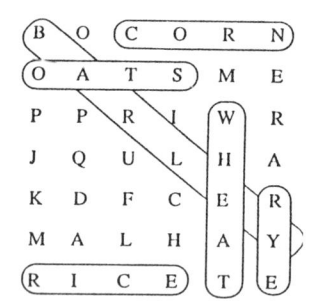

| B | O | C | O | R | N |
|---|---|---|---|---|---|
| O | A | T | S | M | E |
| P | P | R | I | W | R |
| J | Q | U | L | H | A |
| K | D | F | C | E | R |
| M | A | L | H | A | Y |
| R | I | C | E | T | E |

oatmeal    ryebread    ricebran cereal
cornflakes    ricecakes    whole wheatbread
cream of wheat    cornbread    puffed rice cereal
oatmeal bread    oatbran cereal    puffed wheat cereal
wheatbread    wheatsquares    ryecrackers

**7-2. What is Enriched?**
enriched - to make rich or richer, give greater value, better quality

Vitamins and Minerals

**7-3. Pockets for Eating**
Answers will vary

256

## 8. Fruits

**8-1. Try It! You'll Like It!**
Answers will vary

**8-2. Fruit Smart**
orange - citrus
raspberries - berries
watermelon - melons
lemon - citrus
strawberries - berries
cantaloupe - melons
grapefruit - citrus

answers will vary

**8-3. How Fruits Grows**
Fruits that grow on trees
    cherries
    pear
    orange
    apple
Fruits that grow on vines
    grapes
    watermelon
Fruits that grow on bushes
    raspberries

## 9. Vegetables

**9-1. Vegetable Taste Test**
Answers will vary

**9-2. Pizza Smart**
broccoli
mushroom
green pepper
green pepper, mushrooms, broccoli

**9-3. Vegetable Colors**
Not applicable

## 10. Milk, Cheese, and Yogurt

**10-1. Milk Product Maze**

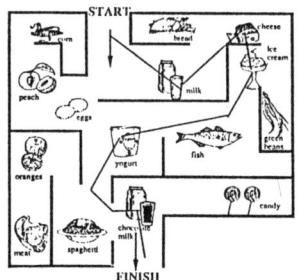

milk, cheese, ice cream, yogurt, chocolate milk

**10-2. Milk Sorting**

| solid | liquid |
|---|---|
| vanilla ice cream | hot chocolate |
| cottage cheese | milk shake |
| cheddar cheese | 2% milk |

**10-3. Milk Products**
ice cream, yogurt, milk, whipped cream, cheese

## 11. Fats and Sweets

**11-1. Food Group Smart**

Food group __milk__   Food group __meat__
Food group __fat and sweet__   Food group __fruit__

**11-2. Smart Choices**
grapes (moving clockwise)
milk
single-dip ice cream
pretzels
carrots
frozen yogurt (example)
any nonfood reward is acceptable

**11-3. Where's the Fat?**
a
b
a
b

# Unit 3: Eating Healthy Foods

## 12. Dietary Guidelines

12-1. Nutrition Smart Guidelines Game
See Directions to the Teacher

12-2. Guidelines Code
1. different
2. fit
3. fat
4. fruits, grains, and vegetables
5. sugar
6. salt

12-3. Keeping Score
Answers will vary

## 13. Eating a Variety of Foods

13-1. Cheeseburger Smart
breads and grains
milk
meat
breads and grains

13-2. Food Diary
Answers will vary

13-3. Varietarian
Not applicable

## 14. Maintaining Healthy Weight

14-1. Good Moves
Answers will vary

14-2. Using Energy
throwing the frisbee
playing the piano
playing basketball
raking leaves
flying a kite
playing with the dog

14-3. Exercise Message
muscles
heart
energy

## 15. Eating Lowfat Foods

15-1. Milk Carton Cutouts
skim (least fat)
1%
2%
whole milk (most fat)

15-2. Clogged Pipes
1. yes
2. yes
3. no, no
4. water could no longer pass
5. blood can not pass
6. eat lowfat foods and exercise

Page 2 -third body has a clogged blood vessel

15-3. Fat Finder
peanuts have fat
green pepper doesn't have fat
raw potato doesn't have fat
bacon has fat
oil has fat
potato chips have fat
crackers have fat
mayonnaise has fat
apple doesn't have fat
cheese has fat
butter has fat
macaroni has fat

page 2
1. no, the potato was fried in fat
2. yes, they are both fried
3. no
4. no
5. no fat
6. yes
7. fruits and vegetables do not contain fat

Unit 3 continues on the following page

## 16. Eating Plenty of Vegetables, Fruits, and Grains

16-1. Starch and Fiber Chains
fruits, vegetables, and grains

16-2. Fiber Foods
grapes
cereal
bread
muffin
carrot
orange
banana

16-3. Fiber Count
4 - pear
3 - broccoli
4 - bran cereal
3 - peanuts
6 - kidney beans

## 17. Using Sugars in Moderation

17-1. Tooth Smart
Foods that stick to teeth
    peanut butter & jelly
    crackers
    caramels
    raisins
    gumdrops
    bread & honey
Foods that do not stick to teeth
    water
    vegetables
    cheese

17-2. Ingredient Smart
a part or combination of a mixture
cereal
    sugar
    brown sugar
    honey
    malt syrup
cake mix
    sugar
    dextrose
cake frosting
    sugar
    corn syrup
    dextrose

17-2. Ingredient Smart (continued)
cookie
    sugar
    molasses
    brown sugar
candy
    corn syrup
    sugar
soda
    sugar

17-3. Sugar Decoder
4 tsps.
9 tsps.
3 tsps.
6 tsps.
3 tsps.
soda pop
jelly beans, pudding pop, and cupcake

## 18. Using Salt and Sodium in Moderation

18-1. Sodium Smart
See Sodium Smart Answer Sheet

18-2. Sodium Inspector
Wheat Snacks - low sodium
Microwave Popping Corn - no statement
Pretzels - very low sodium
Snack Mix - sodium-free

18-3. Sodium Vending
apple - 1 mg
orange juice - 4 mg
chocolate bar - 35 mg
chocolate chip cookies - 182 mg
potato chips - 300 mg
creamed-filled cakes - 378 mg
peanut butter crackers - 422 mg
ham and cheese sandwich - 1025 mg

creamed-filled cakes, peanut butter crackers, ham and cheese sandwich

salty, sodium

# Unit 4: Eating Throughout the Day

### 19. Breakfast

**19-1.** Mystery Message
Breakfast gets me going

**19-2.** Time to Eat
1. 2, 11
2. bedtime snack and breakfast
3. b

**19-3.** Breakfast on the Run

| Circle | X out |
|---|---|
| crackers | crackers |
| grapes | grapes |
| mushrooms | mushrooms |
| tomato | tomato |
| yogurt | yogurt |
| milk | milk |
| lollipop | cheese |
| cake | pizza |
| cheese | bread |
| pizza | |
| bread | |

### 20. Lunch

**20-1.** Bag Lunches
tomato
hot dog
lollipop
banana
ice cream bar
page 2 answers will vary

**20-2.** Menu of Color
Monday
    Tuna salad - red, green, and yellow
    bun - brown
    carrots - green
    red grapes - purple
    milk - blue
Tuesday
    hot dog on roll - red and brown
    green beans - green
    orange slices - purple
    cookie - yellow
    milk - blue

**20-2.** Menu of Color (continued)
Wednesday
    meat loaf & gravy - red and yellow
    mashed potato - green and yellow
    whole wheat roll - brown
    baked apple - purple
    milk - blue
Thursday
    lasagna - brown and green
    bread - brown
    tossed salad - green and yellow
    pineapple - purple
    milk - blue
Friday
    taco - red, green, brown
    corn - green
    pear - purple
    yogurt - blue
    milk - blue

**20-3.** Fill in the Menu
kiwi - fruit
answer will vary - meat
answer will vary - bread
answer will vary - bread
answer will vary - milk

### 21. Supper

**21-1.** Families
Answers will vary

**21-2.** Supper Steps
Answers will vary, but one possible sequence is:
    plan a meal
    do the shopping
    wash hands
    make the food
    set the table
    serve the food
    eat supper
    clear the table
    package leftovers
    do the dishes

Unit 4 continues on the following page

21-3. <u>Microwaving</u>
 1. frown
 2. smile
 3. smile
 4. smile
 5. frown
 6. smile

## 22. Snacks

22-1. <u>Choosing Snacks</u>

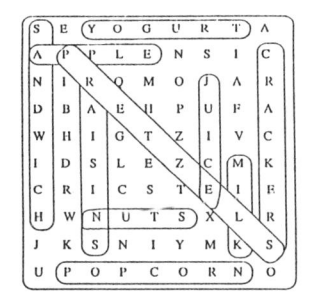

22-2. <u>Snack Track</u>
 Answers will vary

22-3. <u>Popcorn Percents</u>
 1. hot-air-popcorn
 2. ready-to-eat popcorn
 3. stove top
 4. stove top is popped with oil
 5. answers will vary

## 23. Convenience Foods and Vending Machines

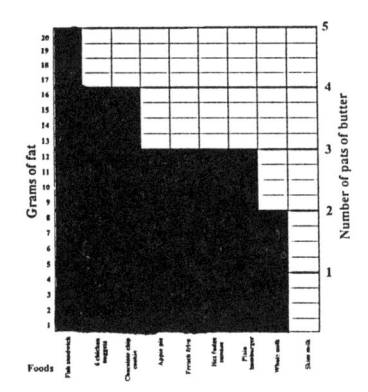

23-1A. <u>Fat Pats</u>

 1. fish sandwich  2. skim milk

23-1A. <u>Fat Pats (Continued)</u>
 1. 0    6. 3
 2. 9    7. 3
 3. 4    8. 4
 4. 1    9. 3
 5. 8   10. 3

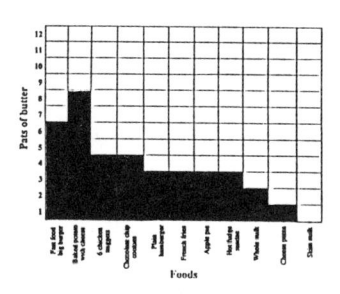

23-1B. <u>Fat Pats</u>

 1. quarter-pound hamburger
 2. 8
 3. 36

23-2. <u>Shopping</u>
 1. pretzels
 2. juice
 3. milk
 4. gum
 5. chips
 6. cookie

 circle - pretzels, juice, and milk

23-3. <u>Snack Cents</u>
 peanuts - 49¢
 milk - 70¢
 string cheese - 69¢
 yogurt - 89¢
 pretzels - 69¢
 animal crackers - 79¢
 candy bar - 45¢
 chips - 69¢
 pie - 65¢
 soda - 69¢
 brownie - 65¢
 cupcakes - 65¢
 cookie - 59¢
 doughnut - 49¢
 beef jerky - 99¢

Snack Cents page 2 continues on next page

23-3. Snack Cents (continued)
1. milk
2. processing and packaging increases the cost
3. string cheese, milk, yogurt
4. animal crackers
   because it is in the bread group not the fats and sweets group
5. candy bar
doughnut
raisins
apple
raisins and apple are nutrition smart

## 24. Advertising

24-1. Commercials
fruit
   Gummy fresh Raisins
vegetables
   none
meat
   Freddie's Fast Food
milk
   Milk for My body
bread
   Happy Morning Cereal
   Crunchy, Munchy Cereal
   Ready, Set, Go Cereal
fats and sweets
   Gooey, Chewy Cookies
   Kool-Man Drinks

1. bread
2. no

24-2. Slogan Power
Answers will vary

24-3. Ads, Ads, Ads
Answers will vary

## 25. Cultural Foods

25-1. Favorite Food Flags
Answers will vary

25-2. Cultural Foods
1. Chili
   meat - beef and pinto beans
   fruit/ vegetables - onion, tomato, and chilies
   breads/cereals - none
   milk - cheddar cheese

   Lasagna
   meat - beef
   fruit /vegetable - tomato, parsley
   bread/cereal - noodles
   milk - ricotta cheese, mozzarella cheese, and Parmesan cheese

   Rice
   meat - beef
   fruit/vegetable - bell peppers, onion, and tomato
   breads/cereals - rice
   milk - none

2. corn bread or rice
   milk, cheese, or yogurt

3. beef and tomato

4. America - Cheeseburger
   Spain - Rice
   Mexico - Chili
   Italy - Lasagna

Unit 4 continues on the following page

## 25-3. Cultural Foods Search

### Mexican

| high in fat | low in fat |
|---|---|
| chimichangas | beans |
| chips | chili |
| deep fried | rice |

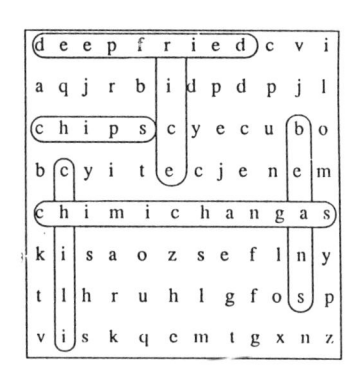

```
d e e p  f r i e d  c v i
a q j r b i d p d p j l
c h i p s c y e c u b o
b c y i t e c j e n e m
c h i m i c h a n g a s
k i s a o z s e f l n y
t l h r u h l g f o s p
v i s k q e m t g x n z
```

### Chinese

| high in fat | low in fat |
|---|---|
| battered | chop suey |
| crispy | lomein |
| deep fried | rice |

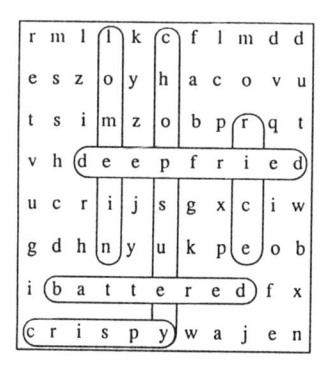

```
r m l l k c f l m d d
e s z o y h a c o v u
t s i m z o b p r q t
v h d e e p f r i e d
u c r i j s g x c i w
g d h n y u k p e o b
i b a t t e r e d f x
c r i s p y w a j e n
```

### Italian

| high in fat | low in fat |
|---|---|
| alfredo | marinara |
| cream | tomato |
| sausage | |

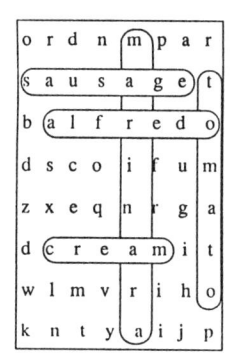

```
o r d n m p a r
s a u s a g e t
b a l f r e d o
d s c o i f u m
z x e q n r g a
d c r e a m i t
w l m v r i h o
k n t y a i j p
```

# Selected Nutrition Education Materials for Grades K-3

## Curriculum and Activity Guides

The American Heart Association Heart Treasure Chest, hands-on activities kit. Order #64-500A. Order from local American Heart Association or contact National Center, American Heart Association, 7320 Greenville Ave., Dallas, TX 75231. $36.00. 800-527-6941.

"Getting to Know Your Heart" The American Schoolsite Program, Lower Elementary ($39.00). American Heart Association, National Center, 7320 Greenville Ave., Dallas, TX 75231. 1988. Contact your local American Heart Association.

Nutrition Comes Alive, Level K-6, Cornell University, Division of Nutritional Sciences, Ithaca, NY. 1986. Grades K,1,2,3,4,5,6, individual grades are $7.00, prices include shipping. Order from: Health Educ. Service, P.O. Box 7126, Albany, NY 12224. 518-439-7286.

Learning About Nutrition through Physical Education Game Activities, Ohio Dept. of Education, Nutr. Educ. Program, 65 South Front Street, Rm. 410, Columbus, OH 43266-0308. Free. 614-466-8251.

Food...Your Choice, (Grades 1 through 6). National Dairy Council, Rosemont, IL 60018. 1987. Contact your local Dairy Council. Each separate grade $26.00.

The Organic Puppet Theatre, Childrens' Activities in Health Awareness, Terry Schultz and Linda Sorenson. Night Owl Press, 1997 Spillwater St., White Bear Lake, MN 55110. 1983. $15.95 plus $1.50 postage. 612-653-1032.

Choose Well, Be Well, A Curriculum for Preschool and Kindergarten, and Primary Grades, NET, California State Dept. of Education, Publication Sales Office, P.O. Box 271, Sacramento, CA 95802-0271. 1982. $8.00 each. 916-445-7608.

Fit It Together, S.E. Buhr, G. Gunderson and T. Corwin, Sharon E. Buhr, Mercy Hospital, Valley City, ND 58072. 1987. $35.00. 701-845-0440.

Eat, Think, and Be Healthy, Creative Nutrition Activities for Children, Paula Klevan Zeller and Michael F. Jacobson. Center for Science in the Public Interest, 1501 16th Street, NW, Washington, D.C. 20036. 1987. $8.95. 202-322-9110.

# Children's Books

The Berenstain Bears and Too Much Junk Food, Stan and Jan Berenstain. Random House, 400 Hohn Rd., Westminster, MD 21157. 1985. $1.95. Also available on cassette, $4.95. 301-848-1900.

Arthur's Thanksgiving, Marc Brown. Little, Brown and Co., 200 West Street, Waltham, MA 02254. 1984. Paperback $4.70. Hardback $14.45. 617-742-2600.

Cloudy With A Chance of Meatballs, Judi Barrett. Atheneum/Alladin Publ., Macmillan, Inc., 866 3rd Ave., New York, NY 10022 or Front and Brown Sts., Riverside, NJ 08075. 1982. Paperback $3.95. Hardback $13.95. 609-461-6500.

The Popcorn Book, Tomie de Paola. Holiday House, Inc., 18 East 53rd St., New York, NY 10022. 1978. $5.95. 212-688-0085.

Strega Nona, Tomie de Paola. Simon & Schuster c/o Prentice Hall, Inc., 200 Old Tappan Road, Old Tappan, NJ 07675. 1987. $13.95. 201-767-5937.

The Giant Vegetable Garden, Nadine B. Westcott. Little, Brown and Company Publ., 200 West Street, Waltham, MA 02254. 1981. $14.45. 617-742-2600 or 800-343-9204.

Mr. Rabbit and the Lovely Present, Charlotte Zolotow, Harper and Row Publ., Keystone Industrial Park, Scranton, PA 18512. 1962. $3.50. 800-982-4377.

Potato Pancakes All Around, A Hanukkah Tale, Marilyn Hirsh. The Jewish Publication Society, 60 East 42nd St., Rm. 1339, New York, NY 10165. 1982. $6.95. 212-687-0809.

Having a Picnic, Sarah Garland. The Atlantic Monthly Press, (distributed by Little, Brown and Co., 34 Beacon St., Boston MA 02108). 1985. $6.95. 800-343-9204.

The Very Hungry Caterpillar, Eric Carle. Philomel Books, Putnam Publishing Group, 200 Madison Ave., New York, NY 10016. 14th printing, 1981. $14.95 Hardback. $3.95 mini-version. 1986. 800-631-8571.

What Happens to a Hamburger, P. Showers. Thomas Y. Crowell, Junior Books, c/o Harper & Row Pubs., Inc. Keystone Industrial Park, Scranton, PA 18512. 1985. $4.95. 800-242-7737.

## Audiovisual Materials

The Best Breakfast, (filmstrips or videocassette with support material), Cambridge Home Economics, One Players Club Drive, Dept. HE3, Charleston, WV 25311. 800-468-4227 $79.00-video $69.00-filmstrips. 1989.

The Most Important Person, (Nutrition film set #6735). Encyclopedia Britannica, 310 S. Michigan Ave., Chicago, IL 60604. Avg. 5 minutes each. Topics: Tasting Party, Have A Snack, What's for Breakfast, Foods Around Us. $450.00-films, $300.00-videotape, $155.00-filmstrips. 312-347-7900.

Nutrition Around the Clock, (5 filmstrips). Coronet MTI, Film and Video, 108 Wilmont Rd., Deerfield, IL 60015. Avg. 7-10 minutes. $215.00 + $5.50 shipping. 800-621-2131.

Nutrition: Who Cares? You Should!, (4 filmstrips, 4 cassettes teacher's guide and processing kit), Guidance Associates, Communications Park, Box 3000, Mount Kisco, NY 10549-9989. 800-431-1242. 1989. $139.00.

Seeing Through Commercials, (film). Barr Films, PO Box 7878, Irwindale, CA 91106-7878. 1977. $340.00. 818-338-7878.

Snacking Mouse, (filmstrip). The Polished Apple, 3742 Seahorn Drive, Malibu, CA 90265. Avg. 5 minutes. 1977. $49.75 + $3.50 shipping.

Winnie the Pooh, Nutrition and You, (6 filmstrips). Walt Disney Educational Media Co., 500 S. Buena Vista Street, Burbank, CA 91521. 1977. Avg. 10 minutes. $205.00 + $5.50 shipping. 800-621-2131.

You Are What You Eat, (film). Avg. 10 minutes. Barr Films, PO Box 7878, Irwindale, CA 91106-7878. 1976. $220.00. 818-338-7878.

## Posters

Chew, Chew, Slo-o-owly. . ., San Bernadino County Child Health, 351 N. Mt. View, Rm. 305, San Bernardino, CA 92415-0010. $2.50 + $2.50 postage. 714-387-6299.

Try Eating Something New, Robert Jacobson. Design. Department P, P.O. Box 8909, Moscow, ID 83843. $3.50 plus $2.75 postage (minimum order 3 posters). 208-882-3749 or 800-441-8558. (The company will send brochure.)

## Food Composition Books

Fast Food Facts (3rd. ed.), M.J. Franz. Diabetes Center Publishing, PO #739, Wayzata, MN 55391. 1990. $6.95. 800-848-2793.

Food Values of Portions Commonly Used, 15th ed., J. A. Pennington, J. B. Lippincott Co., East Washington Square, Philadelphia, PA 19105. 1989. Spiral bound, $18.50.

The Fast-Food Guide, Michael Jacobson. CSPI 1501 16th St., N.W., Washington, DC 20036. 1986. $4.95. 202-332-9110.

## Computer Software

Compute Well, Be Well Computer Activity for Preschool/Kindergarten and Grades 1-3 for use with Apple II computers. Developed to be used with the Choose Well, Be Well Program. Nutrition Education and Training Program, California State Department of Education. Order from Publication Sales, California State Department of Education, P.O. Box 271, Sacramento, CA 95802-0271.1985. $12.50 each.

Food Encounters, Grades 3-6. National Dairy Council, Rosemont, IL 60018-4233. 312-696-1020. (Contact your local Dairy Council to order). $45.00.

What I Usually Eat, Grades 3-6. National Dairy Council, Rosemont, IL 60018-4233. (Contact your local Dairy Council to order). $37.00

Food Facts - for Apple II - 48 K computer. Minnesota Educational Computing Consortium, 3490 Lexington Ave. North, St. Paul, MN 55126. 1983. $35.00. 800-228-3504.

## Teacher Reference Books

How to Get Your Kid to Eat...But Not Too Much, E. Satter, Bull Publishing Co., P.O. Box 208, Palo Alto, CA 94302-2855. 1987. $12.95.

No-Nonsense Nutrition for Kids, A. Nataow, and J. Heslin, McGraw-Hill Book Co., 1221 Ave. of Americas, New York, NY 10020. 1985. $15.95.

## Teacher Reference Newsletters

Environmental Nutrition Newsletter, Environmental Nutrition, Inc., 2112 Broadway, Suite 200, New York, NY 10023, (212) 362-0424 ($24 for 12 issues a year)

FDA Consumer, Food and Drug Administration, 5600 Fishers Lane, Rockville, MD 20857, (301) 443-3220 ($12 for 10 issues a year)

Tufts University Diet and Nutrition Letter, 53 Park Place, New York, NY 10007, ($20 for 12 issues a year)

## Teacher Reference Resource Organizations

American Dietetic Association, 216 W. Jackson Blvd., Suite 800, Chicago, IL 60606-6995, (312)899-0400

American School Food Service Association, 4101 East Iliff Avenue, Denver, CO 80222, (303)757-8555

Center for Science in the Public Interest, 1501 16th Street, N.W., Washington, D.C. 20036, (202)332-9110

Penn State Nutrition Center, 417 E. Calder Way, The Pennsylvania State University, University Park, PA 16801-5663, (814) 865-6323

## Teacher Reference Government Groups

Center for Health Promotion and Education (HHS), 1600 Clifton Rd., Bldg. 14 Atlanta, GA 30333 (404) 329-3235

Consumer Information Center, Pueblo, CO 81009, (202)566-1794

Food and Nutrition Information Center (FNIC), National Agricultural Library Building, Rm 304, 10301 Baltimore Bvd., Beltsville, MD 20705, (301) 344-3719

National Health Information Clearinghouse, ODPHP/NHIC, PO Box 1133, Washington, DC 20013-1133, (800) 336-4797; in VA (703) 522-2590

National Heart, Lung, and Blood Institute, Information Center, 4733 Bethesda Ave., Suite 530, Bethesda, MD 20814, (301) 496-4000

National Institute of Child Health and Human Development (HHS), Bldg. 31, Rm. 2A-32, 9000 Rockville Pike, Bethesda, MD 20205, (301)496-5133

## Teacher Reference Local Voluntary Health Associations
(check your local listings)
American Cancer Society
American Diabetes Association
American Heart Association
American Red Cross
March of Dimes